Also by Joel Makower

The Green Consumer
The Green Commuter
Going Green: A Kid's Handbook to Saving the Planet
50 Simple Things Your Business Can Do to Save the Earth
(with The Earthworks Group)
Trend Watching *(with John E. Merriam)*

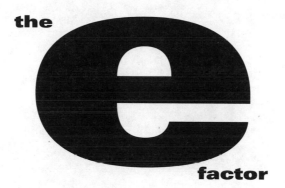

the **e** factor

the

factor

THE BOTTOM-LINE APPROACH TO ENVIRONMENTALLY RESPONSIBLE BUSINESS

JOEL MAKOWER

A TILDEN PRESS BOOK

TIMES BOOKS

RANDOM HOUSE

Library of Congress Cataloging-in-Publication Data

Makower, Joel.
    The E–factor: the bottom-line approach to environmentally
responsible business / Joel Makower. — 1st ed.
         p.   cm.
    Includes bibliographical references and index.
    ISBN 0-8129-2057-0
    1. Social responsibility of business. 2. Industry—Environmental
      aspects. 3. Decision-making. 4. Green marketing. I. Title.
      HD60.M344   1993
      658.4'08—dc20   92-50504

Manufactured in the United States of America

9 8 7 6 5 4 3 2

First Edition

For my father,
a true friend of the earth,
in loving memory

contents

the 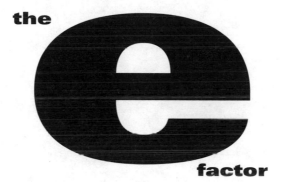 factor

preface

THIS BOOK BEGINS with the premise that being in business need not be an inherently polluting activity.

At first blush, that may seem a startling statement for some companies. These days, just about everyone in business is burdened with some kind of environmental challenge, from properly disposing of toxic-laden wastes to cutting landfill disposal costs to simply educating employees and customers not to toss out things that can be recycled. Nearly every company, it seems, is saddled with pressures from regulators, environmentalists, customers, and others to change their products and processes to better accommodate these earth-sensitive times. And those pressures seem to get stronger every year.

The fact is, all of us in business affect the environment in two ways every working day: We consume energy and other resources, and we create wastes that must be disposed of. All of us, from the hourly wage earner to those with golden parachutes, do these two things. It's a fact of life for everyone in every sector. And that makes everyone in business a party, however unwittingly, to environmental degradation.

But it's *how* you do these two things that can make a difference—to the earth as well as to your company's environmental record and its productivity and profits. In coming years, the distinction between being a "green" or "ungreen" company may become a critical factor in how your stakeholders—be they stockholders, regulators, environmentalists, competitors, employees, or the consuming public—view your company's image. Ultimately, it could make the difference between your company's ability to remain competitive in the twenty-first century.

The truth is that no matter how environmentally responsible, few companies will ever be truly *good* for the earth. The most we can hope is for companies to do the least damage in the pursuit of productivity and profits. But that doesn't mean that you and your company can't have a positive impact on the fate of the earth, or become a powerful agent for persuading others, both individuals and other companies, to play positive roles, too.

That's what this book is all about: incorporating environmental thinking in positive and profitable ways throughout your company's operation. Specifically, it is about what I call the E-Factor, a part of doing business that affects both the environment and your bottom line. As you'll see, the E-Factor encompasses many parts of your business, from the things you make to the things you buy to the relationships you have with your employees, suppliers, customers, regulators, the media, and the communities in which you do business.

If you've already given thought to your company's relationship to the environment, or perhaps already taken some steps to make changes, you are familiar with the challenges and confusion that face those who try to address these issues in a responsible fashion. The challenge is to integrate these green ideals into your corporate culture on a day-to-day basis—not simply to do a few symbolic and well-publicized things every third week in April around Earth Day. The confusion sets in when you confront the overwhelming amount of seemingly conflicting information out there about the real problems and their purported solutions.

Let's be honest: Understanding environmental issues is no easy matter. Considering the environmental implications of something so simple as a polystyrene foam coffee cup compared to a paper cup—or even a washable mug—requires digesting a fair amount of technical data, some of which is contradictory, most of which isn't conclusive. Much of the data out there conflict with other data. It's easy to come away with more questions than you started with. Can you really get employees to tune in to cutting waste? What's the environmentally correct way to package your product? What environmental claims can you make to your customers? (And how much do your customers even care?) Should you disclose your company's environmental performance to the public, regulators, environmentalists, and investors? How much should you change your company in the name of Planet Earth? Will the changes require huge investments of time and money? And on and on.

Time and money are big issues, of course. There never seems to be enough of either for everything else, making it all the more difficult to allocate additional resources to deal with environmental issues. And then there is the sheer scope of the subject matter: With so many serious environmental problems, how can one company make a difference?

Add to this mix the daily pressures faced by most of us in business—from employees, bosses, customers, suppliers, stockholders, regulators, politicians, lenders, and the rest—and it's easy to see how "saving the earth" can take a back seat to simply saving the day. The result, at least as far as the environment is concerned, can be organizational paralysis. When you're sufficiently confused, sometimes it's simply better to sit still and do nothing at all.

In the chapters that follow, we'll take a look at how cutting-edge companies are applying the E-Factor, in the hopes of sparing you some of that organizational paralysis.

Let's begin with a couple of key points.

At its essence, being "green," for all the many things it entails, boils down to two basic goals: reducing waste and maximizing resource efficiency. "Waste," in this case, is not just in raw materials, but can also be found in human effort, energy expenditures, facility use—and, of course, money. "Resources" refers to both your company's resources (raw materials, energy, supplies, facilities, inventory, capital, people) and the earth's resources (water, air, plants, animals, land). That brings us to the first key point, which hits on a theme we'll pursue throughout this book: When you reduce waste and maximize resource efficiency, it doesn't matter whether you are running a business or simply shopping for groceries, you can't help but be more competitive and get a better return on investment over the long run.

So integrating the E-Factor can be as economical as it is ecological. Not every time, but more often than not.

Another important theme is the link between environment and quality. You no doubt have heard a great deal in recent years about "total quality management" or TQM. It's likely your firm has some kind of TQM program, although they go by different names at different companies. Most try to view company operations in a new light, as an integrated system rather than a series of independent parts, and the company itself is part of a larger societal system involving customers, suppliers, communities, stockholders, and others. For the system to work, each part not only must do its part, it must work closely with all the other parts. If one part of the system fails to operate effectively, it can impede the entire operation. It is not coincidence that this same systemic view could—and should—be applied to the environment.

We won't delve deeply into the basics of "quality" in this book—there are dozens of other books that cover this material in considerable detail—but we will look at some common themes between the E-Factor and TQM. For example, both:

- aim to improve a company's final output, whatever it may be, thereby improving productivity and profits;
- require some new definitions of leadership, both by top management and those lower down the organizational ladder;
- emphasize long-range planning over short-term improvements;
- involve changing relationships between companies and their various "publics," including employees, customers, suppliers, and the communities in which they do business;
- strive for cultural change, not just new programs;
- attempt to break down artificial barriers within organizations, involving every department, facility, and organizational level in the pursuit of their goals;
- stress improved information, communication, training, and accountability; and
- demand continual self-assessment and improvement.

As you will see, there are several other close connections between TQM and the E-Factor. One of the most important connections brings us to another key point: In the pursuit of quality, the goal is to continually decrease waste, pollution, defects, and inefficiencies. Considering that waste and pollution are defects (in that they result from inefficiencies in the system), it follows that an ultimate goal of environmental quality is to achieve zero waste and pollution.

To be sure, achieving "zero waste" or "zero pollution" is no mean feat, but companies in some of the dirtiest industries are finding ways to do this, at least in some parts of their operations. We'll look at some of those efforts later in this book.

The E-Factor is really a rather simple concept. It starts with the understanding that nearly everyone in your organization makes decisions every day that take any number of factors into consideration. There's the bottom line, of course, but there are also your company's goals and objectives, the competition, the marketplace, the economy, and other considerations. And each business decision is driven by a different combination of factors. Research and development uses different factors than the sales department. Marketing is driven by different factors than personnel. The factors you consider when designing a product aren't necessarily the same ones you consider when manufacturing or marketing that product. And the factors you consider when hiring an employee aren't likely the same ones used when bringing in an outside consultant. Despite Americans' conventional wisdom about business, not everything is determined strictly by the impact on the bottom line.

This book is about incorporating one additional consideration into some of your decisions: the E-Factor—the environment. It, too, won't govern all your thinking, perhaps not much at all at first. But as you begin to incorporate the E-Factor, you will see that it can play an important role in a growing number of your decisions—from finance to facilities management, manufacturing to marketing. It may not be the driving force in most of them. But even if it influences only a few choices you make, you are well on your way to becoming a greener company.

That leads us to one final key point: The E-Factor is not about turning your company's finely honed policies, products, or processes topsy-turvy in the name of Planet Earth. It is a normal part of daily business to fine-tune one's operations. The E-Factor is simply another part of that fine-tuning process.

As you begin to examine the links between business and the environment, you will see the many things your company does that can have a positive or negative effect on the environment. In fact, "environment" is just one of the many things for which "E" stands. It also means such things as economics, empowerment, efficiency, education, ethics, excellence, and, of course, the earth.

This book is laid out in three basic parts. In the next chapter, we'll take a look at the changing roles of business and the environment, and how each is increasingly affecting the other. In chapters 2 and 3, we'll examine the rationale behind the new green consciousness—both the carrots and the sticks. We'll look at the growing costs to companies for environmental inertia and neglect, and look at some of the economic benefits that companies and society can achieve from new "green" thinking. In chapters 4 through 7, we'll look at specific aspects and applications of the E-Factor, seeing how other companies have tried, with varying degrees of success, to infuse their operations and their culture with environmental consciousness.

This book represents, admittedly, a rather whirlwind tour through the many complexities of doing business in an era of increased environmental awareness. Its purpose is not to offer the final word on the subject. That view is constantly changing, as a growing number of individuals and organizations around the world solve additional pieces of this puzzle. Rather, this book is intended to provide a starting place for understanding—a statement on what we know about business and the environment at this time. It has been the lack of such a cohesive picture that has made it difficult for managers, investors, regulators, customers, and others to view our environmental problems as a set of opportunities for companies, rather than simply a threat to business as usual.

Those opportunities are considerable. Your company's investment in the environment can yield dividends far beyond the bottom line, and far beyond the good it does for the earth. Your efforts will be leveraged, sending a loud and clear message to employees, customers, suppliers, competitors, and the communities in which you do business. That makes your company, and everyone in it, a key player in our planet's future.

introduction

FROM GREED TO GREEN

CONVENTIONAL WISDOM HAS it that if you scratch the surface of just about any environmental problem, you'll find the corporate world lurking as its root cause. And there's sound basis for this assumption. The most sensational environmental tragedies of recent years, from Three Mile Island to Love Canal to the Exxon *Valdez*, are connected to one or more large companies. That idea fits neatly with most people's overall cynicism about corporate greed and social irresponsibility.

Consider a few recent polls that point up the public's dismal opinion of the business world's concern for the environment, and the tremendous credibility gap between companies and their customers. According to a 1991 survey by Decision Research, based in Lexington, Massachusetts, only 7 percent of Americans believe companies are taking appropriate steps to protect the environment. Fully 58 percent were unable to name a single company they considered to be "environmentally conscious." When a company was named, the one most frequently mentioned (by only 8 percent of respondents) was McDonald's Corporation, followed by DuPont, Procter & Gamble, and Dow Chemical Company. However, when respondents were asked to name companies they felt were *creating* environmental problems, three of these—Dow, DuPont, and McDonald's—were among the five most frequently named.

Another study, conducted by Deloitte & Touche and the Stanford University Graduate School of Business Public Management Program, found that "American businesses are realizing that their future success in the marketplace will be directly affected by the public's perception of their environmental activities." Gary Brayton, head of Deloitte & Touche's environmental division, adds, "Consumer and competitive pressures, along with regulatory action, are pushing environmental issues to the core of the corporate strategy and policy-making process."

Even more to the point was another 1991 survey, this one conducted by Arthur D. Little, Inc., the Cambridge-based consultants. It found that Americans rank corporate environmental crimes as more serious than insider trading, antitrust violations, and worker health and safety abuses. Three-fourths of those surveyed said executives should be held personally liable for their companies' environmental offenses, up to and including serving jail time. When the executives were polled on the personal liability issue, just under half agreed. As you'll see in chapter 3, criminal liability for environmental misdeeds is becoming a growing reality for company managers and executives. The trend is clear: The public wants to hold companies accountable, and regulators, courts, and politicians are slowly but surely responding.

A TICKING TIME BOMB EXPLODES

All of this seems to have happened so suddenly. Or has it?

Until recently, the idea of environmentally responsible businesses was largely an environmentalist's pipe dream. When it came to the environment, few companies did much beyond what was mandated by federal and state laws, and many didn't even do that. It wasn't that the captains of industry deliberately tried to harm the earth, but companies had few incentives—financial or otherwise—to take proactive measures. It was often less expensive and far more expedient to pollute and suffer the consequences than to take concrete and costly action to reduce or eliminate pollution and waste. More often than not, those "consequences" were limited, or took so long in coming—if they came at all—that they were worth the short-term risk. With fast-paced economic growth and hands-off regulation throughout most of the 1980s, the environment ranked low on most companies'—and many citizens'—priority lists.

The complacency came to an abrupt end in the late 1980s with the resurgence of public environmental concern. As the twentieth anniversary of the first Earth Day approached—stimulating a new wave of environmentally concerned citizens, politicians, recording artists, and movie stars—companies found their environmental performance undergoing unprecedented scrutiny by a wide range of interests.

Suddenly, customers were asking companies to fill out environmental disclosure forms, to send out environmental information packets, and were holding their products and operations to a new set of "green" standards. Investors began asking questions and the answers had the potential to affect companies' stock prices and disrupt annual meetings with contentious shareholder resolutions. Governments around the world responded to the public's concern with a flurry of sweeping new laws, the cumulative financial impact of which could only be roughly estimated in the hundreds of billions of dollars. Bankers, insurers, and lawyers checked in, too, each with their own sets of questions, concerns, and informational burdens. And, of course, the environmentalists and the media, both national and local, began probing with renewed vigor into sometimes sensitive areas of corporate operations, from products to processes to policies.

Many companies were caught off guard. Unprepared for this wave of environmental concern, and often underestimating its significance, they resisted, stonewalled, or dismissed it all as yet another passing fancy, a set of slogans that would quickly join the ranks of "Whip Inflation Now" and "Just Say No" as short-lived testaments to the meteoric rise and fall of the public's attention span. But that was not to be.

Astute companies might have seen it coming. Issues managers—those people within companies who are in charge of tracking mid- to long-term trends—had watched environmental issues maintain a small but steady level of interest throughout the 1980s. According to John E. Merriam, whose Alexandria, Virginia–based National Media Index tracks corporate issue coverage in the major U.S. media—which, he maintains, mirrors public interest in those issues—environmental matters garnered about 2 percent of media coverage throughout most of the '80s, rising to between 4 and 5 percent by the end of the decade.

Two percent may not seem like much, but even blockbuster stories like a Chernobyl accident or an Alar apple scare typically receive only 10 to 12 percent of media coverage, and then usually only for a few weeks. Smaller but persistent levels of coverage, says Merriam, who previously served as public information director for Robert McNamara at the World Bank, create what he calls public memory of a subject, a kind of hypersensitivity that lies dormant but can spring to action when events warrant. Merriam says this kind of coverage is similar to a persistent drip of water on a rock: It may not move the rock, but over time it will make an indelible impression.

In the case of the environment, only a handful of the stories covered during the 1980s were dramatic, but the overall subject never went away. While environmental reporting beats were scarcer at major news organizations prior to 1990 than they are today, stories about air pollution, acid rain, water pollution, even global warming did find their way into print and on the air. And that, says Merriam, helped the public keep a sort of subconscious vigil on the environment as a whole, if not on the specific aspects of the problem.

All that was needed for this public subconscious to spring to the forefront was an environmental disaster. One such event occurred on March 24, 1989, when the oil tanker Exxon *Valdez* ran aground in the icy waters of Alaska's Prince William Sound.

The events of the next few days and weeks may have had as much to do with the resurgence of environmentalism as anything else. As some 11 million gallons of crude oil gushed from the stricken tanker, the Exxon Corporation, along with the federal government—not to mention the state of Alaska—faced a barrage of attacks from a wide range of fronts. For starters, both Exxon and the government reacted badly. Because there were insufficient personnel and equipment available to contain the slick, currents carried the oil far south into the Gulf of Alaska. Within weeks, the slick had fouled more than a thousand miles of shoreline, including beaches in three national parks and five wildlife refuges.

In September, Exxon officials announced that pollution no longer threatened marine and animal life and the company halted cleanup operations. Nearly everyone else—including Alaskan citizens, government investigators, and environmentalists—contended that the problem remained far from solved. Scientists are still debating the long-term damage to certain varieties of sea birds, salmon, trout, and other marine life.

The *Valdez* was only the first of what would be a horrific three months for the oil industry—and for the environment. On June 23 and 24, three more large oil tanker spills occurred, coincidentally, within twelve hours of each other, and all off the North American coast. These spills added another 850,000 gallons of crude oil into the world's oceans—into the Atlantic off the coast of Rhode Island, into the Delaware River, and into the Houston Ship Channel near Galveston Bay.

This surge of oil disasters tapped—indeed, rapped—the public memory, bringing forth a flood of images from recent history, from previous oil and chemical spills to other events known largely by their shorthand media-driven names: Amoco *Cadiz*, Chernobyl, Bhopal, Three Mile Island, Love Canal, Lake Erie, gas lines, windfall profits, and the burning Cuyahoga River. Those thoughts commingled with other contemporary images of the business world: the unraveling of the financial markets, the loss of esteem of American companies in the global marketplace, and the loss of faith in technology brought about by the *Challenger* space shuttle disaster.

Amid all this, the earth's environmental problems seemed to be getting worse. For one thing, there were new problems that didn't even exist—or at least were not widely known to exist—a decade or so before. We began hearing that our rain may be poisonous, that our summers could be getting hotter, and that we could risk skin cancer with our suntans. It was no longer just the local air and water, we learned—it was a global crisis. And the issues were and are far more frustrating: At the same time that the problems seemed to be getting much more serious, they were also getting much more removed from our control. They were at once far more remote and much more personal, potentially affecting more people far more directly. Many of them—global warming, ozone depletion, overpopulation, vanishing rain forests—seemed out of control, beyond anyone's ability to remedy within foreseeable generations. The situation has been likened to the ominous Cold War threat of imminent thermonuclear destruction many of us believed we faced during the 1950s and 1960s. Individual citizens had precious little control over that simmering situation, short of duck-and-cover air-raid exercises at school and at work. Similarly, many people today say they feel frustratingly helpless, that the solutions to today's environmental problems are less within our grasp than ever before.

And so the public resurgence in environmentalism brought about by Earth Day 1990 was there waiting to happen. Nor would it be short-lived. While the dramatic media attention paid to the subject in 1990 faded soon after Earth Day, public concern remains relatively high—or at least higher than the pre-1990 levels—and continued even through a deep recession and a war in the Persian Gulf. And corporate concern has grown, too.

Today, environmental policy and performance is near the top of many companies' agendas—as well as those of citizen and environmental groups and state and federal government agencies. But the mandate is not merely for companies to clean up their acts. Indeed, the mandate isn't even limited to polluting companies. The pressure is growing for all companies to take an active and positive role in a wide range of environmental issues, regardless of whether they are directly linked to those problems. Interestingly, the strongest pressures aren't necessarily coming from Washington, D.C., or even from state capitals; many plant managers and company executives don't see overworked and underpaid regulators as a serious threat to their livelihoods. Rather, the pressure is coming from customers—other businesses and the consuming public—and competitors, many of whom are striving for a "greener-than-thou" image. That's speeding up change and raising the level of discourse from the symbolic to the substantive.

Have the 1980s—the decade of deregulation, mergers and acquisitions, and obscene paper profits—given way to a new era of corporate enlightenment? Perhaps not entirely. But the attention paid by businesses to social responsibility, including the environment, has gone from zero to sixty in a matter of a few short years, not by all companies, but by a growing number of both large and small ones. Greed is still around, but it has been tempered by a new reality, that corporate survival is linked in part to a company's attention to its responsible role in society. Part of the new reality is a growing understanding that a healthy environment is a vital link to a healthy bottom line. That in itself represents a quantum leap in thinking.

BEYOND ZERO SUM

For years, most discussions about business and the environment amounted to a zero-sum game: profits and productivity versus the birds and the trees. Protecting the earth meant reducing a company's ability to do business. Saving resources meant losing jobs. Conserving resources at home meant sending business abroad. You simply couldn't have it both ways.

Only recently have those assumptions begun to crack and crumble. Increasingly, "doing well" is being associated with "doing good" for the earth. Conservation is no longer being seen as an inhibitor to growth, but as a stimulus for efficiency. Environmental responsibility is no longer just a corporate feel-good issue, but an obligation—to society, customers, investors, and others. To that extent, corporate environmental responsibility can be a win-win proposition, with salutary effects on both business and the earth.

For most of the past two decades, the business-environment debate has centered on "what business is doing to the environment"— the litany of corporate abuses on the air, land, and water done in the name of productivity and profits. That debate certainly hasn't disappeared—indeed, it has intensified—but it has been joined by an equally perplexing discussion: what effect a degraded environment and the increased public environmental concern may have on business's ability to be competitive and profitable. A quick glimpse at the current environmental scene begins to tell the story:

• Environmental regulations in the industrialized world have mushroomed, levying a sort of de facto tax on companies, which must devote significant resources just to fill out the paperwork. The number of pages of federal environmental regulations in the United States stood at around fifteen thousand at the end of 1992, larger than even the federal tax code. Experts believe that the cumulative number of pages of state and local environmental laws may be even greater, a multiplied burden for companies doing business in many states.

• Equally troublesome is the patchwork quilt of laws companies encounter throughout the United States and around the world. Firms doing business in several states may face different packaging laws in each jurisdiction. Similarly, companies selling products throughout Europe encounter a wide range of requirements, from Germany to Greece. When it comes to product packaging, for example, the former has the continent's most severe rules, limiting packaging to a bare minimum; in the latter, as in Japan, packaging is often seen as a sign of affluence, the more the better.

- Some of these laws require companies to disclose far more information about their operations and environmental performance than ever before. For example, in the United States, thousands of companies must report precise figures on use and emissions of nearly two hundred chemicals on a plant-by-plant basis. The implications of such disclosure are staggering. Investors, activists, regulators, media, competitors, and others now have ready access to understand a company's efficiencies and inefficiencies, and perhaps some insight into its proprietary processes. And any company can be instantly—albeit not always fairly—ranked with other companies in the same region, industry, nation, or the world as a whole.

- Cleanup costs are growing, too. The U.S. Superfund law, which requires companies that buried toxic wastes in landfills over the years to spend millions in cleanup costs, is estimated to cost at least $300 billion—two to three times as much as the savings and loan scandals of recent years. But even that number may be conservative. The handful of companies that years ago sought other means of hazardous waste disposal—involving technologies that seemed needlessly expensive at the time—are quietly smug at their prescience, having saved themselves untold millions in cleanup and liability costs.

- Increased pollution has lowered the quality of life substantially in some areas, causing workers—and sometimes businesses themselves—to move to cleaner climes. This has made it more difficult for companies to find and retain valued workers. Moreover, companies in heavily polluted areas are being forced to change their manufacturing processes, change their workers' commuting habits, and install costly new equipment. In many cases, it's far cheaper to get out of town—or get out of business altogether.

- The information requirements brought about by environmental concern have become staggering, too. Many of those requirements result directly from government regulations, but some result simply from sound business practices. For example, requirements for companies to track carefully the nature and use of manufacturing chemicals and materials are forcing valuable knowledge workers to spend their time filling out forms, often by hand, thereby keeping them from the research and development (or production, marketing, or distribution) functions they were hired to do. To reduce wasteful behavior, some companies are finding it desirable to create complex data bases pulling together information from a wide range of functions and departments; often, such information is analyzed using sophisticated artificial intelligence technology. The costs to a company in equipment and training alone can be tens of millions of dollars a year, although such investments can yield dividends in the form of such things as higher compliance, less waste, and reduced employee health claims.

That scarcely skims the surface of what's going on. But what is implicit if not explicit is that when it comes to the environment, business may be its own worst enemy. While it may be convenient to lay the blame for some of these business burdens on the hands of overzealous regulators and misguided environmentalists, the environmental buck still stops in the executive suite. At least that's what the citizenry believes.

This is not to argue that the citizenry is wrong, or to suggest that all of the above is necessary and appropriate. But reasonable or not, the price of pollution has gone up astronomically in recent years. And those costs are only a taste of what's to come: As international consensus grows that significant changes are necessary to spare the world from environmental catastrophe, new and increasingly harsh laws, taxes, and penalties will become commonplace, even in countries that historically have been easy on polluters.

PERCEPTION VERSUS REALITY

Whether or not you agree with this international consensus is largely academic, because perception far outweighs reality. Regardless of your company's record on the environment, a sizable and increasing portion of the public is looking to companies like yours to change their practices and pay for their past environmental abuses. If companies won't do it voluntarily, the public seems ready to make them do it—either directly through their purchases or indirectly by forcing harsh government action. It matters little whether either type of solution makes sense. In some cases it may. In others, the proposed solutions may be far more symbolic than substantive.

Consider the much-celebrated 1990 decision by McDonald's to ban polystyrene "clamshell" packaging in favor of paper-based wrappers in its 8,500 U.S. outlets. Previously, McDonald's had been relying on a study—"a cursory literature review," according to one insider—conducted by the Stanford Research Institute during the mid-1970s, which determined that polystyrene was environmentally preferable to paper packaging. McDonald's had tenaciously defended this position, but was under intense pressure from a relatively small group of consumers and environmentalists—including some well-organized school-group boycotts of the company—to stop using foam. In the end, the protesters prevailed. In making the announcement, McDonald's president admitted that "our customers just don't feel good about [polystyrene], so we're changing."

The foam-switching decision came just four months after McDonald's forged a relationship with the Environmental Defense Fund (EDF), intended to "identify and report on new options to reduce, reuse, recycle, and compost solid wastes produced by more than 11,000 McDonald's restaurants worldwide," in the words of the organizations' joint press release. The new EDF-McDonald's partnership caught most environmentalists and fast-food competitors of McDonald's off guard.

McDonald's decision to ban polystyrene may have been a giant leap for green consumerism—the ability of relatively few shoppers to move a large corporation—but was it, as the plastics industry maintained, not even one small step for the environment? Was the turnaround by McDonald's a function of good science or an exercise in marketplace expedience? Was EDF's motivation to change McDonald's policy that of environmental improvement or a well-publicized dragon-slaying? Both parties contend that the decision was based on years of McDonald's developing and testing new materials, on its very disappointing real-world experience trying to recycle polystyrene in its restaurants, on environmental studies done on related (though not identical) packages, and on the enormous potential to reduce solid waste that would result from the switch.

In reality, it is likely that both good science and smart marketing played a role. Few could argue that public perception of polystyrene as an environmental evil was key to both parties' motivation. Why else would a progressive organization like EDF go out on a limb, joining forces with a controversial company that for some symbolizes a wasteful, use-

The Most Serious Environmental Problems

Scientists	Citizens
Ecological Risks	• Hazardous waste sites
• *Global climate change*	• Industrial water pollution
• *Stratospheric ozone depletion*	• *Occupational exposure to chemicals*
• Habitat alteration	• Oil spills
• Species extinction	• *Stratospheric ozone depletion*
	• Nuclear power plant accidents
Health Risks	• Industrial accidents releasing pollutants
• *Criteria air pollutants (e.g., smog)*	• Radioactive wastes
• *Toxic air pollutants (e.g., benzene)*	• *Air pollution from factories*
• Radon in homes	• Leaking underground tanks
• Indoor air pollution	• Coastal water contamination
• *Drinking water contamination*	• Solid waste and litter
• *Occupational exposure to chemicals*	• *Pesticide risks to farm workers*
• *Application of pesticides*	• Water pollution from agricultural runoff
• *Stratospheric ozone depletion*	• Water pollution from sewage plants
	• *Air pollution from vehicles*
	• Pesticide residues in foods
	• *Global climate change*
	• *Drinking water contamination*

it-and-lose-it society that has squandered many of its resources? And why else would McDonald's even bother to team up with a group of activists and subject itself to this risky exercise? Obviously, both parties saw the potential for furthering their respective agendas, a potential that was handily fulfilled by their innovative and synergistic relationship.

The reality-perception gap may seem a mere annoyance or indulgence that companies must grant consumers, but there may be greater ramifications to public misperception of environmental issues. Consider a pair of 1990 surveys. One, conducted by the U.S. Environmental Protection Agency (EPA), asked a group of scientists that constitute EPA's

Scientific Advisory Board to rank the most serious environmental problems. The scientists ranked ecological and health risks separately (although one item, stratospheric ozone depletion, appeared on both lists). Another poll, from the Roper Organization and sponsored by S. C. Johnson & Son, asked a similar question of the American public. The chart on the previous page shows how each group responded, with problems named by both groups in italics.

What can we make of this mismatch in perception? What is the significance of the public's clear-cut concern for hazardous and radioactive wastes, and the scientists' absence of concern over these issues? And what about the similar public concern and scientists' lack of concern over industrial accidents, such as oil spills, nuclear power plant accidents, and leaking underground storage tanks? What about the public's apparent overreaction to the landfill and litter problems? And how can we interpret the public's apparent *under*reaction to the deleterious effect of modern society on habitats and species?

Even more important: How should your company react to these findings? Should you stick with the hard science, even if it flies directly in the face of public sentiment? Or should you give the customers what they want, even if it means exacting a higher cost on the environment? In this case, is the customer always right?

Let's zero in and take a look at the pharmaceutical industry. Here is a group of companies clearly concerned about public health, and yet involved in manufacturing processes that can involve significant releases of toxic chemicals into the environment. Moreover, some pharmaceuticals are also engaged in manufacturing other health care products, including diagnostic equipment and medical devices, which may involve potentially harmful processes and materials, including nuclear radiation.

The dilemma quickly becomes evident: Should a pharmaceutical company attempt to turn around public concern over toxic chemicals or radiation with an intensive informational campaign about plant safety and environmental practices, thereby risking forging a link in some consumers' minds between the company and environmental problems? Would an increasingly cynical public even believe the company's attempt to right the misunderstanding? Would silence on these issues be more prudent, or would that risk a costly loss of face should it be reported that a company's plant ranks high in releases of toxic chemicals among local firms?

It's hard to ignore the fact that selling ideas to the public these days is a risky proposition, especially when it comes to the environment. Consider the case of the so-called degradable trash bag.

In 1990, in the wake of Earth Day, several companies introduced plastic garbage bags they claimed were biodegradable—that is, over time they would break down into elements that caused little or no harm to the environment. The public responded enthusiastically. For example, Mobil Chemical Company's Hefty degradable trash bag, introduced in 1989, quickly picked up nearly a third of the trash bag market.

But Mobil's and others' marketing claims were subsequently refuted; practically nothing, it turns out, effectively degrades in landfills. Several companies, including Mobil and First Brands (maker of Glad Bags), were subjected to heavily publicized retreats, forced to pull their products off the shelves; they were also sued by a coalition of state attorneys general for misleading the public. In a related situation, disposable-diaper companies making degradability claims faced a similar fate—again, with considerable government scrutiny and media attention.

Since then, a wide range of TV shows, print articles, brochures, and other materials have counseled consumers not to seek out products that were claimed to be biodegradable or photodegradable. And yet polls show that a surprisingly large number of citizens—including many otherwise worldly reporters, educators, and environmentalists—still take a product's degradability into account when shopping for environmentally responsible products, and counsel others to do the same.

Why, in spite of all the publicity and information to the contrary, would consumers still believe in the myth of degradability? It's difficult to know for certain, but the idea that adding a few teaspoons of corn starch to the ingredients of a simple plastic trash bag would simply make all of our landfill problems melt away in the noonday sun is undeniably attractive. The public may have liked the idea so much they didn't want to let it go. Such a collision between the irresistible force of public opinion and the immovable object of scientific reality presents an apparent no-win situation for companies. But that doesn't have to be the case.

According to people in communications, advertising, and consumer affairs, when it comes to the environment, consumers are capable of coping with imperfect data and solutions that aren't necessarily aimed at the lowest common denominator. This school of thought claims that companies continually underestimate consumers' ability to adjust to uncertainty and change. Average citizens can deal with imperfect answers as long as they are aware of the imperfections, the thinking goes.

They can respond favorably to changing data, as long as they feel they are let in on the process.

Others disagree, countering that consumers consistently reject solutions that require a significant change of habits or are difficult to understand or implement. Indeed, the degradable trash bags were among a small handful of successful mainstream products during the first rush of "green" marketing centered around Earth Day 1990. Nine out of ten consumers were telling a succession of pollsters that if they knew Product A was kinder and gentler to the planet than Product B, they would surely choose Product A, even if it was slightly more expensive. But by the time they rolled their shopping carts to the checkout line, their purchases looked much as they always had. In other words, most American consumers balked when it came time to turn their professed environmental concern into actual shopping choices. Were they purposefully misleading the pollsters by overstating their environmental concern? Were they displaying a resistance to change? Were "green" products lacking in quality, performance, or cost competitiveness? Or were they merely confused and frustrated at the conflicting information they encountered along the aisles?

Perhaps more significant are the 1992 survey findings by the Roper Organization, which found that about one in five consumers seeks products made from or packaged in recycled materials, one in four avoided buying aerosols, and that an equal number sought out biodegradable low-phosphate detergents. Whether people actually shopped the way they say they did is another matter. In any case, they were at least aware of what they *should* be doing. That's hardly a revolution, but it does reflect a sea change in shopping criteria, if not actual purchases.

THE DELICATE DANCE OF DISCLOSURE

Companies will find themselves increasingly coping with other such delicate perception-reality disparities between themselves and their customers—not just the end users of their products and services, but a wide range of other "customers" as well: vendors, community groups, the media, environmentalists, investors, regulators, and their own employees. Each of these entities—sometimes referred to collectively as "stakeholders"—plays some role in any company's environmental performance. And each contributes to, affects, and/or is affected by a company's environmental image and impact.

This is nothing new. The media, environmentalists, and regulators have long been vital to the way a company's environmental record is perceived by the public. The kind of goods a company buys from its suppliers has always affected the quality of that company's goods and services. Community groups—which can include at least a few company employees—have always had a stake in the way plant performance affects the quality of life in the surrounding region. And investors have traditionally helped to steer the corporate ship of state, their fortunes dependent on the smoothness of the waters.

But things are changing. As these stakeholders have increasingly recognized the relationships between corporate environmental performance and the quality of their lives and fortunes, they are demanding more and better information about company operations, and are making that information more widely available than ever before.

Consider the implications of just one American law: Title III, Section 313 of the Emergency Planning and Community Right-to-Know Act of 1986, also known as the Superfund Amendments and Reauthorization Act, or SARA. That law requires U.S. manufacturers to report annually to the federal government precise data reflecting the amount of certain hazardous substances they release into the environment from their facilities. The accumulation of that data, known as the Toxics Release Inventory (TRI), is a data base that describes companies' releases to air, water, and land. Companies that must report under this act are manufacturing facilities in the United States with ten or more employees that use one or more of the TRI chemicals above certain threshold amounts.

TRI has been a boon to those desiring a peephole into how, and how much, companies are emitting potentially toxic chemicals. With the TRI came a plant-by-plant, chemical-specific, quantitative analysis of company operations. It didn't take a great deal of imagination to see how such data could become a potent tool for a variety of stakeholders to assess companies' environmental performance. Citizen groups could now rate and rank the biggest polluters in their areas. The information could become the basis of in-depth TV and newspaper reports, or simply a quick-and-dirty story listing the "dirty dozen" companies of a given area. Environmentalists, investors, and regulators each could glean their own facts and conclusions from the disclosed data.

At the same time, the data provide the companies themselves with a new tool—and plenty of incentives—for their own pollution prevention or waste reduction efforts. In fact, more than one CEO has said that until the TRI data were released, he had no idea how much waste his company was generating in the form of pollution. From there, the data became the basis for setting efficiency goals and improvements.

The Toxics Release Inventory is only one of several types of disclosure with which American companies must comply. And as the mountain of public data grows, it is finding its way into the computers of a host of organizations, each of which uses the data to suit its own agenda.

For example, the Council on Economic Priorities (CEP), a New York–based public interest group interested in corporate disclosure, used the TRI as a key part of its Environmental Data Clearinghouse, a computerized reporting service on corporate environmental performance. CEP focuses mostly on consumer-products companies. Among other things, the group rates more than two thousand consumer products in its annual guide, *Shopping for a Better World*. (In the guide, CEP rates each product on twelve social responsibility criteria, including the environment.)

For a modest sum, the Environmental Data Clearinghouse, launched in 1991, will provide a detailed analysis of a company's operations and performance to almost anyone who asks. The data are gathered from a variety of sources, including the companies themselves, and each company has a chance to respond to the report and correct inaccuracies before it is issued. A typical report offers a description of the company, its operation, products, facilities, and environmental policy. There's a section detailing environmental fines and liabilities, as well as another describing environmental awards and commendations. And, of course, there is a summary of the company's TRI emissions. Among those to whom CEP makes the data available at little or no charge are news reporters. (A more detailed description of a typical CEP report appears in chapter 3.)

There are other such services, most notably the Environmental Information Service operated by the Investor Responsibility Research Center (IRRC), a nonprofit group supported by institutional investors—insurance companies, university endowments, pension funds, and other large portfolios managed by organizations—committed to using some type of social responsibility criteria in choosing investments. IRRC's service offers environmental analyses of the Standard & Poor's five hundred companies.

The delicate dance for many companies is not in compiling this information—it is required by law—but in whether and how to voluntarily release data not required by law. For example, should a company's environmental performance be aired in its annual report? No law says it should be, but there may be some value in doing so. In line with the notion that the best defense is a good offense, a small but growing corps of companies is finding that publishing annual warts-and-all environmental reports ultimately solves more problems than it causes. They may not head off protests, litigation, and legislation, but such disclosure inevitably fosters a dialogue between companies and concerned parties, more often than not leading to improved understanding and compromise by all parties involved.

In the end, never before has so much information about company operations been so readily available directly to such a wide range of stakeholders. The potential for disclosure—voluntary or otherwise—may be one of the most powerful agents for improving companies' environmental performance.

HOW GOOD IS "GOOD ENOUGH"?

Clearly, this ongoing amassing of data about environmental performance creates new pressures and challenges for managers and executives. One big challenge is that the standards for environmental excellence are a moving target, to say the least.

This is not about the government's standards, which will always be shifting, it seems, creating ever-changing definitions of compliance and liability. This is about stakeholder standards, the usually unwritten (sometimes unconscious) and widely varying standards held by consumers, investors, competitors, and others about what makes a company "green."

There is good reason for this lack of consensus. As you will see throughout this book, the most innovative companies are leapfrogging over one another with state-of-the-art environmental policies, products, and processes. For instance, something that a few years ago seemed to be "good enough" for most people—being in compliance with most, if not all, government regulations—may now be viewed as an inadequate, bare-bones effort. In 1990, if your company recycled office waste paper, it would have been viewed as being at the forefront of corporate environmental practices. Now paper recycling programs are commonplace; indeed, you may be singled out for *not* having one. Today's forward-thinking companies have moved beyond recycling, striving to reduce waste to nothing—or at least to a bare minimum. Someday soon, such zero-waste goals will be the norm and the state of the environmental art will have moved on to other matters.

The challenge to stay current on environmental issues is enormous. Coping with regulations alone can consume the full-time attention of a small army of lawyers, engineers, and support staff. Keeping up on the technologies of your industry is another matter. And staying on top of what other companies—your competitors in particular—are doing is yet another challenge.

The good news is that companies have much to gain from successfully meeting these challenges. As you will see in later chapters, investments in cutting waste, streamlining processes, redesigning products, and educating employees and others on the environment can yield big dividends in reduced costs and increased sales and productivity. There is a small but growing body of empirical evidence showing that companies with the most proactive policies are also among the most profitable, as measured by a variety of standard measures of economic performance.

One obvious reason is that many of the efficiency measures save money. Another reason is that a leading-edge company often becomes the standard against which all companies in its industry are measured. When those measurements are being taken by federal and state regulators, that can result in a company leading regulators rather than following them. More than one progressive company has stated, privately as well as publicly, that remaining far above compliance is for them a competitive advantage. While many of their competitors scramble to install costly equipment or undergo expensive redesigns to meet tough new codes, the progressive companies are ahead of the game, doing what they do best.

None of this is a simple matter, to be sure. Forecasting is always a risky business, especially when trying to predict government action well into the next presidential administration. There's always the possibility you could over- or underanticipate the regulations, spending millions in needless costs in the process. But forecasting isn't—or shouldn't be—done in a vacuum. Few companies if any are in business simply to stay ahead of the government. Forecasts are merely a tool, to be used in collaboration with other programs and policies.

Ultimately, an important part of any company's success will be the vision of its leaders and their ability to foment change. Without that vision, backed by leadership and action, even the most well-meaning environmental initiatives are doomed to fail. Middle managers, already buffeted by a whirlwind of directives and demands, read the signals offered by senior executives as a guide to which company pronouncements require attention and action, and which are done primarily for the record. As Robert Kennedy, chairman and CEO of Union Carbide Corporation, put it: "An organization's ability to resist and defeat a direct order to do something difficult is just about infinite."

He goes on: "One doesn't change that mentality by issuing harsher directives. We do it by sharing and talking frankly about problems, showing what's at stake, removing obstacles to change, making people discontent with what is, and showing them a vision of what should be. That's being called empowerment today."

THE NEW RELATIONSHIPS

Leadership and empowerment are just two of the principal concepts that are part and parcel of the new corporate environmental consciousness. There are others, many well known to those who have dabbled in organizational development, change management, and total quality management: cross-functional teams, bottom-up leadership, systems thinking, benchmarking, continuous improvement, and so on. Each of these, worthy of entire books themselves, will be more fully discussed in subsequent chapters.

In the end, most of these concepts boil down to communications and relationships—the ability of individuals, and companies themselves, to foster a new breed of positive and proactive partnerships that benefit the environment as well as business. Many of these partnerships are ones you likely grapple with on an ongoing basis—for example, forging a partnership with your own employees that gets them to think and act like owners, or working with suppliers to improve the nature and quality of their products and services. But that's just a beginning. When it comes to integrating environmental thinking throughout your organization, some new and different kinds of partnerships may be in order—with regulators, environmentalists, customers, competitors, and communities, among others.

This is far easier said than done, and there are a myriad of land mines hidden along the way. Forging links with environmentalists, for example, can open your company to unexpected criticism, even litigation. So, too, working with regulators. And getting in bed with the competition can be fraught with difficulties, from acrimony to antitrust. Many aspects of the openness that comes with these partnerships will no doubt raise a few legal eyebrows among your organization's counsel and could incite a fractious debate among its leaders. The risks of such actions are incalculable.

But doing nothing is even riskier. There is a strong likelihood that one or more of your competitors are embracing some of these ideals, putting one or more of these green business tools to work. Your customers may well be eyeing your operations in a new light, looking to reduce their liability, improve their image, and satisfy their own constituencies by seeking products and services from companies with a demonstrated commitment to environmental excellence. Many of your corporate and institutional customers already have policies requiring them to consider the environmental implications of their purchases—including the performance of their suppliers. And as their standards rise, simply complying with the law will no longer be enough.

The choices may be tough ones, but the potential rewards are significant.

ENTER THE E-FACTOR

Reaping the rewards takes some time and effort. Exactly how much and what kind depends a great deal on the nature of your company—its leadership, its corporate culture, and its awareness of and interest in the relationship between business operations and the environment. Not every company approaches this subject from the same perspective, uses the same tools, or experiences the same outcomes.

But an examination of dozens of the companies leading in environmental excellence shows that there are several keys to success. In the chapters that follow, you will hear from and about some of these companies and the policies and processes that have enabled them to integrate environmental thinking into their operations—from strategic planning to manufacturing to marketing and sales.

The remaining chapters are arranged into six key concepts. The first two, chapters 2 and 3, provide the rationale for total environmental quality; the last four chapters describe the steps companies have taken to get there. The key concepts are:

The Rationale

1. **Economics**—the new understanding of the relationships between economics and ecology. Now that we are able to quantify the costs our actions have on the environment, there is a new basis for company actions. Increasingly, the marketplace, not the government, will drive a growing number of environmental decisions.

2. **Enforcement**—the growing pressures on companies to improve their environmental performance and the consequences resulting from their failure to do so. Those consequences are driven not just by government regulators but by a wide range of others, including customers, lenders, insurers, employees, and local communities.

The Process

3. **Empowerment**—the importance of leadership and corporate vision in fostering change. Behind nearly every successful effort is a leader whose commitment to environmental excellence creates the foundation for positive action. Such leadership provides the basis for a company policy and action plan, and the incentives—and disincentives—for change.

④ **Education**—the need for communication, openness, and new partnerships between companies and their customers, suppliers, regulators, stockholders, and the general public.

⑤ **Efficiency**—the need for companies to integrate the ideas of pollution prevention, waste reduction, energy efficiency, and process redesign throughout their operations. This is the goal of most "greening" efforts, where the biggest bottom-line savings take place.

⑥ **Excellence**—the need to merge Total Quality Management principles with environmental practices, including measuring and accounting for environmental improvements, using traditional TQM and accounting measures. To do this often requires creating new kinds of information and accounting systems.

It is important to point out that few if any of the organizations profiled in this book could be deemed perfectly "green" businesses. Indeed, few show up on lists of the most socially progressive companies. Several are in industries that the public perceives as being among the most notorious polluters. Nearly all of these forward-thinking firms have environmental skeletons in their corporate closets and some, despite their environmental leadership, still rate high on lists of the biggest emitters of toxic substances. Many companies are grappling with the consequences of careless actions taken decades ago, when they followed then-traditional business practices for manufacturing or waste disposal. In other words, when it comes to the environment, practically no one's perfect—not by a long shot.

But that's less important than the fact that these companies have started on the long journey toward environmental excellence, cleaning up their messes, improving efficiencies, and fomenting cultural change—one step at a time. All have experienced successes, often quantified in the form of dramatically decreased wastes, emissions, and costs. Few of these firms will ever reach environmental perfection, but that hasn't stopped them from trying. How far they ultimately get is irrelevant.

What's important is that they have taken some good, green steps toward the twenty-first century.

economics

2

HOW MUCH IS A CLEAN EARTH WORTH?

IF A TREE falls in the forest and no one's around to claim it, does it have a value?

This is more than a mere twist on a classic conundrum. Measuring the economic value of the earth's resources—trees, fresh air, clean water, and a diversity of animals, insects, plants, and microorganisms—has become both a cause and a challenge for some economists. And though the science of ecological economics is nascent, companies are increasingly feeling its impact. In coming years, the manner by which we as a global society choose to value resources—and devalue them when they become expended or polluted—could affect tax rates, energy costs, balance sheets, and the prices of just about everything, from life's basic necessities to its most indulgent luxuries. The inevitable shifts in corporate accounting practices may well be felt throughout the world's economies.

Consider that falling tree. Essentially, the question posed above asks whether the tree becomes more or less valuable when it is cut down or dies and falls, compared to its worth when it is stands healthy in a forest.

To understand the economics of our tree we need to take a brief inventory of a tree's value and to look at both the conventional and ecological economists' view of a tree—when it is standing and after it has fallen. For that, we'll turn to Robert Costanza, a biologist at the University of Maryland, and a founder of the International Society of Ecological Economics.

"The conventional economics view is that unless something impinges on people's preferences—unless someone is there to hear the tree fall—it has no value," says Costanza. "That's what we're trying to get away from. There are physical things going on that we can point to. We're trying to get beyond bringing everything back to market valuations. Not that we should ignore the market, but we can't be limited by the places to where the market extends. There's a lot going on in the world that's not covered by market interactions."

As an example, Costanza points to a variety of services performed by that standing tree customers generally don't perceive as valuable, though scientists do. Such services include trees' role in erosion control, in moderating global carbon dioxide cycles, as habitat for wildlife, and as a source of recreational opportunities for humans—camping, hiking, picnicking, and so on. "Recreation values are the closest we come to the market," says Costanza. "And that's where a lot of those with conventional economics backgrounds spend time worrying because that's something that people do perceive as a valuable product, although it's generally not marketed. If you asked the standard consumer, 'How much is having the forest there to prevent soil erosion worth to you?', that's just not a well-posed question, and not one you'd get a very interesting answer to, mostly because that consumer is not consuming that service directly."

Of course, a fallen tree has value, too—as lumber, as firewood for chilly campers, or, when decomposing, as a source of nutrients that will be returned to the soil and taken up by other plants and trees. Theoretically, one could calculate the value of these things as well.

So, the route to determining the value of a standing or fallen tree is to examine the forest, tracing the trees' physical and biological impacts.

Are such calculations possible? Not really—yet. Says Costanza: "I think we're getting pretty close. We do have some ideas. The models are there to begin to do that, although they could be vastly improved. But I also believe the whole issue of uncertainty is going to remain a critical one. The fact is, we're never going to know with a very high degree of precision the answer to these sorts of questions because there's so much uncertainty inherent in the problem. We could reduce the range of uncertainty, but it will always be there."

Costanza and three colleagues took a stab at one set of calculations in 1988, when they tried to establish market and nonmarket values of forest and other lands within the state of Georgia. To do so, the group relied upon two relatively simplistic approaches to assessing value. One approach, which has been used for years in conducting cost-benefit analyses for dams built by the U.S. Army Corps of Engineers, seeks to measure nonmarket values by determining through surveys what people would be willing to pay for natural resources and services if a suitable market existed. So, for example, consumers might be asked, "How much would you personally be willing to pay to have a forest in which you can hike?" A similar technique was used in 1990 by the Bonneville Power Administration, which canvassed 3.6 million consumers to learn that they would be willing to pay an average of $13.30 each, or a total of $48 million, to avoid having a nuclear power plant built near them. In contrast, the consumers said they would pay only about $5.50 each to avoid a new hydroelectric plant. That $7.80 differential represents the relative values of the nuclear and hydroelectric plants to that group of consumers. And because it also mirrors the relative value of the environmental disruption each might cause, it provides some rough insight into the price the public places on certain environmental benefits.

Another method of valuing the natural environment is somewhat more complex. It measures the total amount of energy captured by natural ecosystems (in the form of sunlight, among other things) as an estimate of their potential to do useful work for society. That involves estimating the amount of energy, converting that number to the equivalent in coal or oil, and placing a dollar value on these fuels. All of this calls upon certain economic assumptions, each of which is subject to debate and further refinement.

As you can see, both methods have their drawbacks, and both offer only partial pictures of the actual value of a tree, forest, or other natural resource. Still, using these admittedly flawed systems, Costanza and colleagues were able to peg the value of an acre of undeveloped forest in Georgia. Indeed, both methods yielded similar estimates of around two hundred dollars per acre per year. For the state as a whole, these natural and undeveloped ecosystems were valued at $2.6 billion, a number roughly comparable to the annual marketed production of agriculture ($2.8 billion) and timber ($4.5 billion), both very important industries in Georgia. The researchers did not attempt the micro view in this study by attempting to calculate the value of a single tree.

All of this is more than mere academic noodling. Resolving such issues could be key to designing sustainable forestry programs, in which companies can harvest some of the forest's products in a way that does not undermine the forest's other assets—its recreation value, soil conservation value, global gas balance value, and all the rest. Proper valuation could also help create government programs that are different from the ones we have now, which are based primarily on the value of timber. In short, placing our values more in line with real environmental costs will help us view both the forest and the trees in more complete economic and ecological terms.

TAKING NATURE INTO ACCOUNT

O.K., so the minutia of arboreal economics may have little to do with day-to-day life in the corporate trenches. Much like traditional economics, few senior executives and top managers will need to be well versed in this stuff. But—as with traditional economics—that doesn't mean that these theories won't affect their jobs in profound ways. To explain further requires delving a bit more into the sometimes arcane world of economics. While all of this may seem mostly theoretical, and more than a little mysterious, the journey is well worth the effort. Nearly anyone seeking to be a key corporate player in the twenty-first century will need a working knowledge of the emerging theories behind ecological economics. What follows is a layperson's overview of the subject. There is a growing body of literature on the subject for those interested in pursuing it further. (Please refer to the resources in the back of this book for additional information.)

Let's begin with what we know. Conventional macroeconomics deals almost exclusively with money—what we make and what we spend. Whether we look at an individual's monthly income and expenses or the sum total of monetary flows throughout nations or the entire world, the theories and measurement tools remain fairly consistent. Most theories focus on individual, firm, or societal behavior—the flow of a nation's monetary wealth among the citizenry, regardless of whether that wealth is equitably distributed.

A small but increasingly influential school of economic theory says that measuring and tracking money alone isn't enough. For one thing, the old way assumes that bigger is better, and that more is always desirable. That may be true to an extent—some of the poorest Third World nations are also among the most polluted—but Costanza, World Bank economist Herman Daly, and other ecological economists say that such thinking ignores some very important points. For starters, it overlooks the fact that, much like the nonmarket value of the forest, a sizable piece of any nation's "wealth" can be found in such things as air quality, energy reserves, viable wetlands, and the diversity of flora and fauna.

Consider the gross national product, or GNP. As nearly every college graduate knows, GNP represents the sum total of all goods and services bought and sold in a country over a given time—food, shelter, clothing, haircuts, funerals, vacations, forklifts, bar tabs, plumbing contractors, consultants, car washes, and so on. Originally designed to measure war production, GNP considers only *paid* production, omitting unpaid labor (such as housework) and the impact of economic decisions on future generations. Still, GNP has become a conventional measure of a nation's wealth: The higher the GNP and the faster its rate of growth, the better off the citizenry, at least in theory.

But is that really the case? Consider the notorious Exxon *Valdez* oil spill. Estimates put the cost of cleaning up the mess—in the form of jobs, equipment, and supplies and resources needed to accomplish this Herculean task—at around $2.5 billion, not including repair of the ship itself (or of restoring Exxon's tarnished public image) or the $1 billion settlement Exxon negotiated with claimants. That $2.5 billion cleanup tab became part of the gross national product of the United States over several years.

But was the nation an economically healthier one as a result of the *Valdez* spill? Certainly not. GNP figures may not fully reflect the loss of fishing by Alaskan natives, the loss of the spilled oil, lost tourism, the effects the oil may have over the years in the form of depleted plant and animal populations, and the biological value these creatures would have provided to the larger ecosystem. And what if there were a thousand

Valdez-like spills a year, each adding another several billion dollars to the economy? While the nation's wealth, as measured by GNP, would grow significantly, it is doubtful that such growth would be desirable in the larger scheme of things. Indeed, over time, such incidents and their resulting expenditures could lead to a decrease in real GNP to the extent that they divert resources from the production of more desirable things. If our money, in the form of taxes and higher gasoline prices, is tied up in oil-spill mitigation, we will have less to spend on Christmas presents, college tuition, industrial expansion, and everything else.

Simply put, using traditional GNP measurements, a nation could rape its forests, plunder its energy reserves, render its water undrinkable and its air unbreathable, and hunt and fish its wildlife to virtual extinction—and still show signs of economic health in the form of a growing GNP, at least for a while. But chances are, such a nation would not remain competitive, or even viable, for long.

Clearly, a nation can suffer hangovers from its economic binge: congestion, pollution, depleted resources, social inequities, and other manifestations of a large, complex system out of balance. So, GNP alone is an inadequate measure of economic wealth and health.

Or consider the law of supply and demand. This law—the fundamental building block of any free-market system—states that price is relative to supply. As supply decreases, prices go up; they drop when supplies become bloated. So, a car dealer with excess inventory at the end of a model year will dramatically cut prices, but will raise them if there is a shortage of a particularly popular model. Such market machinations also affect our behavior outside the marketplace: If something is in short supply, we will use it more carefully than something that is in abundance—our leisure time, for example.

But what if something has no known price, or is perceived as "free"? That's certainly the case with clean air and water, healthy wetlands, and other natural resources. If they are taken for granted because we do not fully appreciate their value, logic would dictate that these "commodities" won't be adequately protected and conserved. In other words, when a resource has no known "price," it is likely to be squandered. (Again, consider leisure time.)

So, some type of improved measurement system may be in order, one that more accurately values these things. Currently, economists, ecologists, and others are debating what type of system we need. Ideally, it should account for such things as ecosystem services (the economic value of plants' ability to clean the air, for example, or of trees to reduce soil erosion) and natural capital (such as the value of untapped energy reserves, forests, minerals, and wildlife). In short, it should recognize that "the ecosystem constitutes the primary asset base of a country and is the hinge upon which successful development will turn," says Thomas A. Robertson, a Washington, D.C., consultant and former coordinator of the Energy Center at the University of Florida.

Such thinking has already worked its way into the national accounting systems of a few countries. In Norway, for example, the gross domestic product reflects the value of petroleum, minerals (copper, iron, lead, titanium, and zinc), forest products, fish, and hydropower resources. Their value may be negatively offset by the discharge of selected air and water pollutants. France has been trying to create a national accounting system known as "patrimony accounting," intended to analyze and describe the natural environment in its three principal functions: economic, ecological, and social. Germany is attempting to quantify its "gross ecological product," employing statisticians and economists at its Federal Statistical Office to merge the country's natural resource accounts with its national income accounts, with the aim of creating a methodology for measuring ecological costs. And the World Bank is working with the United Nations in Mexico and Papua New Guinea to create a system of "environmentally adjusted economic accounts" to derive gross domestic product statistics. In doing so, these countries' assets have been expanded to include such things as soil, wetlands, and biodiversity, and liabilities now include the costs of degradation of these resources as the result of productive activities.

There have been several attempts to create such measurement systems in the United States, though none has yet become widely accepted. In their 1989 book, *For the Common Good*, Daly and John Cobb proposed an Index of Sustainable Economic Welfare (ISEW), which attempted to adjust GNP to account mainly for depletions of natural capital, pollution effects, and income distribution. They concluded that while the United States' GNP grew between 1956 and 1986, its ISEW had remained relatively unchanged since about 1970, if one takes into account such things as the loss of farms and wetlands, the effects of acid rain, devalued tourist locations, species loss, and pollution-related health costs.

Such factors, says Tom Robertson, "when seen from a more complete and coherent perspective, represent a degradation of a nation's total asset base, and a loss in the ability of the country to produce to meet its needs. In other words, degradation of the environment means far more than the loss of species and diversity, or polluted air, land, and water. Environmental degradation means the loss of productive capacity, a decline in the ability of a nation to support its population, and growing resistance to the ability of a place to achieve satisfying, sustainable standards of living." In the end, he says, the degradation results in the "loss of an ability to compete in the larger scale of regional and global economies."

That's serious stuff, but how does it relate to the activities of a single company? Surely, over the long term, any companies would be affected by the larger community's ability to assimilate and neutralize its wastes. The quality of an area's local sewer system, water supply, and air are just three of the criteria companies consider when investing in new or expanded facilities. When any of these criteria are inadequate, a region's attractiveness to business declines. Witness the exodus of businesses from Southern California or Mexico City in recent years, as those regions' unhealthy air quality increasingly hindered daily life. (One observer, writing on the *Wall Street Journal* editorial page, even suggested that Southern California's air pollution, having led to increased unemployment, was a principal cause of the 1992 Los Angeles riots. Meanwhile, the mayor of Mexico City proposed that the city solve its smog problem by having two thousand huge fans blow it away—propelled by fossil fuels.) And in Eastern Europe, high levels of environmental contamination are scaring off investors. Agfa, the German photographic film manufacturer, turned down the opportunity to recover its old plant near Bitterfield, which was confiscated under Communism in what had been East Germany. "Agfa has said the place is too dirty," a German government official told *The New York Times.*

In the shorter term, the concepts underlying ecological economics may show up in a variety of government regulations that could significantly, sometimes dramatically, affect company operations. Los Angeles is just one of many polluted American cities in which employers are, or soon will be, faced with the unenviable task of having to force employees out of their cars. Specifically, under state and federal regulations, they must increase the average number of employees in each vehicle by 25 percent, based on regional averages. Mandatory company plans will be incorporated into state plans, which must be submitted to the federal government. Companies that fail to attain the mandated "average vehicle ridership" by targeted dates could be subject to federal, state, or local fines. As a result of all this, companies are scrambling to induce—or force—employees to change their daily habits using any number of carrots and sticks.

The commuting challenge is just one of many demands made on companies doing business in regions with polluted or diminished resources. And for many companies, such intrusions raise the cost of doing business enough to drive them from the area. Even nonpolluting companies, or those that have already instituted greener policies, can be swept up in this kind of eco-dragnet.

One far-reaching proposal, from Costanza, Daly, and others, could more fairly balance the costs. It has to do with a "flexible environmental assurance bonding system designed to incorporate environmental criteria and uncertainty into the market system, and to induce positive environmental technological innovation," as Costanza describes it. The basic idea is to link the costs of pollution more closely with the polluters, and their products and services. As Costanza and Daly describe it in the introduction to the textbook *Ecological Economics*: "In addition to direct charges for known environmental damages, a company would be required to post an assurance bond equal to the current best estimate of the largest potential future environmental damages; the money would be kept in interest-bearing escrow accounts. The bond (plus a portion of the interest) would be returned if the firm could show that the suspected damages had not occurred or would not occur. If they did occur, the bond would be used to rehabilitate or repair the environment and to compensate injured parties." In doing so, the burden of proof would be shifted from the public to the resource user and a strong economic incentive would be provided to research the true costs of environment damaging activities and to develop cost-effective pollution control technologies.

Is it really feasible to account for environmental inputs and outputs in a way that would be meaningful for chief financial officers, stockholders, and others? Some think so. Since the 1970s, scholars have been proposing some kind of corporate environmental accounting systems (CEAS) based on a company's inputs and outputs. One such system, described in 1975 by Arieh A. Ullman, a Swiss academic, would measure the "annual environmental effects connected with regular business operations: consumption of materials and energy, generation of solid waste,

[and] discharge of pollutants into air, water and soil," he wrote in the journal *Accounting, Organizations, and Society.* "Since there are many materials and various sorts of pollutants, a special account should be established for each."

Ullman's plan would institute a series of Equivalent Factors, established by governments, equating various environmental impacts— how much water pollution equals how much air pollution, and so on. This would enable a company to assess the net environmental benefit of, say, installing air pollution abatement equipment that might result in increased water pollution, or to compare the energy and pollution involved with recycling a material to that involved with creating virgin materials. Multiplying Equivalent Factors with relative inputs and outputs of physical units—tons of coal, cubic feet of water, kilowatt-hours, etc.—would result in CEAS-units.

Those CEAS-units would in effect become a company's environmental stock in trade. Combined with government credits granting each company a given number of units, it would establish a baseline amount of energy consumption and pollution creation.

Key to Ullman's thinking are what economists call "externalities"—the costs and benefits of production or consumption that are not borne by producers and consumers. These costs are "external" because they are not reflected in the market price of goods and services. (Market prices are said to reflect only "internal" or private costs and benefits.)

For example, though a gallon of unleaded gasoline might be priced $1.25 at the pump, the actual cost may be significantly greater. If you consider that gasoline's externalities—the environmental impact of drilling and shipping the crude oil and refined gas, for example, or the cost of cleaning up damage to air that results from burning the gas in an internal combustion engine, perhaps even the military costs of protecting and defending strategic oil reserves—the true cost of that gallon could be many times greater than the pump price. Indeed, the estimated $60 billion the United States and its allies spent on the 1991 Persian Gulf war alone would nearly double the actual cost of each barrel of oil imported from that region during the year.

Ullman and others suggest that companies and consumers begin to incorporate some of these external costs into the prices of goods and services so that they more fairly reflect their impact on the environment. That will make environmentally destructive products and services far more expensive than their more benign counterparts.

This brief examination into the world of ecological economics begins to describe the complex economic calculations inherent in nearly any pollution-prevention initiative. It also suggests other factors that have to be considered: political ramifications, the effects of decisions on the marketplace, how competitors and customers will view actions, and the real benefits to be derived from any given strategy. These are not just matters for the accounting department, of course. They will require input from a variety of sources inside and outside the company. And they must be coordinated, synthesized, and analyzed so as to make them understandable by key individuals who happen to be neither accountants nor scientists.

Slowly, very slowly, companies are beginning to appreciate the direct impact of what has so far been a largely academic debate on proper valuing of the environment. And as the twentieth century closes, the speed of change will accelerate, as companies increasingly find it necessary to accurately account for the environmental costs of just about everything they do.

For most companies, now is the time to begin because, already, environmental costs to business are spiraling out of control. In 1992, U.S. companies spent $115 billion complying with environmental regulations, according to EPA, about 2.1 percent of the gross national product. By decade's end, that portion of GNP could rise to as high as 2.8 percent. Whatever the number, it would suggest that chief financial officers and business managers at affected companies will need systems in place to account for and allocate these costs in order to keep them within reasonable bounds. Unfortunately, few companies have a handle on the environmental impacts of their operations, let alone on their individual plants, products, and processes.

Just talk to Tony Dorfmueller, a retired worldwide group vice president at Ashland Chemical, who now works with companies in the process industry on environmental, health, and safety (EHS) issues. "When I go into a company, I ask the CEO two questions," says Dorfmueller. "The first is, 'How much are your EHS efforts costing you?' I have yet to find one executive who knows the answer to that question. The answer to the second question, then, will be obvious, but I ask them anyway: 'Are you allocating your EHS costs to each product you sell?' Of course, there's always an embarrassed silence."

Dorfmueller contends that the ignorance behind that silence will be increasingly costly to companies. Without sufficient analysis of costs and benefits, companies may be spending more than necessary on environmental initiatives that bring little benefit, and not enough on others that could produce substantial improvements. Without this information, it's difficult to tell where the laws of diminishing returns kick in. Is it more cost effective to outfit your widget factory with state-of-the-art emissions control devices? Or would it make more sense to reformulate your widget recipe to reduce emissions, even if it raises the unit costs and lowers profit margins? Perhaps the most cost-effective move would be simply to manufacture fewer widgets. You can't make the right decision unless you have the right data.

All of this points up the need for better ways to measure and analyze the things companies do. In chapter 7 we'll examine some of the ways companies are evaluating their operations and measuring their improvements, two key elements of most successful total quality management programs.

ACCOUNTING, FROM CRADLE TO GRAVE

As economists slowly begin to address how environmental concerns can be factored into accounting practices, companies will eventually be asked, if not required, to translate these concepts into balance sheets, profit-and-loss statements, and other standard indicators of economic performance. Doing so will be no mean feat. For a company to fully account for the environmental costs of its operations will require that each product or service be analyzed for its inputs and outputs: the nature and amount of resources that go into a product or service (as well as into the company itself) and wastes and by-products that result from products' manufacture, use, and disposal.

Such cradle-to-grave thinking is known as life-cycle assessment (also called life-cycle analysis), or LCA. A basic definition of an LCA is "a method to holistically evaluate the consequences associated with the cradle-to-grave life cycle of a product or process," according to an EPA task force studying this topic. Put another way, LCAs are where ecological economics meets the factory floor—and the accounting department.

The subject of life-cycle assessments is not entirely new, but it is just beginning to gain some consensus among both ecologists and some economists. Until recently, most efforts to identify and measure inputs and outputs were incomplete, examining only a part of the product or its life cycle. And the information used in the analyses rarely ventured outside the factory gates—where the raw materials were generated, and where the wastes ultimately are disposed.

For example, Migros-Genossenschafts-Bund, a Swiss cooperative that is that country's largest retailer, several years ago created a computer program to evaluate the "eco-balance"—the life cycle—of product packaging. With a few clicks of the keys on a standard personal computer, nearly anyone could compare two or more products' packaging, calculating the kinds of resources needed to make and dispose of the package. For example, using its *Eco Base 1* computer program, Migros determined that when compared with a cardboard milk carton, a returnable glass milk bottle used only about 40 percent as much energy and created only 40 percent of the air burden and just 20 percent of the water burden. When using a polyethylene "tubular bag" to package milk, the energy consumption and air and water burdens fell to about 20 percent of that needed for cardboard cartons. But the computer program has its limitations. For one thing, it "does not allow any general statements to be made about individual packing materials," according to a Migros document. "It is rather a question of elaborating various alternative solutions." Moreover, "some packing materials have very special properties which for individual packaging tasks are so important that one cannot do without them. . . . This is the reason why Migros does not in principle close its eyes to any packing material."

Migros's pioneering effort is beginning to pale in comparison with some of the newer LCA models. Consider the following analysis of a typical bar of household soap, described with the help of Tim Ream, an EPA environmental protection specialist in Research Triangle Park, North Carolina. Ream is part of a team of researchers in government and the private sector working to fine-tune and standardize the LCA process.

Ream says that a basic LCA model of a soap bar shows four kinds of inputs—resources that go into manufacturing the soap—and five kinds of outputs—waste, pollution, and usable products that result from the manufacturing process. The inputs include tallow, sodium hydroxide, additives (such as pigments or perfumes), and the energy and labor used in the process. At the other end, the outputs include usable products (mostly the soap itself), air emissions, liquid wastes, solid wastes, and other environmental emissions.

That's a simple LCA inventory of inputs and outputs, but it's not useful because it is only a summary of the entire direct process and doesn't tell the whole story. To be useful, this inventory must be expanded to include a more comprehensive range of resources and processes. "Ideally, you would be able to draw a dotted line around each of the life-cycle stages," says Ream. "It's important to do that because later on you want to be able to say, 'Of all the impacts that a bar of soap has on the environment, which ones are the ones we should be most concerned about? Which are the areas where we have the greatest opportunity for improvement?' That's why the simplified diagram won't help you. With the simplified diagram you might not be able to say, 'Hey look, all of our negative impacts are coming from the use of tallow. If we can only find a substitute for the tallow we're using, then we could make a much lower-impact product.' "

Tallow comes from the fat of cattle. Incorporating it into a soap-making LCA requires accounting for the various materials and processes involved with cattle raising: the preparation of soil, the planting of seeds, and the application of fertilizer and pesticides needed to grow a crop that can be fed to the cows. The cows will eventually be slaughtered and rendered into tallow, all of which takes energy and uses other resources.

Another aspect of soap production requires the use of chlorine and sodium hydroxide. Chlorine is used in pulp mills to produce the soap's paper package; the sodium hydroxide is used in the actual soap production. Making sodium hydroxide requires taking salt water and running an electric current through it; the process yields chlorine as a by-product. Accounting for the process requires the inputs for the electricity itself, which likely is generated by coal or oil. But there are practical limitations. Says Ream: "There's always a question in LCA about how far back you should go. In this case, you'd go back as far as the coal that fired the electric plant. You probably don't go back as far as forging the metal to build the machine that dug the coal. But it's very important to lay out that entire process so that any end user of the information that produced the LCA can very clearly see where the boundaries are drawn."

Paper making is next. Tracing that would likely lead from the seedlings planted in the forest to the harvesting of the trees, which are then fed into a pulp mill along with the chlorine and other ingredients. The finished product, paper, is then wrapped around the bar of soap. Ultimately, it will be disposed of by the consumer, where it will be sent to a municipal landfill or incinerator; in some cases, it may be recycled.

Simplified Life-Cycle Analysis for a Bar of Soap

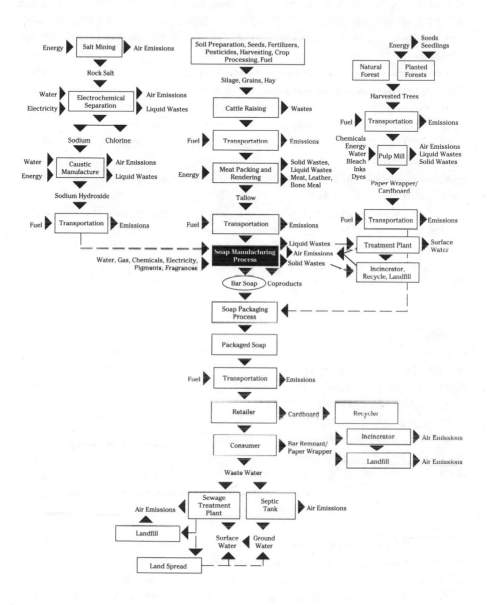

Each of those processes will have additional inputs and outputs.

And then there's the distribution process, which takes the soap from factory to market, where it's taken home by the consumer. The principal input here is the fuel needed for transportation. The "product" of this stage is really the movement of the soap from one place to another.

Finally, the soap is used by the consumer. In the case of soap, there are few emissions other than the soap dissolving in water and heading off to a water treatment plant, where treating it—along with other waste water—involves additional chemicals and energy.

With all of these processes quantified, an analyst can isolate discrete portions of the process, adding up all the inputs and outputs. But the value of the flow diagram that results from all this information has a lot to do with how it is used. The raw numbers alone provide little help. It takes rigorous interpretation and analysis to turn the numbers into meaningful information that can ultimately be used to reduce waste and maximize resource use.

The point here is the complexity of analyzing something as simple as a bar of soap, a small solid brick of relatively pure ingredients, with no moving parts, and requiring little energy to use. Contrast this with a washing machine, a relatively sophisticated machine made of various metals and plastics, whose use involves sizable quantities of water, energy, and detergent. Or even a can of freeze-dried chicken noodle soup, with a dozen or more ingredients and several layers of paper and plastic packaging.

Says Tim Ream: "You can see that making even a bar of Ivory soap, which is ninety-nine and forty-four one-hundredths percent pure, is still not a very simple process to describe. That really is the crux of life-cycle assessments. On one hand, you want to come up with an analysis that describes all the possible impacts. On the other hand, there is such an interrelatedness and interconnectedness of both natural and industrial processes that the drawing of the lines in an LCA is a difficult thing to do."

Obviously, analyzing even the bar of soap could go on and on—to include, say, the gas used to power the chain saw that cut the tree used to make the paper wrapper. And where to draw the boundaries of LCA is one of the issues that must be resolved before LCAs can be widely used and relied upon. If too many factors are included, the equations may be too complex, inhibiting widespread use. Too few factors might omit key components of a product's life cycle, yielding inaccurate results. The challenge for Ream and his colleagues is to analyze the quantity and quality of data to establish a workable methodological framework. That process will be an ongoing one. LCA experts describe a triangle showing the three "I's" of the LCA process: Inventory (measuring the inputs and outputs), Impact (evaluating the data), and Improvement (fine-tuning the first two steps). LCA, then, is the embodiment of the continuous improvement process key to total quality management.

To make LCAs work, they must be accessible at the plant level, where much of the key data needed for LCA exists. Chances are, you can't easily approach your plant manager and say, "Give me all your input and output information for this plant," without getting escorted politely to the door. Still, it isn't necessary for the process to be perfected before LCA can be put to use. The technology exists now to do simple life-cycle analyses that can be used for such things as strategy tools and to optimize manufacturing practices.

For example, an LCA sponsored by Procter & Gamble in 1990 examined the impacts of disposable and reusable cloth diapers. P&G, of course, is maker of Pampers and Luvs brand diapers, which command roughly half the $4 billion-a-year disposable-diaper market.

The Procter & Gamble LCA, which was conducted by Arthur D. Little, Inc., concluded that manufacturing and using disposables consumes more raw materials than cloth diapers and generates more solid waste, while making and using cloth diapers consumes more water and energy and releases higher levels of water and air pollutants than do disposables. On balance, the researchers concluded that "the specific health, environmental, and economic advantages of disposable diaper products appear to outweigh the more limited advantages of the reusable diaper products."

That may not be a surprising finding for a study sponsored by a disposable-diaper maker, but Little's Karen Blumenfeld, who helped conduct the study, says it was all aboveboard. "If a company chooses to publicly release a life-cycle report, anyone can attack it and pull it apart to figure out whether they agree with the assumptions or not. P&G's life-cycle study was attacked left and right, but its conclusions stood up."

Blumenfeld, a senior consultant in the firm's Environmental Business and Strategy Unit, points out that few people are likely ever to agree on the methodology of a life-cycle analysis. "It would be very difficult to get every expert to agree on what the right boundaries are and what the right assumptions are for a particular study. There are no perfect data bases. I think that the state of affairs of life-cycle assessment being what it is, you have to look for an organization that is experienced and whose judgment you trust, because there are a lot of judgment calls, and there always will be. EPA tried to come out with the how-to cookbook approach. They realized you can't, because every case is different—every case has its own unique considerations. There are certain aspects you can standardize, but many things just have to be decided on a case-by-case basis."

Danger lurks for those who use LCA casually or carelessly. Says the EPA's Timothy Mohin: "If you use LCA data, you must be prepared to show your methodology and open it up to peer review. If you can't stomach that possibility, you're not ready."

SMOG FUTURES AND GREEN TAXES

The ability to more precisely quantify the inputs and outputs of daily business is the first step to better controlling them. And if some emerging trends continue, companies will have strong economic incentives to have a handle on such data.

Consider a brave new experiment created by the 1990 Clean Air Act that aims to bring the price of electricity more in line with the impact that generating it has on the environment. Although still in its infancy, this experiment already appears to be the wave of the future. And it sheds a bit of light into how polluters will increasingly be forced to pay for the pollution they create—and how pollution prevention could become a profit center for some companies in the near future.

This experiment contrasts with the past two decades or so of environmental regulations, which have used the command-and-control approach to reduce pollution. Much like General Colin Powell's quotable military strategy for defeating the Iraqi army during the Persian Gulf war—"First we're going to cut it off, then we're going to kill it"—this style of regulation aims to isolate the individual pollutants associated with specific companies or industries, with the intention of controlling, and eventually reducing or eliminating, those emissions.

That is the ultimate goal, of course, but command-and-control regulations have their limits for most pollutants. (Some pollutants, such as CFCs, polychlorinated biphenyls, and the pesticide DDT, are so detrimental that they require command-and-control efforts for them to be phased out or banned.) Such regulations provide companies with little incentive to go beyond compliance and develop innovative technologies or manufacturing practices. They don't encourage the greatest amount of pollution reduction technologically feasible. And they require constant and expensive monitoring by regulatory officials. Simply put, they strive for mediocrity, not excellence.

The new U.S. experiment aims more toward excellence. It has to do with the relatively abstruse world of sulfur dioxide (SO_2) emissions. SO_2, a key ingredient in the production of acid rain, results primarily from the burning of high-sulfur coal by electric-generating utilities. Once in the air, SO_2—along with nitrogen oxides, which also result from utility-generated combustion—combine with other airborne chemicals (such as automobile exhaust) and water to form sulfuric and nitric acid, and undergo further chemical reactions to become sulfates and nitrates. When these chemicals mix with rain, sleet, snow, hail, or fog, they fall to earth, where they can wreak havoc on everything from the lives of water-borne organisms to human respiratory systems to the high-gloss finishes on expensive cars.

However devastating this so-called acid rain may be, the cost of reducing its emissions isn't cheap. And the 1990 clean air law aims to cut SO_2 emissions in half by the year 2000. Using existing pollution-control technology, the utility industry variously pegs the price tag of compliance at between $4 billion and $7 billion annually, mostly in new pollution-control equipment. Those are staggering costs by any measure.

Prior to the 1990 law, companies had little incentive to seek alternative means of generating electricity, or of increasing efficiency to reduce electricity demand (although a few forward-thinking utilities deemed it worthwhile to engage in both activities during the 1980s). But the clean air law included a provision to establish an incentive program that might do just that. It's called "emissions allowance trading."

Here's how it works: Beginning in 1995, the federal government will grant utilities authorization to emit an annual allowance of SO_2 in the form of emissions credits. The hitch is that each utility will get only enough credits to cover about half of what it has usually been polluting. So a utility will either have to find ways to reduce emissions or purchase additional credits on the open market. For example, to emit more SO_2

than legally allowed, a utility must pay for that right by buying excess allowances from other companies, at whatever price the market will bear. Much like an overdrawn check writer, companies that use more allowances than they have in their accounts will face severe penalties. Conversely, if a utility uses less than its full allowance—that is, if it emits less SO_2 than the government permits—it can sell its excess allowances to other utilities that aren't able (or willing) to comply.

But companies aren't waiting until 1995 to begin trading emissions allowances. The first publicly disclosed trade took place in 1992, when the Tennessee Valley Authority purchased the right to emit 10,000 tons of SO_2 from Wisconsin Power and Light, a utility hundreds of miles away. The history-making deal, worth about $3 million, or about $300 a ton, required the Wisconsin company to reduce its emissions to a level 10,000 tons below what the law then required. For TVA, it meant literally buying additional time to install smokestack scrubbers or replace high-sulfur coal with cleaner fuels.

Although it is too early to tell, it is likely this system will spur additional marketing opportunities for both utilities and their largest customers. For example, the law encourages utilities to decrease their production of electricity, thereby releasing fewer emissions. To do so, utilities could step up already existing efforts to increase the efficiencies of their customers—through new energy-efficient motors, lighting, manu-facturing processes, and other means. That, in turn, could stimulate technological improvements, thereby reducing pollution control costs. And customers that have their own cogeneration facilities—turbines that produce electricity from surplus heat from manufacturing opera-tions—could sell this relatively "clean" excess power back to utilities, requiring them to burn even less SO_2-emitting coal.

And then there is the possibility for marketplace quirks. Environ-mental and citizen groups could raise funds to buy emissions allow-ances, with no intention of reselling them, as a means of reducing acid rain in their area. Such a move could further squeeze the market for emissions allowances, raising their price, and stimulating even greater efficiency measures by utilities and their customers.

The concept of emissions trading isn't entirely new. Under fed-eral law, companies since the 1970s have been able to earn credits for installing pollution-prevention equipment. And those credits can be sold within a region. But deals were complex and required a great deal of time-consuming permitting and paperwork. The SO_2 allowances represent the first national marketplace for a single pollutant.

In the process, polluters themselves increasingly will be putting a price on pollution. That price—in this case, the value of the right to emit SO_2—will be standardized and traded—like coffee, chicken, and corn—in such futures markets as the Chicago Board of Trade and the New York Mercantile Exchange. So, alongside hog futures will be what we might call "smog futures." Specifically, the futures contracts will be traded in units of "25 one-ton sulfur dioxide emission allowances." One can imagine the contracts being traded by pollution arbitragers, or "poll arbs," in the argot of the futures pits. If poll arbs think the value of SO_2 allowances will rise—that is, if they believe the cost of complying with SO_2 regulations will increase or the supply of emissions allowances will shrink—they will buy more permits now to sell later. If it is anticipated that the cost will drop or the allowances will be plentiful, they will sell futures now, buying them back later at a lower price.

Don't fret if you don't grasp the nuances of selling something you don't really own; few folks truly understand futures trading. But the bottom line is crystal clear: Suddenly, polluting has a nationally agreed-upon price tag.

Emissions trading is not without its critics, who argue that the allowances are immoral because they give companies the right to pollute. But others counter that companies have long had this right, if only by default in the form of government inaction or the lack of deterrent penalties, and it has cost companies little or nothing for this right. Smog futures, then, add at least a modicum of reality to the marketplace. Another shortcoming of emissions credits is that they fail to deal with the largest cumulative source of air pollution: automobiles. No one has yet devised a scheme to grant consumers emissions credits they can apply to driving, heating their homes, or whatever. However effective such a program might be in reducing pollution, it's not likely to happen in the foreseeable future.

Whatever the critics think, the market-based pollution bandwagon is rolling. Even before the first smog future was traded, other pollutants were being considered for marketplace regulation, including carbon dioxide and chlorofluorocarbons. Regulators in Southern California also have approved a plan to let firms trade pollution rights in that region, beginning with nitrogen oxides. And in 1992, a United Nations group proposed a worldwide pollution market as a means of controlling global carbon dioxide emissions. Under the system, quotas would be set for how much each country would be allowed to pollute.

The idea makes some sense. For the first time, it gives companies incentives to beat, not just meet, pollution regulations. But it is far from the last word in pollution control. Some companies believe that more could be done.

Consider 3M. The company has pledged to "retire" its excess pollution allowances—that is, not to sell them to anyone at any price. "If what we're doing is creating a program for environmental improvement, our upper management decided that any credits we would not need for our own expansion at a facility would be donated back to the state agency for improvement in air quality," says Thomas Zosel, manager of 3M's Pollution Prevention Pays program. "So, when we make an environmental improvement, it will really be an environmental improvement." That policy may cost 3M tens of millions of dollars, but Zosel and his colleagues see a larger mission in all this: Not just transferring pollution around the country, but actually reducing it.

There is also potential for economic and social chaos in companies' ability to trade pollution allowances. Some companies, for example, may find it more profitable to sell their emissions allowances, then take the money and run, shutting down operations, packing up and moving to states or countries with cleaner air—or at least less restrictive policies. The result could be a king's ransom paid for business flight, with the community—and former employees—left paying the price tag of increased unemployment and a decreased tax base. Clearly, that's not what the law's authors had in mind when they set out to find market-based methods to control pollution.

Indeed, such shortsightedness may be the biggest potential obstacle to the success of smog futures and other market-based incentives: Amid all the excitement over yet another means of making paper profits, companies must keep in mind that the ultimate goal is a cleaner world.

Another emerging policy tool is "green taxes," which refers to a rather broad array of fees levied on activities that pollute or reduce resources. A green tax might be one placed on materials at their source—oil as it is pumped out of a well, coal as it is mined, freshwater as it is extracted from underground—and on other materials as they are manufactured, sold, or released into the environment. There might be a green tax on paper made from virgin pulp, sulfur dioxide emissions from factories and utilities, or hazardous wastes at the time they are disposed.

"Taxes are appealing because they offer an efficient way of correcting for the market's failure to value environmental services," says the Worldwatch Institute in its 1991 report, *State of the World*. "Taxing products and activities that pollute, deplete, or otherwise degrade natural systems is a way of insuring that environmental costs are taken into account in private decisions—whether to commute by car or bicycle, for example, or to generate electricity from coal or sunlight."

Proposals for green taxes abound. One would raise gasoline taxes by $1 or more to reduce fuel demand and lower emissions of global warming gases. Another would tax freshwater withdrawals to encourage conservation, and still another would tax oil spills by their amount—at, say, $20 per gallon discharged. That, say proponents, would give oil drillers and shippers an incentive to minimize their risks. At least one proposal would *remove* a tax in the name of the environment. Stephen Hanke, a Johns Hopkins University economics professor, has advocated eliminating property taxes based on the value of private timber stands. This, he says, effectively amounts to taxing each tree, as opposed to the land on which the trees stand. The current practice encourages premature harvesting of trees in order to reduce taxes. It would be better to levy the tax on the land value alone, he says.

Robert Costanza and Herman Daly, for their part, have proposed a "natural capital depletion tax," levied on products and services that deplete a nation's stock of natural capital—fish and wildlife populations, topsoil, trees, mineral deposits, fossil fuels, and other resources.

The political feasibility of such taxes is questionable, to say the least, even if they were offset by reductions in income or sales taxes. Few countries will be eager to place a tax burden on their nation's companies that isn't matched by their foreign competitors. And if enacted, these particular green taxes would cause a shift in consumption habits, which could affect markets, industries, and jobs. Implementing them would represent a sea change in the way we value the world around us. In effect, they would shift some of the tax burden to companies and consumers based not on how much they earn but on how they spend what they have. If they spend it on products, processes, and services that cause little degradation of the environment, they will pay fewer taxes than if they spend it in ways that consume a disproportionate amount of resources or create needless pollution. Obviously, such a scheme would be a powerful incentive for companies to instigate a wide range of pollution prevention and waste reduction measures.

This idea isn't entirely new. Modest green taxes already exist in

Europe. Taxes levied on the carbon content of coal, oil, and natural gas already are in effect in Finland, Sweden, and the Netherlands, although critics say the taxes are not high enough to spur major changes in energy use. And there is a green tax in the United States: a per-kilogram tax on chlorofluorocarbons, levied in 1989 to encourage industry to find effective and affordable alternatives to this ozone-depleting gas. The gradually increasing tax could raise about $5 billion a year by 1996.

A simpler form of green taxes comes in the form of advance disposal fees, or ADFs, which aim to build the cost of waste disposal into a product's purchase price. The actual amount of the fee might be based on the product's (or its package's) weight or volume, or it might be a per-item charge—$5 per automobile battery, for example. At the other end of the process are graduated trash pickup fees now being levied in some communities. In such a scheme, placing a single trash can at curbside for pickup might cost little or nothing, while the second can would cost a few dollars more, and the third and subsequent cans increasingly more. Such fees provide weekly incentives to consumers to reduce purchases of goods whose waste can't readily be reused or recycled.

Still another example of green taxes comes from the state of Delaware, which in 1992 issued tax incentives designed to help the state recruit industries that use recycled materials. Eligible manufacturers include those that derive at least 25 percent of their raw materials from recycled materials removed from the waste stream. Also eligible are manufacturers that process recycled materials for resale to other manufacturers, those that collect materials to recycle and distribute, and those that voluntarily reduce waste by set amounts. Besides tax incentives, manufacturers in Delaware could be eligible for other incentives from the state. Says Philip Cherry, director of pollution prevention in the state's Department of Natural Resources and Environmental Control: "It's an environmental program that both sides of the coin can get behind."

Proponents of green taxes point out that they are eminently fairer and less disruptive than the alternative: an outright ban on activities, such as driving gas-guzzling cars or manufacturing products not made from the highest possible amount of recycled content. With a gradually increasing green tax, they say, individuals and industries can slowly adjust their behavior to accommodate the new environmental reality.

Whether or not green taxes gain in popularity, they are worthy of further debate. At the very least, they could create opportunities for policymakers to examine the underlying concepts. After all, it is the almost complete lack of understanding of these notions that has contributed to a marketplace in which prices appear to be out of line with true environmental costs.

THE SUSTAINABILITY SCENARIO

Green taxes are among the many concepts being hotly debated around the world as countries grapple with ways to address the notion of "sustainable development." That term, coined in the mid 1980s, refers to a form of development or progress that "meets the needs of the present without compromising the ability of future generations to meet their own needs," as defined in *Our Common Future*, a 1987 report from the World Commission on Environment and Development, a United Nations group. What those words actually mean to companies and countries began to become more apparent five years later, during the 1992 United Nations Conference on Environment and Development—the Earth Summit—held in Rio de Janeiro.

At the core of sustainable development thinking is an increased emphasis on the value of the environment—the natural environment as well as the one created by human activity. Another fundamental notion is that the economy is not separate from the environment in which we live, that the health of each is dependent on the other. In other words, the environment's carrying capacity must be as fundamental a component of business decisions as are cash flow, market demand, and raw-material availability.

However simple these ideas may seem, they become more complex as they filter down into company and government policies. For one thing, integrating this notion into company and national economies will requires implementing some of the ecological accounting practices being advocated by some economists, something few countries or companies are prepared to do. Implementing these ideas will require higher levels of efficiencies—in manufacturing, agriculture, transportation, and energy—than have typically been reached. And as was demonstrated at the Rio summit, it will also mandate a wide range of radical political shifts involving such things as population control, women's rights, trade restrictions, tax incentives, and foreign aid. Clearly, each of these issues presents a potential hornet's nest of conflicts, pitting the environment against a host of economic interests, religious tenets, cultural practices, and political convictions.

The issues are no less thorny inside boardrooms. Many sustainable development policies fly in the face of traditional business thinking, from strategic planning and R&D to marketing and accounting. A national goal of reducing carbon dioxide emissions, however laudable and however much it would engender operating efficiencies over the long term, will still require significant investments in new equipments and processes, money that must be diverted from new-product development, expansion plans, marketing efforts, and dividend payouts. Changing over to sustainable agriculture techniques—with fewer pesticides and fertilizers, more efficient use of water, and crop rotation—for whatever environmental benefits it might bring, would send shock waves through agribusiness. Senior executives, not to mention stockholders, no doubt squirm at the breadth of the sustainable development agenda. Integrating these ideas into public policy and corporate governance will be one of the ongoing challenges of the early twenty-first century.

But some countries and companies aren't waiting to embrace the sustainability challenge, seeing far more opportunities than threats in the concept. Japan clearly sees the potential. In 1990, the Tokyo government unveiled a hundred-year plan for sustainable development, launching it with a Research Institute of Innovative Technology for the Earth, backed with a $37 million annual budget. Much like its high-tech counterpart, the Ministry of International Trade and Industry (MITI), which helped pool knowledge and other resources to turn Japan into an international technological force, this new organization sees the future of international markets dependent on environmentally sound technologies. (MITI, meanwhile, has pledged to create a model "eco factory" that mixes environmental harmony with production efficiency, doing such things as using high-speed robots to dismantle used cars, and turning industrial waste into reusable steel and plastics.) Japan already has made great strides in making itself competitive in this arena. During the past twenty years, it has increased its manufacturing efficiency to the point that it uses just half the energy and raw materials as the United States to produce one unit of GNP. According to some experts, such efficiency translates into a 5 percent cost advantage on some products. A few U.S. companies have also begun to see the competitive edge that can be derived from more sustainable business practices. For example, officials at 3M predict that if it reaches Its goal of reducing air and water emissions by 90 percent and solid waste by 50 percent from 1990 levels, it could cut its inflation-adjusted cost per unit of most products by 10 percent.

HOW MUCH FOR THIS POUND OF POLLUTION?

Ultimately, smog futures, green taxes, and sustainable development amount to a search for the lowest-cost method of reducing the greatest amount of pollution. That search is at the heart of some of the most bitterly fought battles between economists and environmentalists. For the latter, the cost of reducing or eliminating pollutants isn't as important as that the deed itself be accomplished; for the former, cost is key. Politicians and regulators, caught in the middle, often find that sorting out the economic analyses offered by each side's experts is all but impossible. And succumbing to political pressures to do *something*, they are prone to creating laws whose impact on companies sometimes involves far more dollars than sense.

Consider clean air. In recent years, companies, environmentalists, and regulators have grappled with the most cost-effective ways to reduce the damage cars have on the air quality in our most polluted cities. The 1990 clean air law targeted nine regions and established a set of Draconian measures intended to improve those regions' air quality.

Hydrocarbons, the direct result of burning gasoline and other fossil fuels, are one of the chief problems associated with auto exhaust. They mix with sunlight and other ingredients in the atmosphere to form photochemical smog. Thanks to such innovations as the catalytic converter (a product of 1970s regulations), today's cars emit substantially fewer hydrocarbons than those made two decades ago. But a funny thing happened on the road to cleaner air: The nation's automobile population grew by about fifty million during that same period. And those cars are driving more miles each year than ever before. So, automobile-borne hydrocarbons remain a thorn in the side of air quality, though nowhere near as big a problem as would be the case without catalytic converters.

Reducing hydrocarbon emissions beyond current levels could

be an expensive proposition. It could require retrofitting existing sources of the pollutant—mostly cars and factories. That could mean recalling millions of cars as well as adding end-of-pipe controls to thousands of plants. Opponents of such sweeping measures say the cost is prohibitive to both consumers and companies. They say a cleaner environment would simply put them out of business. Proponents disagree, saying that the cost of not doing so could be greater in terms of lost taxes (as companies move elsewhere to get away from smog-choked areas), productivity (as employees spend more time out sick from respiratory ailments resulting from poor air quality), even lost human lives (from cancer, emphysema, and other pollution-related diseases).

All of which begs the question: How much does it really cost to remove hydrocarbons from the air? And how much *should* it cost? The answer to the second question stems largely from the answer to the first. And the answer to the first question is inevitably, "It depends."

Consider the findings of studies done for the oil industry on the cost of reducing hydrocarbon emissions through the use of reformulated gasoline. The studies were conducted for the Western States Petroleum Association in 1991 to analyze the impact of proposals by the California Air Resources Board to require new fuels to meet the state's air quality goals. The study begins with the understanding that existing emissions controls—primarily catalytic converters—reduce about 95 percent of hydrocarbon emissions at the cost of about $1,000 per ton of pollution.

Reducing emissions further—from about 1.56 grams per mile to about 0.24 grams per mile—would add about six cents to the cost of a gallon of gas. Running the numbers reveals that those six extra cents would raise the cost of hydrocarbon emissions tenfold, to just over $10,000 per ton. Meanwhile, as automotive pollution-prevention technology improves, further reducing tail-pipe emissions, the cost per ton of reduced emissions will increase even more. For example, under the existing law, gasoline will have to be reformulated again in the year 2000 at a cost of about 15 cents per gallon. At that price, the cost per ton of hydrocarbons removed jumps to more than $200,000. And by the year 2010, the last turn of the regulatory screw will result in the cost per ton reaching about $800,000. One could make a reasonable case that those last few incremental changes just aren't worth it.

Now, the above figures were compiled by the oil industry for use in arguing against proposals that would require them to reformulate their fuels—at no doubt considerable costs to the refiners. As such, they are politically loaded and must be scrutinized for their scientific methodology and assumptions. But the point they make is indisputable: A law of diminishing returns is in effect here. At some point, the price of "clean"—however subjective that term may be—becomes prohibitive.

There are faster and cheaper ways to cut emissions: Simply eliminate the most polluting vehicles. For example, consider SCRAP, an experimental project conducted in 1990 by Unocal Corporation, an oil company. The project's goal was to induce owners of pre-1971 model automobiles in the Los Angeles area to sell their cars to Unocal for $700. Unocal would then take the cars to a scrap yard to be crushed and recycled, removing them permanently from the roads.

The rationale behind SCRAP—for South Coast Recycled Auto Project—was that these older cars have little or no pollution-control equipment. As a result, studies revealed that these cars are the worst polluters on the road, with hydrocarbon emissions more than 90 times greater than comparable new model vehicles. Getting rid of them would be a quick way to reduce the source of up to 15 percent of all emissions from mobile sources, according to Unocal's estimates.

For the 1990 experiment, Unocal budgeted $5 million, enough to purchase and scrap 7,000 cars. To their surprise, other interested parties chipped in additional funds. For example, Ford Motor Company contributed $700,000, the local air quality management district added $100,000, some local Lincoln-Mercury dealers gave $63,000, and one hundred or so individual benefactors sent checks totaling around $100,000. According to Unocal, the CEO of a Silicon Valley firm hundreds of miles north of Los Angeles sent a check for $700 with the comment, "Buy and bury one for us, too." With the extra contributions, Unocal had enough money to scrap 8,376 cars.

Among the biggest surprises of the program was that the purchased cars were far dirtier than had been predicted. One car in five exceeded the measuring capabilities of the smog-check machines. The worst car tested emitted enough unburned gasoline from its tail pipe to run a 1990-model car getting thirty-two miles per gallon. All told, Unocal estimated it removed 12.8 million pounds of pollutants from Southern California's air—"the equivalent of removing about 150,000 brand-new cars from the road," the company reported. The cost was relatively low—about $937 per ton of pollution removed—and the speed far exceeded that of other programs. The company received more than three thousand calls the day the program was announced, with fifteen hundred old cars registered within the first forty-eight hours.

SCRAP so impressed federal officials that in 1992 the Bush administration proposed a "Cash for Clunkers" program, based on Unocal's prototype. In this case, the buyers of the vehicles would be companies that wanted relief from the financial obligations of federal air-quality standards. In other words, by buying old cars, a company might relieve itself from the burden of having to undertake more drastic pollution-prevention measures.

Not everyone was impressed, however. For example, the Ralph Nader–founded Center for Auto Safety called the proposal "an ineffective and costly clunker" because it allowed companies to continue polluting the air. Such a swap would do little to clean up the environment, they contended.

The point is well taken. At best, Cash for Clunkers is a stopgap measure. Among other things, it doesn't alleviate the fact that more and more drivers are traveling more and more miles. Far more dramatic measures must be taken to effect long-term air-quality improvements. The idea has its merits, not the least of which is eliminating some of the more potent polluters. But the Nader group was right: The deal did not forgive companies their other environmental responsibilities. Still, SCRAP and its imitators demonstrated that cost-effective pollution reduction need not involve prohibitive investments over long periods of time. Some things can be done virtually overnight.

MONEY TALKS

The ability of companies to make the most economic choices in reducing pollution and waste will be of increasing interest to employees and managers. The reason: Companies are beginning to peg the salaries of executives, managers, and even the rank and file to such things as pollution prevention, waste reduction, and energy savings.

One of the first companies to make the move was ICI, the British chemicals conglomerate. In 1990, it began to link managers' pay to performance in meeting environmental targets. For some of ICI's most senior managers, whose pay was already performance-based, the environment was moved to the top of their list of priorities.

Another believer in pay for performance is Browning-Ferris Industries (BFI), the Houston-based operator of landfills and recycling and trash-disposal operations. During its 1991 fiscal year BFI initiated a comprehensive incentive program for managers of its one hundred or so landfills, designed "to make environmental compliance an integral part of running their business," according to Bruce A. Gantner, BFI's director of environmental compliance.

Simply put, BFI's program rewards managers for taking risks. The "risks," in this case, mean that managers must tackle problems at the local level, including, if necessary, a decision to shut down an operation altogether. "Without empowerment, managers wait for someone else to make a decision or pass the issue off to a higher authority," says Gantner. The company's goal, then, was to push power and authority down to the local level.

The BFI incentive plan involves a rather complex 100-point scoring system with thirty "performance goals." Ten goals are worth 5 points, ten are worth 3 points, and ten are worth 1 point. A 5-pointer, for example, has to do with "staffing and assigned responsibilities, including backup coverage." To satisfy this goal, a manager must "identify the environmental compliance issues relevant to the site including, but not limited to, groundwater monitoring, on-site generated waste . . . stormwater management, methane monitoring . . . and health and safety. . . . For each issue, a backup person should be identified to perform the tasks in the absence of the primary coordinator."

Those thirty goals add up to ninety points. The remaining ten points were set aside, "to be awarded at the discretion of regional management for other performance measures," says Gantner.

Under the system, compensation of BFI's facility managers has two components: base salary and a performance bonus linked with environmental compliance performance. The environmental component was created, says Gantner, because BFI wanted managers to go beyond standards required by law whenever the circumstances warranted. As stated by Bruce E. Ranck, BFI's president: "If a landfill manager is going to make a mistake, we want him to err on the side of being overly cautious."

Ultimately, each manager is evaluated under the hundred-point system and, using an intricate formula involving no fewer than three multipliers, managers received their score—and their pay.

Does it work? BFI thinks so. According to Gantner, during fiscal 1991, the number of enforcement violations and penalties for BFI's active landfills decreased over 75 percent.

Money talks, indeed.

What's good for the bosses may also be good for subordinates: rewards for employees who find ways to improve a company's environmental performance. After all, the idea of having hundreds or thousands of pollution preventers, waste watchers, and energy savers in every department and facility can't help but have a salutary effect on the bottom line.

That's what 3M discovered in 1975, when it inaugurated its Pollution Prevention Pays, or 3P, program. At its simplest, 3P is a glorified employee-suggestion box. But the suggestions, in this case, have to do with things the company could do that would have a demonstrable effect on reducing emissions of toxic materials, whether in the air, water, or ground.

"Typically, 3P projects are initiated when employees recognize a specific pollution or waste problem and a possible solution," says Tom Zosel, manager of the program. "An employee team is then developed to analyze the problem and develop solutions. Such a team might consist of employees from several disciplines, including engineering, research, marketing, and legal. A proposal is then submitted to the affected operating division and a decision is made on whether to commit funds, time, and other resources to it."

Projects that are accepted are eligible for awards. To qualify for an award, a 3P project must fulfill certain criteria. It must actually prevent pollution, not control it. It must result in cost savings to 3M and meet an acceptable return on investment. And it must involve a technical accomplishment, innovative approach, or unique design. For their ideas, employees can receive $500 gift certificates. In addition, 3M encourages other forms of recognition, including from peers. The company runs internal seminars where technical papers are presented; if the information is not considered proprietary, it also may be presented to other companies as well.

The result: Since the program began in 1975, 3M estimates that it has saved the company $573 million, and has reduced the company's pollution by about half.

"Pollution prevention doesn't always pay," admits 3M vice president Robert P. Bringer. "But it does pay in a lot of cases. And there was enough evidence over a few years that we think maybe people's attitudes in the company started to change a little bit. Instead of just looking for cost-reduction opportunities, some of them are looking at pollution-prevention opportunities, knowing that most of them would have cost benefits, also. It's a very slight change in thinking, but a very important one."

Of course, pay-for-performance makes perfect sense in companies with some kind of profit-sharing plan. At companies like Herman Miller, the office furniture company, and Quad/Graphics, a printer of magazines and catalogs, profit-sharing plans become huge incentives to cut wasteful and polluting practices.

At Quad, for example, a $500 million company with some 5,300 employees, a group of press operators began to examine the amount of waste ink being discarded from the pressroom of its main plant in Pewaukee, Wisconsin. They were taken aback by what they found: more than seventeen fifty-five-gallon drums of ink were being wasted every month at the plant. Besides the cost of the ink itself, there were additional costs inherent in this waste, including those needed to handle, label, and transport the ink-filled drums. Companywide, it turned out that Quad pressrooms generated nearly one thousand drums a year of waste ink in 1988, each containing four hundred pounds of toxic ink that could not be put to productive use.

John Disch, press manager of Quad's Pewaukee plant, drove the message home to employees one day when he called a meeting of press crews, rolled out seventeen drums of ink, and asked the workers to guess how long it took to accumulate that much waste ink in one pressroom. When they learned that it took only a month, they sprang into action. By setting up Recyclable Ink Stations and implementing other simple changes in processes but no new technology, Quad's Pewaukee plant has since reduced its production of waste ink to less than one drum per month. Other Quad plants had similarly impressive results. The cost to start the program: nothing. The payback: more than $500,000 a year to the company's bottom line. Says John Imes, Quad/Graphic's environmental manager: "When $3 million to $3.5 million is going into profit sharing, a half-million dollars is some serious costs."

But employees of greener companies aren't the only ones who benefit financially from pollution prevention, energy efficiency, and the like. Consider, for example, a study conducted in 1991 for Citizen Action, a consumer and environmental group based in Washington, D.C. The study examined the employment and other economic development impacts that might result from an accelerated investment in energy efficiency and alternative energy technologies.

The study used the state of Virginia as the laboratory for the following programs: the introduction of a variety of lighting and heating, ventilation, and air-conditioning efficiency investments in the commercial sector; a 10 percent reduction in the present consumption of natural gas within the residential sector through weatherization, insulation, and furnace efficiency improvements; and the supplemental use of solar heating to displace electric water heating in 100,000 homes. Among the assumptions were that the investments would be made over a ten-year period and the payback periods for the investments would be ten years for residential weatherization and solar water heating projects and five years for commercial efficiency improvements. It was also assumed that the energy utilities involved would be allowed a rate of return on the actual investment in efficiency improvements, which is permitted in about half the states.

The economic impact of all this included payments to contractors to carry out the improvements (a positive impact), re-spending of the energy savings by households and businesses in the Virginia economy (also a positive impact), and slightly higher utility rates and the initial outlays by homeowners and businesses to finance the improvements (a negative impact).

The bottom line: Even with the initial outlays and higher utility rates, the residential improvements would generate nearly $10 million (in 1991 dollars) in net total economic activity each year for twenty years. Moreover, total employment would be increased by an average of 465 jobs a year for twenty years. And personal income in the form of increased wages and salaries were projected to increase by about $8 million a year for twenty years. The commercial efficiency programs showed similar positive economic impacts.

Looking at the bigger picture offers even more impressive numbers. A 1992 study by four environmental groups, coordinated by the Union of Concerned Scientists, concluded that aggressive action to curb carbon dioxide emissions by 70 percent over forty years could cost the economy about $2.7 trillion. But it could also save consumers and industry about $5 trillion, yielding a net savings of $2.3 trillion. Even the federal government—whose political leaders waged a constant battle during the 1980s against environmental measures on the grounds that they would hurt the economy—has its own rosy scenario. Environmental Protection Agency analysts concluded that the gross national product would rise, not fall, over the next twenty years if emissions were reduced through a carbon tax, assuming the tax revenues were "recycled" back into the economy through investment tax credits for industry, which would stimulate capital investments.

It's all speculation, of course, and based on assumptions that are debatable at best. But both projections suggest that the macro- and microeconomic effects of reducing pollution could pay off big in the long run.

DOING WELL, DOING GOOD

There's a growing body of evidence showing that the benefits of environmentally responsible management policies involve more than the tangible economic benefits that come just from reducing emissions and waste. Companies with the best environmental records are being smiled upon by a growing number of constituencies. For starters, resource-starved regulators are demonstrating that they are pleased to leave alone companies that proactively comply with the law. The Occupational Safety and Health Administration (OSHA) has a formal name for these—the Voluntary Protection Programs—in which they agree not to routinely inspect companies that have ongoing OSHA approved safety programs. The Environmental Protection Agency is moving toward a similar hands-off policy for companies that adequately demonstrate that they are well in compliance and taking proactive measures.

But there's a more immediate bottom-line payoff, according to one study. Stephen E. Erfle and Michael J. Fratantuono, economics professors at Dickinson College in Pennsylvania, analyzed the links between companies' social performance and their profitability. Their finding: A positive correlation exists between financial performance and several dimensions of social performance—including a company's environmental record.

In their study, Erfle and Fratantuono compared standard financial indicators for eighty-four companies to their ratings by the Council on Economic Priorities in *Shopping for a Better World*, an annual best-selling guide that rates more than two thousand consumer products by examining their manufacturers' records on ten key social issues, from charitable giving to family benefits to advancement of women and minorities to attitudes about nuclear power and South Africa—and, of course, environmental performance. The end product is page after page of product names and ratings, aimed at providing readers "with the information necessary to tell one kind of product from another, so you can select products from companies whose policies and practices you support," as the book's introduction explains.

The professors found that there was indeed a link between profitability and five of the ten categories tracked by the book: environmental performance, advancement of women, advancement of minorities, charitable giving, and community action.

Companies with the highest environmental ratings were those with "positive programs, such as the use and encouragement of recycling, alternative energy sources, waste reduction, etc. A record relatively clear of major regulatory violations," according to the researchers. Those with the lowest ratings had "consistently poor public record of repeated violations and/or major accidents. . . . Relatively little effective positive enforcement." Of the companies examined, 22 percent were rated "high" and 41 percent were rated "low," with the remaining 37 percent rated "medium."

Here is how the companies with the top-rated environmental records compared with those with the worst records:

The top-rated companies were found to have

- 2.2 percent higher return on assets
- 4.5 percent higher return on equity
- 3.9 percent higher return on investment
- 4.4 percent higher earnings-to-assets ratio
- 13.3 percent higher sales-to-assets ratio
- 9.3 percent higher sales growth
- 1.9 percent higher asset growth
- 16.7 percent higher operating income growth

Concluded the professors: "Good social performers may find it easier to win concessions from workers; draw customers; and attract investors, given the reduced probability of costly, government-imposed, sanctions. In this light, strong social performance may contribute to long-run profitability."

Of course, such results beg a chicken-and-egg question: Are companies more profitable because they are environmentally responsible, or vice versa? Says J. Ladd Greeno, vice president of Arthur D. Little and managing director of its environmental, health, and safety practice: "I have seen time and time again that it's often easier to strive for environmental excellence when a company is reasonably profitable and it's often extremely difficult when operations are not profitable." On the other side of the equation is whether increased attention to environmental performance can lead to improved efficiencies, cost reductions, and increased profitability—thereby strengthening a company to implement even more ambitious environmental initiatives. Ultimately, Greeno points to a diagram depicting a continuous cycle in which each kind of improvement leads to others.

In any case, the Dickinson College results weren't what Professors Erfle and Fratantuono expected. "When I originally saw *Shopping for a Better World*, I thought it would be an interesting data source to measure the cost of being socially responsible," says Steve Erfle. "But what we found weren't costs, but benefits. That was a big surprise."

Consider it a wake-up call for a new era.

enforcement

HEEDING THE LAW OF THE LAND——AND THE MARKETPLACE

ON MAY 23, 1990, a federal jury convicted Borjohn Optical Technology, Inc., and its president, John Borowski, of illegally discharging toxic metals and dangerous chemicals into the local sewer system, endangering company employees in the process. Borowski had been charged with ordering employees to discharge nickel plating and nitric acid solutions containing illegal concentrations of nickel into the sewer system in Burlington, Massachusetts. The system is tied into the Massachusetts Water Resource Authority's treatment plant, which in turn discharges into Boston Harbor.

At the sentencing five months later, Borowski received twenty-six months in prison, to be followed by two years of probation, and a $400,000 fine. Borjohn Optical was fined $50,000 and was ordered to make a lump-sum payment of $15,500 for medical bills of two employees. As a consequence of the conviction, Borjohn Optical was placed on the List of Violating Companies maintained by the federal government, making the firm ineligible for federally funded contracts, grants, or loans. The case is under appeal.

three: enforcement

Just a few short years ago, the prospect of someone serving a prison sentence for a company's environmental misdeed seemed highly unlikely. The John Borowskis of the world, if they were caught, indicted, and convicted, were more likely to receive a fine and a stern warning. In many cases, the fines for illegal dumping or excessive emissions cost the company far less than it might have paid to reduce emissions or dispose of the waste more responsibly. Between 1987 and 1991, for example, the average fine levied by the federal government for environmental crimes was about $149,000. That's far less than the typical cost of designing, building, and implementing a system for proper treatment of hazardous wastes, which can run into the millions. So, it was perhaps understandable, albeit shortsighted, for some companies to find the least costly disposal method—however illegal, however many people or other creatures it might imperil—and suffer the consequences. With a little bit of luck, there wouldn't be any.

Luck is considerably more difficult to count on these days. Federal and local government agencies are finding that it is politically popular—as well as in the public's interest—to crack down hard on polluters. And they are less inclined than ever to let some low-level manager take the fall. Today's midnight dumpers and emissions scofflaws are more likely than ever before to have their senior executives dragged into court, perhaps sent to jail, face stiff fines, and lose the prospect for receiving federal funding or favors.

In the United States, many of these changes occurred during George Bush's watch. During the first three years of the Bush administration, the U.S. Department of Justice set all-time records for criminal prosecutions of environmental crimes. Between 1989 and 1992, Justice increased its budget for this mission considerably, adding lawyers to its environmental crimes division. Bush administration officials boasted that their actions resulted in more prosecutions between 1989 and 1992 than during the preceding eighteen years. Similar rises in enforcement were seen at the state level.

Political posturing aside, the numbers are frighteningly real for several hundred corporate environmental wrongdoers. Between 1982 and 1992, the Justice Department handed up roughly eight hundred environmental indictments. Those indictments led to the conviction of 578 corporate presidents, officers, and other managers, resulting in the sentencing of over 350 years of jail time, of which over 150 years were actually served. During fiscal 1991 alone, EPA assessed almost as many criminal penalties as it did during the previous twenty years.

During the early 1990s, the pace of prosecution quickened, with EPA's enforcement levels reaching record levels. In fiscal 1990, for example, the agency referred sixty-five criminal cases to Justice. Fifty-five individuals and corporations were convicted and sentenced to over sixty-two years of imprisonment for environmental crimes. The average sentence was 1.8 years, roughly equal to the average sentence for first-time possession of heroin.

Still, the cumulative indictments and resulting sentences are relatively infinitesimal. To put things in perspective, those sixty-two years of jail time pale when compared to the sentences meted out on any single day in a typical urban courtroom. And the twenty-seven Justice Department lawyers investigating and prosecuting environmental crimes would represent scarcely a blip on the legal radar screen in the private sector. Sidley & Austin, a Chicago-based law firm that claims to have the largest environmental practice in the United States, has sixty-five lawyers working full-time on environmental matters. Another problem is that most federal enforcement efforts have focused on relatively small-time polluters.

But the government's increased efforts are not to be discounted, and further action is inevitable. In recent years, memorandums of understanding have been signed between the EPA and the Securities and Exchange Commission (SEC), the Occupational Safety and Health Administration (OSHA), and the Internal Revenue Service (IRS). Each is intended to pool governmental resources to catch and penalize companies not in compliance with any of a dozen or so key laws. For example:

- EPA has agreed with the SEC to report each quarter the identity of every company named as a potentially responsible party (PRP) under Superfund. A PRP is one of several categories of past or present owners or operators of a hazardous waste disposal site deemed by the government to be responsible for cleaning up mishandled waste. (More on that later in this chapter.) EPA will also identify defendants in filed criminal cases and companies that are facing corrective action for other waste-disposal problems. The SEC wants this information in order to ensure that companies make appropriate disclosures about liability and potential liability in accordance with its strict reporting requirements. (More on this, too, later on.)
- EPA's agreement with OSHA allows the two agencies to identify

and share information about potential environmental and workplace health and safety problems. For instance, if during a health and safety inspection, OSHA officials encounter a situation they believe may be of interest to EPA, they have a formal means of passing along the information. Similarly, EPA inspectors can report evidence of health and safety abuses encountered during environmental-related inspections to OSHA. Increasingly, the two agencies will share and exchange data, training, and technical resources.

• EPA has agreed to report quarterly to the IRS the identity of any civil or criminal defendant who has been assessed a penalty of $5,000 or more. The IRS wants to ensure that such environmental penalties are properly reported in company tax returns as punitive sanctions, which cannot be deducted as business expenses.

If that weren't enough, a growing number of cases are being brought against companies on the basis of whistleblowers, disgruntled employees and union officials who provide defamatory information. Such cases represent a growth industry for regulators, especially during tough economic times, when layoffs are common, raises are few and far between, and overall morale and commitment can drop. And government enforcement agencies cultivate such whistleblowing relationships. For example, an investigation of Bristol-Myers Squibb, the pharmaceutical manufacturer, began in 1988 after one of the company's environmental specialists quit in frustration because her recommendations for complying with the Clean Water Act were not heeded. As a result of the investigation, the company pleaded guilty in 1992 to violating clean water laws by discharging chemicals that polluted a lake in upstate New York. In one of the largest environmental penalties ever assessed, Bristol-Myers agreed to pay a $3.5 million fine and spend another $30 million to build a waste-water treatment plant.

There are other signs of a continued boom in investigations and prosecutions. The Environmental Protection Agency's criminal investigative team is expected to grow from about 70 people in 1992 to around 250 by 1995. And the Federal Bureau of Investigation (FBI) has quietly stepped up its efforts in investigating environmental crimes.

The FBI? Actually, the FBI has been involved with environmental crimes since 1982, when it signed a memorandum of understanding with the EPA that places environmental matters within its jurisdiction. In 1992, the two agencies renewed their agreement, further expanding the relationship. Now the FBI has its full complement of some 9,800 agents in fifty-six field offices available to deal with environmental matters, using the full range of techniques for which it has become legend: surveillance, wiretaps, informants, undercover agents, and all the rest. According to Robert J. Chiaradio, supervisory special agent in the white-collar crimes section, who heads the environmental operations, FBI involvement multiplied fivefold between 1986 and 1992 and was expected to increase by at least another 50 percent by 1994.

If you need any evidence of the kind of clout the FBI can bring to an environmental crime, consider the Rocky Flats nuclear weapons plant near Denver. The plant is a Department of Energy facility that had been operated by Rockwell International Corporation since 1975. Its primary mission is to fabricate plutonium triggers for nuclear bombs, and it has facilities to recover plutonium from the wastes of other Energy Department operations and from "retired" nuclear weapons. It is located just sixteen miles from Denver, a metropolitan area of more than two million people.

After allegations about the illegal disposal of both chemical and mixed radioactive and hazardous waste, the EPA referred the case to the FBI. Both the Energy Department and Rockwell International were suspects. Among other things, the FBI flew aerial surveillance missions to gather evidence that plant personnel were using an obsolete, unpermitted incinerator to treat hazardous wastes. After gathering information for more than a year, the FBI and EPA sent in a team of 120 agents with a search warrant in 1989. Before it was all over, the FBI had seized over a million pages of internal documents for review; ultimately, some 3.5 million pages would be examined. The FBI alone had fifty agents at Rocky Flats around the clock for three weeks. That's something the EPA alone wouldn't have had the resources to do.

The result: In 1992, Rockwell, which had ceased operating the plant in 1989, pleaded guilty in federal court to five felony and five misdemeanor violations of the Clean Water Act, and agreed to pay $18.5 million in fines—the largest amount imposed to date in a hazardous-waste case. At the time of settlement, a Justice Department official noted that "the investigation revealed a pattern of conduct which took place over days, weeks, months, and sometimes even years." The official added that the fines were levied despite the fact that "no significant environmental damage appears to have occurred as a result of the conduct. . . ."

It's not just the United States that is pursuing companies and their leaders for environmental misdeeds. Consider the case of Warren Anderson, who was chairman of Union Carbide Corporation during the 1984 gas disaster in Bhopal, India, in which more than 4,000 people died and at least 200,000 were injured following a toxic-gas release at a pesticide factory—the worst industrial accident in history. In 1989, Union Carbide agreed to pay $470 million to cover liability in the case.

In 1992, nearly a decade after the accident, Anderson, who stepped down as chairman in 1986, was still being chased by the Indian government to face trial on homicide charges. Plant officials in India also were charged. Among other things, the courts there ruled that Anderson "committed an offense of culpable homicide." Although it is unlikely that Anderson will ever face an Indian court, his plight has sent a tremor through corporate boardrooms around the world, as corporate leaders begin to recognize that they are personally liable for their companies' environmental actions. Insurance companies are responding in kind, with a never-ending series of rate increases for "D&O" policies covering company directors and officers.

Governments aren't the only source of environmental "enforcement" companies must deal with. A host of other enforcers are out there—among them, community groups, environmentalists, customers, suppliers, stockholders, and the media. Each has joined the growing chorus of individuals and groups demanding that companies abide by both the letter and the spirit of environmental regulations. And each has become increasingly willing to use a variety of tools at its disposal—from lawsuits to boycotts to media manipulation—to tighten the screws for compliance. Clearly, the potential impact on company operations is enormous.

FROM PINSTRIPES TO JAIL STRIPES

Whatever wag once mused that golf was the great social equalizer had obviously never been to prison. Where else could a corporate executive live so close to burglars, con artists, and thugs? The mere thought of it—the loss of freedom, dignity, possessions, and ready access to the outside world—can send chills down the spine of even the most hardened businessperson, which is just what the government wants. Prosecutors are finally recognizing that bringing criminal charges against individuals, particularly senior corporate executives, is a far stronger deterrent than even the most severe financial penalties. And new laws have made it considerably easier for the government to prosecute—and prevail.

From the government's perspective, prosecuting the boss makes perfect sense. After all, corporations cannot go to jail, and they can readily pass along any fines to consumers in the form of higher prices. As one federal prosecutor, wishing anonymity, put it: "We know that the sight of one guy being carted off to jail will deter at least a hundred others from breaking the law. Nothing hits home stronger than the thought of doing time and having a criminal record."

At the same time, the penalties for polluting have become more severe. For example, the 1990 Clean Air Act Amendments radically restructured the criminal provisions for violations. Before 1990, there were four basic categories of pollution violations, all of them misdemeanors; now, there are seven—one misdemeanor and six felonies. "Prosecutors really like felonies," explains Paul G. Wallach, senior partner with the Washington, D.C., law firm Hale & Dorr, himself a former prosecutor. "If you have five felonies, you get a raise. If you have five misdemeanors, your boss asks you why you bothered."

What's most distressing for company officials is that the 1984 Sentencing Reform Act required judges to refer to a "sentencing table"—which calculates prison sentences using a formula that considers the level of the offense and the defendant's criminal history. The more serious the crime, and the more recalcitrant the defendant, the greater the mandated term. The sentencing law also abolished the practice of imposing a sentence and immediately suspending it; now courts have little authority to suspend sentences except in unusual circumstances. Sentences may be reduced only in the form of time off for "good behavior."

Chapter Two of the law contains guidelines for offenses involving the environment. There are five categories of environmental crimes, the most common being 2Q1.2, "Mishandling hazardous or toxic substances, pesticides, recordkeeping, tampering, and falsification." Sentencing guidelines for this offense start at 2 to 8 months for those with no previous criminal history or other aggravating circumstances. At the other extreme, sentences call for 18 to 24 months. The most severe sentencing provision is 2Q1.1, "Knowing endangerment resulting from mishandling hazardous or toxic substances." Penalties start at 51 months, climbing up to more than ten years for the worst offenders. (The only exceptions to the above is when an environmental law—say, the Clean Water Act—specifies penalties that are less than called for under the federal sentencing guidelines. In such cases, the provisions of the law prevail.)

In addition, all the major environmental laws have civil penalties that can be levied on violating companies. Most call for fines of at least $25,000 per violation per day. In fiscal year 1991, for example, the EPA obtained $73.1 million in civil penalties, a record, representing a 21 percent increase over the year before. More than $28 million in penalties came under the Clean Water Act and Safe Drinking Water Act, nearly twice that assessed the year before. About a third of that came from just two cases: a $6.1 million fine against Wheeling-Pittsburgh Steel Corporation, and $3.1 million against Pfizer Pigments, Inc. These penalties were on top of court-ordered mandates to install required pollution control equipment to meet regulatory requirements. In the case of Wheeling-Pittsburgh, those costs alone exceeded $20 million. And, of course, there were legal fees, which in some cases have been known to exceed the penalties themselves.

Even those who make their living defending companies against such actions believe the system has gone too far. "With the governments' new initiative, the distinction between criminal and civil enforcement has become blurred, leaving good corporate citizens and their employees wide open to overzealous prosecutors, who in many instances are seeking little more than the potential benefit of an indictment in the high publicity area of environmental crimes," says Wallach.

Few executives and managers appreciate the potential risks they face. "The statistics demonstrate that the bulk of the government's cases involve otherwise upstanding businessmen who generally have never been in trouble before," according to a memorandum from the Chicago law office of Chapman and Cutler. It describes the case of the president of a "well-known New England company" who was indicted for an environmental crime almost simultaneously to being nominated to receive his state's Businessman of the Year award. "Typically, such a defendant deludes himself or herself with the false assumption that while people and businesses are indeed being charged and convicted of environmental crimes, only the traditional criminal has to worry."

But, say the lawyers, "One does not have to be evil to do evil. To obtain a conviction the government must only prove that an act which violated the law was done knowingly or absent a mistake or inadvertence. The government does *not* have to prove that the act was done with an evil purpose. Premeditation or malice aforethought are *not* required" [emphasis in original].

One of the biggest potential stumbling blocks for some companies, says Paul Wallach, is the court doctrine of "collective knowledge," in which a company is considered to have acquired the aggregate knowledge of all its employees, even though no single employee has sufficient knowledge to violate a law. So, says Wallach, "If one employee was aware of a discharge, and another employee knew that such a discharge would violate the applicable limitation, then the corporation would be deemed to have knowledge of a discharge in violation of the law, even though no one individual was aware of the discharge and the limitation. This doctrine is particularly troubling because a corporation is liable for all the acts of its employees, so long as the employee intended to benefit the corporation."

If each employee is, in effect, liable for the actions and knowledge of all the others, it doesn't take long to understand why the government believes that company directors and officers—who theoretically know everything that goes on inside their companies—should be taken to task, and to court, on behalf of their firms. Take the case of the United States vs. Pennwalt Corporation, resulting from the 1988 rupture of a steel storage tank, spewing chemicals into Puget Sound in Washington state. A federal court indicted the Tacoma plant manager—along with three senior executives thousands of miles away in the company's Philadelphia headquarters. According to lawyers at Chapman and Cutler, the three officers were indicted for each individual's ability "to have prevented the violation by virtue of his or her position in the corporation and failure to do so." Underscoring the government's position, the court required Pennwalt's CEO to appear personally to enter a guilty plea, rather than allowing corporate counsel to do so. Says Wallach: "This case offers a further example of the extreme type of case that the government is now willing to pursue in the environmental area."

Such a legal climate makes painfully clear the importance not only of compliance, but also of effective leadership, communication, information dissemination, and training. No longer is ignorance bliss; you may be held personally responsible for things you thought you knew but didn't. The result is that every company must view its environmental compliance efforts from the perspective of a prosecutor, judge, and jury.

REGULATION WITHOUT END

Even without the threat of doing time, environmental regulations can be confining enough. During the past quarter-century, no other subject has had a bigger impact on company operations. Nor does there seem to be a limit to government control over companies' impact on the environment: Nearly every sizable company in almost every sector is now, or soon will be, subject to some kind of federal or local environmental controls. Through war, recession, and economic boom times, environmental regulation is a growth industry.

But the effect on companies can be far from growth-producing. In some industries, accommodating the regulations has taken center stage, radically affecting the way companies do business. Sometimes the changes create new efficiencies, at least over the long term, but the cost may be high—too high, some companies believe. In 1991, for example, the Pharmaceutical Manufacturers Association issued a statement that, "if the current trend continues, environmental regulation, not FDA approval, may cause the greatest delay in new drug introductions." That statement should not be taken lightly: The Food and Drug Administration's languid and labyrinthine approval process for drugs and devices has long been a thorn in the side of the pharmaceutical industry.

When you examine major U.S. environmental laws and regulations as a group you begin to understand part of the problem: They approach environmental problems in a piecemeal fashion. This may make sense at first—after all, water pollution and air pollution are distinctly different—but even a cursory look at this reveals how inefficient, perhaps even inept, the system is. For instance, air and water pollution share many of the same pollutants, industrial processes, and emitting industries, companies, and plants. And some chemicals can end up fouling air, water, and land. In some cases, the same chemical is regulated by the Clean Air Act; the Clean Water Act; the Comprehensive Environmental Response, Compensation, and Liability Act; the Hazardous Materials Transportation Act; the Resource Conservation and Recovery Act; the Safe Drinking Water Act; the Superfund Amendments and Reauthorization Act; and the Toxic Substances Control Act. For the government, this regulatory hodgepodge could mean up to eight or more separate EPA offices tracking the same emissions from the same companies. For companies, this could mean a small army of bureaucratic operatives with virtually identical interests breathing down their necks.

That's not all. Under most federal environmental statutes, state and local governments are allowed, even encouraged, to establish their own more stringent environmental laws. As a result, a manufacturing plant that is in full compliance in one state may be in violation of one or more statutes in another state.

If that weren't enough, interpretations and enforcement of all of these laws, federal and state, are always in flux. At the federal level, all three branches can potentially make—or alter—environmental rules. In the executive branch, a presidential commission (such as George Bush's Council on Competitiveness) can scrap or weaken regulations if its members believe the law may be too burdensome on companies—or for any other reason, for that matter. Congress can legislate—overtly, in the form of major new laws, or covertly, with loopholes or exemptions inconspicuously tacked onto other bills—exempting specific companies or classes of companies from some kind of environmental regulation. And the federal courts can adjudicate any of a variety of lawsuits charging regulators with matters ranging from the failure to enforce its own laws to the overenforcement of those same laws. So environmental laws are subject to any number of forces. These things, of course, also take place at the state and local levels.

This is not to argue that federal environmental regulations are unnecessary or even excessive; that debate is best left to policymakers and pundits. The point is that they exist. Depending on who you are talking to in the corporate world, complying with government rules and regulations is anything from an annoying cost of doing business to a suffocating intrusion into corporate life.

Indeed, some laws should be changed. For example, the 1990 Clean Air Act specifies the level of pollutants that manufacturing industries are allowed to emit. But the rules were developed for firms that engage in continuous processing—the assembly-line type of manufacturing in which a given plant or machine continuously produces the same ingredient or product; an example would be an oil refinery or chicken-processing plant. In those operations, emissions are fairly predictable, perhaps fluctuating only on the basis of how much raw material (oil or chickens) is being processed. In that case, setting a permissible level of emissions is fairly easy to do.

But other industries use what is known as batch processing, in which products are produced in batches before switching machines over to another product. That's common, for example, in the pharmaceutical industry, where a succession of sera or pills may be produced by a given plant. Of course, each batch uses different ingredients and yields different emissions, requiring that permit and emissions limitations be more flexible. So the Clean Air Act's rules aren't particularly relevant to the pharmaceutical industry. For that reason, the lobbyists from the Pharmaceutical Manufacturers of America, the industry's trade group, have tried to get the law amended to better accommodate their members' manufacturing methods. As of this writing, the PMA was still trying.

PMA's efforts are just one of dozens of skirmishes in the ongoing battle between the government and the private sector over the goals of a cleaner environment and companies' ability to do business. The level of venom a company executive uses in describing the battle usually has a lot to do with how far ahead (or behind) the company in question is on the regulatory curve. Companies whose strategy is to stay a step or three ahead of the regulators have discovered certain freedoms to conduct business unhampered by matters of compliance. Both the EPA and some state regulators have adopted unofficial hands-off policies, in which companies with good track records get inspected less frequently. From the regulators' perspectives, this is pragmatic in an era of budget deficits and cutbacks.

Take 3M, for example. The $12 billion company, which manufactures sixty thousand different products, uses a significant amount of chemicals and industrial processes. But compared with some of its competitors, 3M has taken a forward-looking approach to regulators. Whenever possible, the company has tried to minimize the impact of regulation by being ahead of its requirements.

Please understand: 3M doesn't like regulations any more than other companies do. In fact, Robert P. Bringer, 3M's top environmental executive, calls regulation "a market force of substantial proportion today." He explains: "It's not only costing companies a lot of money to deal with regulation, but it's starting to affect the flexibility of a lot of operations, whether or not we can do certain things in certain areas of the country, and whether or not we can use certain materials. We're very concerned that some of the regulations on chemical usage might start to impact on our researchers searching for the best possible option to develop a new project. They might reject a lot of options just out of hand because it's too much trouble. To get permission to do something, it's going to eat into the time frame you have set up for yourself."

In combating the impact of regulation, Bringer refers to what he calls his company's "attitude": "If you have a proactive attitude, an anticipatory attitude, that's how you carry out your business. Then you're always looking for those things, you're always asking yourself the question, 'What should we be doing today that's going to prevent us from having problems ten or fifteen years from now?' I think you really have to take that long-term look, which has not been the forte of companies necessarily. 'What the hell is our profit going to be next quarter?'—that's about as far as you get sometimes. But I think the long-term view is necessary when you're dealing with the environmental issue. I just know intuitively that if we meet the goals that we've set for ourselves in the year 2000, and we are manufacturing most of our products that now use coating operations—which is a good share of what we make—with solventless processes, we're going to be making them a lot cheaper, we're going to have a lot less regulatory problems, and we're going to have higher-quality products and processes. A lot of good things are going to happen. So, one of the big reasons for us being proactive and moving out of some of these situations is eliminating the trigger of regulation as much as possible. The further ahead we are, the less impact regulation will have on the way we do business, or would like to do business."

That may seem like common sense, but it's actually cutting-edge thinking. The vast majority of companies—both in the United States and in Europe—have focused mostly on meeting the regulations, and sometimes just barely. For them, looking over their shoulders at the next wave of regulations and deadlines is a way of corporate life. A few others, like 3M, know that such shortsightedness is foolhardy.

THE SUPERFUND QUAGMIRE

The environmental community, perhaps even the general public, sees little wrong with scaring corporate executives into submission. Public opinion polls indicate that they are willing to do this to "save the earth." But when it comes to Superfund, even some environmentalists aren't sure what we've gotten ourselves into.

The Superfund law—known formally as the Comprehensive Environmental Response, Compensation, and Liability Act, or CERCLA—was passed during the lame-duck session of Congress in late 1980, although extensive amendments were enacted in 1986, after the Bhopal tragedy. (In the acronym-laden worlds of government and business, these amendments are known as the Superfund Amendments and Reauthorization Act, or SARA.) Superfund goes far beyond any other federal environmental law, covering air, water, soil, and biological organisms. Its principal purpose is to provide a federal response to the uncontrolled releases of hazardous substances on land or at sea. It covers every type of industrial, commercial, and noncommercial facility—even the federal government's own extensive portfolio of owned or operated properties.

CERCLA has a lot of provisions. Among other things, the law established a trust fund—Superfund—to pay for the provisions of the law. This is unique: Other environmental laws are financed directly by the federal treasury. In this case, the fund was intended to front the money for cleanups, with reimbursement coming from those parties who were deemed responsible. The law requires states to nominate sites with serious environmental problems to a National Priority List. Since 1980, more than thirty thousand sites have been identified and nominated and about twelve hundred have been placed on the list. (These numbers don't include the thousands of sites listed on *state* Superfund lists, or sites covered under other federal laws.)

That sounds simple enough, but complexities quickly set in. CERCLA requires those who contributed hazardous waste to a site—called the "potentially responsible parties," or PRPs—to pay for environmental studies and cleanup. According to the law, companies have "strict liability," meaning a company or individual need not be negligent—it can be held liable even if it complied fully with the law. Also, liability for cleanups was deemed "joint and several," meaning that each party involved could potentially be responsible for the entire cleanup cost, even if the company had played a minor role—or even a nonexistent one—in dumping the actual wastes. The rationale, according to the law's drafters, was that any PRP could sue other PRPs to share in the responsibility. That way the burden of collection would be on the responsible parties, not the government. Finally, the liability was deemed to be retroactive without limit. Companies whose original owners are long gone—and, in fact, which may have been merged with or acquired by a succession of other companies—may be found liable for sites they owned or operated fifty or more years before, when casually dumping chemicals in steel drums (later found to leak) was the state of the art. In 1991, for example, Monsanto agreed to contribute $13 million as its share of cleaning up a site where it had dumped wastes in the 1930s.

One big problem is that there is no clear definition of what constitutes "clean." At a project in Holden, Missouri, in which an abandoned factory contained residues of toxic chemicals, local experts estimated it would take $71,000 to clean it up to the point where it would be highly unlikely the chemicals would ever harm anyone. Another $3.6 million would clean up virtually all residues and bury remaining traces under a blanket of clay. But that wasn't clean enough: state and federal authorities each demanded their own versions of a cleanup costing somewhere between $13.6 million and $41.5 million.

Nearly everyone agrees that something must be done to improve Superfund's abysmal cleanup record. Consider a few statistics. As of late-1992, just over 100 of 1,245 EPA-identified Superfund sites had been cleaned. The rate of completion grew during 1991–1992 from about 20 to about 35 sites a year, with EPA's announced goal to complete one hazardous waste site per week. Even at that accelerated rate, the current list of priority sites wouldn't be completed until roughly the year 2014, never mind the other 30,000 or so lower-priority sites.

Horror stories of the impact of Superfund on business are legend. Critics point to those involving smaller companies, who are affected by the enormous costs of cleaning up a hazardous waste site more than larger companies. Consider the case of someone we'll call Marvin Smyth, head of Smyth Electric, a small secondhand electric machinery company in the Northeast. (He asked that his real name not be used.) In 1977, Smyth sold a used transformer for about $10,000 to a coal company in Kentucky. The transformer contained a small amount of PCBs, an extremely toxic organic compound widely used as an electric insulator. (PCBs were legal until 1978, when they were banned in the United States.) One weekend, the transformer was struck by lightning and severely damaged. The repair cost would have been $6,000, but instead the coal company sold the transformer for $1,000 to a third company that repaired and resold scrapped transformers. That was the last Smyth knew about it.

Fast-forward twelve years to 1989, when Smyth is notified by the EPA that his firm has been identified as a PRP for a Superfund cleanup site in Cape Girardeau, Missouri, about one hundred miles south of St. Louis. "They found our name on a transformer card," says Smyth. "It's very vague, almost like a packing list." It seems the scrapping company dumped PCBs on the ground in their operation. But Smyth's historical connection with the transformer made him liable for the cleanup—potentially equally liable with the scrapper and the six hundred other PRPs who allegedly dumped hazardous wastes at this site. "The EPA simply called and said, 'You're on the PRP list. We strongly recommend that you pay your portion. Your share is over $225,000 and probably rising,' " recalls Smyth. Besides the liability, which remains unresolved, Smyth's comprehensive insurance coverage has been suspended, pending resolution of the case.

There are dozens, perhaps hundreds, of Marvin Smyth–like cases, in which small firms have found themselves snarled in a Superfund imbroglio with $5,000 or $25,000 transactions years earlier turning into six- or seven-figure liabilities. One can debate endlessly whether the punishment fits the crime but when the EPA calls, there's no sense in arguing morality. The situation simply becomes a case for the lawyers.

Besides lawyers' fees, government fines, and cleanup costs, there are other costs. Not the least is compensation to the victims of hazardous waste dumping. For example, in 1992 Monsanto and several other chemical companies agreed to settle a lawsuit by buying up an entire neighborhood as well as paying for the college educations of seven hundred children who lived there—all at an estimated price tag of $207.5 million. The settlement resulted from the companies' involvement with what came to be known as the Brio Superfund site—a fifty-eight-acre former dump twenty miles southeast of downtown Houston. Though the companies admitted to no wrongdoing, they agreed to buy out the mortgages of 212 families still living near the site. It was believed to be the largest settlement to date in a toxic-waste case. Of course, not one cent of that $207.5 million went toward cleaning up the Brio site, which could be hundreds of millions more. Monsanto's experience in the Brio case is telling. For one thing, the company had not owned any of the land, or dumped any chemicals on the site. It merely had sold chemicals to a refinery at that site.

In the world of Superfund, just about anyone, it seems, can be a potentially responsible party: the current owner or operator of a site, the past owners or operators of a site, any person or corporation who contracted for disposal of hazardous waste at a site, or any person or corporation who accepted hazardous waste for transportation to a site.

It takes only a couple of case histories to begin to understand the magnitude of the situation—and the morass that has resulted from Superfund. For example, State Street Bank & Trust Company, based in Boston, became a potentially responsible party in the late 1980s, when some two hundred companies, including IBM, DuPont, and Kodak, sued the bank, charging that it should be responsible for $30 million to $50 million in cleanup costs at a Lowell, Massachusetts, plant. The bank had controlled the day-to-day operations of the plant's prior owner after the company defaulted on its loan. Therefore, the plaintiffs alleged, the bank became an owner and operator under Superfund. In another case, Valley National Bank of Arizona, which had been trustee for an estate that held stock in a landfill, was identified as a PRP after the estate was closed when it was discovered the landfill contained hazardous waste.

A lender needn't even exercise management control over a property to be deemed liable. In a seminal case involving Fleet Factors Corporation, a U.S. Court of Appeals ruled that a secured creditor may be liable by merely participating in the "financial management" of a facility and having a *capacity* to influence the corporation's treatment of hazardous wastes. "Fleet Factors" has become a shorthand in the banking world for the uncertainty lenders now face from potential environmental liability.

This case and others have sent a chill through the banking community. With their deep pockets—after all, banks are where the money is, as Willie Sutton so accurately pointed out—banks and savings and loans recognize that they are sitting ducks for lawyers seeking another party with which to share Superfund cleanup costs. The American Bankers Association and other groups have prevailed upon the EPA to modify the law to exempt lenders who do not actively participate in the management of a facility.

Ironically, another concerned financial institution is the federal government. In the current era of bank and savings-and-loan failures, with such agencies as the Resolution Trust Corporation (RTC) and the Federal Deposit Insurance Corporation (FDIC) taking over failed institutions (and the defaulted properties each controls), the government has become a potentially responsible party. The RTC told Congress in 1991 that it has identified 300 properties that have potential environmental problems; the FDIC controls 238 such assets. Those are added to the government's existing hazardous waste burden, resulting from chemical accidents and neglect on dozens of Defense Department and Energy Department sites.

Not everyone agrees with the extent of the problem. In fact, the number of lender liability cases is fairly small—less than one percent of all PRPs, according to a study by the Southern Finance Project, representing less than one tenth of one percent of the nation's banks, savings and loans, and credit unions. Still, lenders are worried.

Lenders aren't alone in their concern over Superfund's broad reach. The commercial real estate industry has been similarly tarred, with the Superfund law affecting the cost of the vast majority of transactions, despite a 1986 "innocent landowner" amendment. That clause is intended to provide a safe harbor for owners or operators of real property that acquire title after disposal of a hazardous substance—if they can establish through "due diligence" that they did not know, and had no reason to know, about the hazardous release. In other words, to prove this a company must have made appropriate inquiry into a property's previous ownership and uses. However, in passing the law, Congress provided few guidelines for determining what constitutes "due diligence" on the part of such companies. This uncertainty has resulted in a significant number of real estate transactions simply falling apart under the sheer weight of ambiguity.

And then there is the insurance industry, which is inevitably a party in nearly any transaction involving money, liability, and litigation. Actually, the insurance industry had been dealing with these matters long before Superfund, although policies written after 1980 are litigated less often than earlier ones because newer policies are more specific in defining the scope of coverage. Those earlier policies did not foresee Superfund's commandments for retroactive joint and several liability. As a result, insurers' actuaries could not accurately calculate risks and premiums.

Most policies cover sudden and accidental losses, which raises the problem: If a company *suddenly* discovers that it *accidentally* built property on a plot of land that has been deemed a hazardous waste site, and is held responsible for cleanup of the site, is it covered by insurers? This is among the sticky questions being raised both in and out of court. In addition, there are often several, and sometimes dozens, of insurers involved. For example, a suit filed by FMC Corporation in California involved 173 insurance companies (FMC won). But judges and juries have ruled on both sides, sometimes giving partial victories to one side or the other. Complicating things is the fact that the federal government years ago opted out of insurance regulations. So, insurance laws are established by each state's insurance commissioner, resulting in a patch-work of laws, each further refined by the courts.

Clearly, the insurance industry has reason to worry. The General Accounting Office, the investigative arm of Congress, found in 1991 alone that just nine insurance companies had some fifty thousand unresolved claims and were involved with about two thousand pending lawsuits over pollution coverage liability. The outcome of these claims and suits could be devastating to the insurance industry. A report by Standard & Poor's estimated that, even if insurers were forced to pay only 15 percent of cleanup costs, the resulting losses could virtually bankrupt the entire property-casualty insurance industry.

One could make a case that bankers, real estate brokers, and insurers were unfortunate victims of a concerted effort to mitigate a serious and nagging environmental problem. But Superfund isn't exactly getting to the heart of the problem; for instance, no one's been very successful at cleaning up—except for lawyers, that is. With the cost of litigation sometimes meeting or even exceeding the cost of the actual cleanup, the legal profession seems to be the only party for whom Superfund is a success. *Business and Society Review* reported in 1991 that "at a recent first meeting of the fourth group of PRPs to be identified at one major Superfund site where the process had already been ongoing for five years, four hundred lawyers filled the Grand Ballroom of a Grand Hotel, each with their clock ticking. Only a handful of scientific and technical people were present."

Superfund seems to be a lawyer's dream. According to a 1992 study by the Rand Institute for Civil Justice, nearly 90 percent of the money paid out by insurers on Superfund claims has gone for legal and administrative costs; just over 10 percent went for actual site cleanups. The approximately $1 billion that went to lawyers between 1986 and

1989, says Rand, could have funded cleanups at forty polluted sites. All told, Superfund legal costs could top $200 billion, according to Jessica Mathews, vice president of the World Resources Institute.

Mathews, a Superfund critic, is among those calling for reform of the law. She is joined by a host of others, including many in the environmental cleanup industry, who would benefit from the reforms, because they would likely result in more money being spent on bulldozers than legal briefs. A coalition of businesses, calling itself the Superfund Action Coalition, formed in 1992, is seeking technical changes in the Superfund law which would limit retroactive liability to the most egregious, willful violations. That, contends the group, will allow fewer settlement dollars to go to lawyers and more to actually cleaning up sites; another result would be reduced harassment of small, well-intended companies. Other groups have called for a public works approach—some kind of business tax to create a massive fund that would go toward cleanup, eliminating the legal costs altogether. That, proponents say, would at least lend some predictability to the cost of doing business.

Clearly, Superfund's costs are out of line. Consider this cost-benefit analysis, by Jocelyn White, president of Environmental Issues Management, Inc., a Washington, D.C., firm that advises industry on hazardous waste cleanups. White points out that the EPA budgeted $1.75 billion for fiscal year 1993 for Superfund cleanups. That money is intended to alleviate the estimated one thousand cancer cases a year resulting from exposure to hazardous waste sites. In contrast, the National Cancer Institute budgeted a mere $133 million to conduct research on breast cancer, which afflicts an estimated 175,900 Americans a year. Running the numbers, White found that Superfund allocated about $1.75 million for each cancer case, while the breast cancer research program allocated only about $756 per cancer case.

Why does one federal program receive more financing and appear to be more important than another? "Popular opinion generally drives government's spending choices," suggests White. "The press and public exert enormous force to make politicians respond to their concerns about the environment. Legislators and federal agencies design programs and allocate money in keeping with those demands." White admits that "it may not be realistic to think that money will be shifted from the Superfund to breast cancer research." But, she says, "We should spend to mitigate real risks, not waste funds on projects that do so little for the environment and public health."

Not everyone would agree with this analysis—or even that the Superfund law needs changing. In fact, the environmental community has continually pressed the federal government for *stronger* Superfund enforcement. Douglas W. Wolf, a lawyer for the Natural Resources Defense Council, testifying before Congress on behalf of seven environmental groups in 1991, said that Superfund works precisely because it is so frightening to companies. "The very threat that they might be liable for a Superfund cleanup causes many businesses to entirely change the way they operate," he said. "It also gives these businesses an important reason to follow other environmental laws: If they don't, they may succeed only in creating dreaded Superfund liability."

Wolf and other environmentalists emphasize Superfund's benefits, both direct and indirect. Specifically, they point to a 1991 report by the National Research Council, the research arm of the National Academy of Sciences, which described the hazards of unmitigated hazardous waste dumps. The study concluded that abandoned waste sites can pose severe threats to local communities. For example, the council concluded that hazardous waste contamination has caused "a variety of symptoms of ill health in exposed persons, including low birth weight, cardiac anomalies, headache, fatigue, and a constellation of neurobehaviorial problems," and that "some studies have detected excesses of cancer in residents exposed to compounds, such as those that occur at hazardous-waste sites."

But even Wolf and colleagues acknowledge that the current Superfund approach to cleanup could be improved. One type of improvement, which is being spearheaded by the states of California and New Jersey, establishes fixed soil cleanup standards for certain toxic substances often found at abandoned waste sites. According to Wolf, this will give regulators "an answer to the important 'how clean is clean' question at each site they tackle. Using these standards to make cleanup decisions will reduce the need for a complex, site-by-site analysis of potential risks to human health and the environment, something very susceptible to error and manipulation." Not to mention very expensive.

A MATTER OF RECORDS

Superfund may be the most dramatic example of companies' futures being determined by their environmental performance, but it is far from the only one. Consider the mundane subject of accounting—the way companies translate their day-to-day activities into standard numerical reports. Due to increased reporting requirements mandated by federal and state laws, the common, everyday accountant is having a greater role than before in shaping how a company's environmental performance is viewed by a wide range of others who have direct or indirect financial interest in that company. His or her accounting methods increasingly show up in companies' annual reports, and, in turn, may be reflected in their credit ratings, stock prices, tax liabilities, and potential for acquisition and divestiture.

Historically, financial statements have been governed by a set of generally accepted accounting principles, or GAAP, which are widely recognized by lenders, investors, and others, including the government. GAAP tells companies how and when to deduct expenses in the current fiscal year or amortize them over several years. They describe how to assign "soft costs"—such as legal, consulting, and overhead—to each widget coming off an assembly line. From the basic to the arcane, GAAP offers a way to account for just about everything. In the United States, the Securities and Exchange Commission requires publicly held companies to follow GAAP in their required filings.

But when it comes to telling companies how to account for today's environmental realities, GAAP has left some gaps.

The situation has presented some new challenges for companies that are just beginning to need to reflect some of their environmental costs in their accounts. Up until the early 1990s, most companies' environmental accounting did not involve finances. It simply dealt with the need to inventory their emissions and wastes—to account for what was going into their plants and what was coming out. At most, companies were required to note in financial reports that sometime in the future that they might have some expenses when actual cleanup and pollution-prevention measures were implemented.

But today, much of the work is being done, and companies are accounting for those costs on their balance sheets and other financial documents. "The accounting standards are very simple," explains John

P. Surma, director of environmental services for Price Waterhouse. "They merely say that when you think that a loss is probable, and you can estimate how much it is, you record it. That's the rule. It's very simple and sounds very easy to apply. In the case of a product liability, where something explodes and your obligation is to replace it, you can probably figure out how much it can be.

"On the other hand, when you're one party of fifty in a Superfund site that had cost estimates of between \$50 and \$500 million, knowing how much loss to record is a much different question. The accounting standards don't tell you how to do that. And it would be virtually impossible to write any accounting standards that would attempt to answer that question."

Surma points to the site in Holden, Missouri, mentioned earlier—the one where cleanup estimates range from \$71,000 to \$41.5 million. "Picture yourself as the financial officer of that company. What would you do? The accounting standard would say, 'It seems that the company would have a loss.' So they met the first test. How much is it? What would you record? Would you record the \$71,000 and risk having to pump it up to \$15 million or \$30 million? Would you record \$30 million, thinking that if your company gets off for \$71,000 you'll look stupid? What would you do? That's the real crux of the question." Answers to such questions are slow in coming, but some guidance already has been offered by the Financial Accounting Standards Board, the industry group that helps establish GAAP. And additional standards will emerge, each of which will require financial managers and executives to reexamine select parts of company operations.

The reason we must consider these mundane and mysterious matters—which seem to have so little to do with enforcing good environmental behavior—is the magnitude of the costs involved. It will take billions of dollars, perhaps a trillion or more, to resolve the existing environmental problems of U.S. companies alone. Whatever the number, it is significant. And the way those numbers are accounted on companies' ledgers could profoundly affect their bottom lines.

And then there's the matter of timing: Exactly when do you record liabilities for remediating environmental problems? A Price Waterhouse survey of 125 large U.S. companies found eight different practices of recording this information. When it comes to reporting a company's activities on the books, and especially recording environmental liabilities, timing can be everything. A well-timed entry can minimize or magnify a loss, with a concomitant impact on a company's earnings per share, stock price, and tax liabilities.

As you might expect, the Securities and Exchange Commission takes great interest in such activities. Over the last few years, the SEC has created specific environmental disclosure requirements for publicly held companies. Moreover, as stated earlier, the commission has an arrangement with the EPA by which that agency reports to the SEC environmental information on a quarterly basis, enabling the SEC to better monitor companies' reporting of Superfund and other environmental liabilities. Among other things, the SEC requires companies to disclose any "significant" legal or administrative proceedings in which it is engaged, as well as the material effects that compliance with federal, state, and local environmental laws may have on its and its subsidiaries' capital expenditures, earnings, and competitive position.

Companies used to have more flexibility when it came to reporting these things. Only when a liability became "certain" did it need to be recorded on the books. And that gave companies some wiggling room. In the past, a liability could be deemed "certain" only when a final judgment was made by an agency or a court, ordering the company to pay cleanup costs. Now, with Superfund, things aren't that loose. The SEC ruled in 1989 that once the EPA has designated a company as a PRP, the liability becomes "certain" and must be disclosed by management in its annual 10-K filing—unless it determines the amount won't have an adverse effect on the company's financial condition.

Of course, a Superfund action isn't the only thing that requires a company to record and disclose its environmental performance to stockholders and others. Lawsuits over environmental mishaps and misdeeds may also need to be noted, in order to alert investors about any potential judgments. However, management is likely to put its own "spin" on the situation, playing down the suits' merits—and the likelihood of plaintiffs to prevail. Even so, the mere mention of such suits in an annual report is telling, indicating a reasonable chance that the legal actions will cost the company. Consider the following notation in the 1990 annual report of International Paper Corporation:

> In late 1990 and early 1991, several lawsuits were filed against paper products producers by landowners, commercial fishermen, and individual consumers of fish claiming property damage or risk of personal injury allegedly resulting from the

presence of dioxin in mill discharges. This flurry of litigation and the accompanying publicity were spurred by a successful recovery against another paper company in a lower state court. International Paper is named in some of these lawsuits, which request cumulative punitive damages in excess of $2 billion. Considering the aggressive solicitation methods being employed by the plaintiffs' attorneys, the Company believes additional suits, accompanied by maximum publicity, are likely. However, management believes these suits are without merit and expects to prevail upon final resolution.

Is International Paper's management worried? Should its stockholders be? Read between the lines and judge for yourself. Whatever the outcome of this "flurry of litigation," one thing is certain: Thanks to the growing number of organizations that compile and publish data on corporate environmental performance, the circumstances referred to in the above paragraph will be circulated far beyond the people who read the company's annual report. They will become the stuff from which media investigations, stock analyst recommendations, and environmental group actions are made.

WHERE CREDIT IS DUE

If a company's financial records are burdened by a less-than-sterling environmental legacy, it would follow that lending institutions would think twice before extending or expanding a line of credit to that company. But until recently, that wasn't necessarily the case. Because environmental problems weren't generally recorded as long-term liabilities, they were written off as costs of doing business, usually hidden amid the operating accounts of one or more parts of the company.

Thanks to the requirements of increased financial disclosure, it's now a whole new ball game. And banks and other lenders are among those who are peering into these matters more carefully than ever before. A few of these lenders are beginning to recognize that providers of capital must share responsibility for safeguarding the environment with users of that capital.

This may sound like brazen stuff from the traditionally conservative banking industry. In the past, the only interest most banks had in the environment was a bit of cursory information necessary to ensure their loans. But now, burdensome environmental cleanup costs clearly can impair borrowers' ability to repay their loans on a timely basis. And, as discussed earlier, when bankers take over polluting projects by default, they face their own liability. As owners, the banks can be named as polluters, too. So, bankers must engage in a substantial amount of "due diligence" to ensure that they don't become ensnared in such matters.

The cost of becoming ensnared can be substantial. A $200,000 loan at 5 percent interest might earn about $4,000 a year in net profits for the lender. But if the borrower defaults for environmental reasons— for instance, the owner is unable to pay for cleaning up improperly dumped chemicals—the value of the loan could dip to about 30 cents on the dollar, or $60,000, a $140,000 loss for the bank. If the bank, as the new owner of the borrower's property, must pay for the cleanup, the combined losses could easily exceed the original loan value, perhaps by hundreds of thousands of dollars.

Bankers' checklists for environmentally related loans now comprise an increasingly sophisticated number of requirements, from aerial photographs to reviews of geological surveys to in-depth research of government records. Lenders must examine future compliance costs, potential environmental liabilities, and the potential diminution in the value of collateral as the result of environmental problems. They must have a firm grasp on the present and historical uses of the site—and surrounding sites, which may have leached contaminants across property lines. Comprehensive testing of soil and groundwater are often required, as is an examination of any of several categories of environmental permits.

Clearly, this is no longer a case of simply reviewing balance sheets and checking credit references.

But what about the prospect of banks going beyond that—of actually becoming proactively involved with borrowers' environmental responsibility? Observers of that pin-striped profession might think it heretical for bankers to step into the environmental fray beyond ensuring the quality of their loans. But a few forward-thinking companies see the environment as an opportunity for a competitive advantage.

Among them is Bank of America, which has taken a few tentative steps toward integrating environmental criteria into the loan application process. However, as Richard D. Morrison, the bank's senior vice president for environmental policies and programs, will be among the first to tell you, doing so is easier said than done. Nevertheless, he says, the bank has "a strong predisposition to help environmentally beneficial businesses and not support guys that are not doing the right thing with the environment." The company now employs nine people who review potential environmental problems on all new business and commercial real estate loans.

"We have a very simple policy," says Morrison. "It says that we'll take into account the environmental responsibility actually displayed by both customers and suppliers. That means you have to look at each class of loans and you have to make some kind of determination whether they're good for the environment or really bad for the environment. The assumption being that the guys who are sort of in the middle, we're not going to deal with initially. If the guy is really doing something great, then you want to try to help a little bit. If a guy is really doing something horrible, you want to preferably try to get him to stop doing something it. If you just say 'I won't give you any credit,' all he does is go to another bank and you haven't done anything for the environment. The best of all worlds is if the guy is doing something that isn't quite right and you can persuade him to take a few steps in the direction of what you think is right. That's the basic idea."

Figuring out how to apply this in the real world "has proved to be immensely more difficult than I thought it would be," says Morrison. For example, there's the matter of loans made to companies conducting business in the tropical rain forests of Southeast Asia. Says Morrison: "If you're logging in the rain forest in Malaysia or Indonesia or one of those countries, and if you're not doing it in a sustainable manner, you're a bad guy, right? Being a dedicated environmentalist, I would have said that was a definite slam-dunk."

But things were not quite that simple. Following a meeting at the World Resources Institute in 1992, Morrison learned that "it isn't the logging that destroys the rain forest, it's what comes after that. It's the fires that burn out of control for nine months, or it's the agriculturalists that move in there with their slash and burn. So just the act of logging isn't so bad.

"If you go to the guy that's logging and you put on certain conditions—'We'll only finance you if you log in this manner, which is by definition sustainable'—you've got something you can get your hands into. Maybe the best thing you can do is not to go hassle the loggers, but maybe you should be out there trying to finance projects that create enough employment so that these people don't have to go into the forest and do their slash-and-burn agriculture. All they're looking for is a way to make a living. They're poor people, not mean folks, just trying to make it to the next day." All of which, he says, shows, "how very difficult it is, no matter how pure your motives are, to do the right thing, or even find out what the right thing is."

Morrison is well aware that getting involved with companies' environmental policies is fraught with potential pitfalls. Burdensome environmental restrictions could make a bank less competitive in the financial marketplace. Banks *want* to grant loans; that's the business they're in. Large seven- or eight-figure commercial loans are the stuff from which profits are made. But there are only so many of those to go around, and banks engage in hard-boiled competition whenever they arise. So, adding environmental criteria not required by government regulations could jeopardize a bank's competitiveness: a potential borrower, not wanting to be bothered with additional environmental disclosure, could simply shop the competition.

The road to an environmentally improved lending operation has been a bumpy one for Bank of America, and its experience demonstrates the problems many companies are encountering as they shine light on their greener policies, sometimes illuminating their own environmental skeletons in the process. For example, one of the bank's critics is the Southern Finance Project (SFP), a lending-industry watchdog based in North Carolina. In a 1992 paper, "Green Words, Grimy Deeds," the group took Bank of America to task for practices that undermined its environmental policy. Among the charges was that the bank committed billions of dollars in funding to "firms that consistently have racked up some of the sorriest environmental records in corporate America." In its paper, SFP cited a report in *American Banker*, a trade publication, that Bank of America "has been the lead bank on big loans to . . . corporations in industries that are prone to environmental difficulties." In the article, Richard Morrison was quoted as saying, "These are large companies that are in the mainstream of their industry. We are not in a position to tell them what to do."

Moody's Investors Services, the powerful bond rating and financial publishing firm, also has announced its intentions to make companies' environmental performance part of their creditworthiness. In a 1991 report, Moody's noted that "environmental liabilities may pose significant credit risks because of their potential for creating sudden and possibly large financial obligations on past generators of waste materials. In addition, increased regulatory compliance costs may add to operating costs." As a result, Moody's announced that it may downgrade some companies' credit ratings because of future environmental liabilities. That same year, John A. Bohm, Jr., Moody's president, described the cloud of uncertainty hovering over the corporate financial landscape. "Environmental costs which had scarcely been considered yesterday are becoming stark realities today," he wrote in *The Journal of Private Sector Policy*. "Who knows how many apparently sound and prosperous firms are financially dependent upon some modern, yet-unsuspected counterpart to asbestos, soon to be outlawed?"

No one knows, and by the time they do, it may be too late.

IN THE PUBLIC INTEREST

Meanwhile, what about the environmentalists? In the name of "we, the people," they represent an ongoing source of pressure on corporate and government officials. Their prodding, litigation, and ability to influence public opinion and legislation can be considerable. But how much clout do they really have?

There's no simple answer to that. A lot of the answer depends upon the industry you are in and the relationships your company has forged with environmental groups and their leaders—not just at the national level, but at the state and local level, too. In fact, local groups (or local chapters of national groups) often wield far more clout than their larger national counterparts. Environmental groups can deal with companies most effectively at the plant level, organizing boycotts or demonstrations, testifying at local regulatory or administrative hearings, appearing in local papers as well as on radio and television, and otherwise insinuating themselves into the business of firms with whom they disagree. But environmentalists don't have to be the evil empires some companies perceive them to be. As you will see later in this book, even some companies that have national reputations as polluters have maintained good relationships in their local communities as well as with national environmental groups, using time-tested techniques of communication and disclosure.

Who exactly are environmentalists? These days, they can be just about anyone. A 1991 Gallup Poll found that about 75 percent of Americans consider themselves "environmentalists," though another study, from the Roper Organization, showed that only about 9 percent of Americans actually contribute to environmental groups. And while the mainstream environmental movement's leadership remains largely white, middle class, and male, more attempts have been made to involve and empower the dispossessed, particularly at the local level, where some of the most polluted areas are those inhabited by the urban and rural poor. In any case, attempts to pigeonhole environmental groups into neat categories can be frustrating; such exercises often reveal more about the pigeonholers than the environmentalists.

Still, there are some notable differences among environmental groups. Consider this analysis, proffered in the summer 1990 edition of *General Electric EHS News*, an in-house publication. GE noted that "there are two basic types of environmental organizations. 'Full-time' groups make advocacy their daily work, and are generally knowledgeable about and expert in environmental issues. . . . 'Ad hoc' organizations are generally formed by local citizens in response to perceived environmental problems. They generally have less expertise and staff support. . . ."

GE further divided the "full-time" environmental groups into the following clusters:

Conservationists, the largest category, include the Sierra Club, Izaak Walton League, National Parks and Conservation Association, and the National Wildlife Federation, all focusing on conservation, generally moderate in their positions, and generally are known to "give industry a fair hearing." Many of these groups have shifted their efforts from narrow to general environmental goals. For example, Defenders of Wildlife, which once focused primarily on matters of animal cruelty, now works to preserve the entire ecosystem.

Legalists include the Environmental Defense Fund, Friends of the Earth, and the Natural Resources Defense Council, all "skilled lobbyists, pushing Congress to pass one environmental law after another," as well as being increasingly active at the local level. These are the groups most likely to take on corporations and government agencies in court and regulatory hearings.

Grass-roots groups "believe staunchly in the concept of 'citizens' empowerment': getting ordinary people involved in their local environmental problems," using such tools as rallies, petition drives, media events, letter-writing campaigns, and consumer boycotts. Chief among these is Greenpeace, the largest environmental group in the world, with 2.5 million members worldwide.

Eco-philosophers are influential individuals "who are articulating the philosophical underpinnings of the environmental movement." Barry Commoner, biologist, author, and Queens College professor, is one example.

GE's analysis, however instructive, is of limited value. Experience has shown that—to paraphrase a well-known sports caveat—on any given day, any environmental group can beat its opponent. The Sierra Club's so-called moderates, for example, can effectively raise hell in the media over a wide range of matters, taking a no-compromise position on an issue such as saving the spotted owls of the Pacific Northwest. The legalist Environmental Defense Fund was the group that formed a controversial but highly successful alliance with environmental nemesis McDonald's, advising the fast-food chain on ways to "green" its operations. And some of the scrappiest local grass roots groups can wreak havoc in local communities, pressuring government and corporate officials on matters near and dear to their daily lives. Senior executives back at company headquarters often underestimate these groups, which can be far more potent than either the local or federal government at forcing action against polluters or sidetracking construction projects that they think are not in the public's interest.

No matter how you classify them, environmental activists of the 1990s are a different breed from their 1970s' predecessors. Those earlier pioneers lacked the scientific, technical, and legal expertise enjoyed by today's groups. Today's environmentalists are just as likely to take on the World Bank, the European Community, or the Secretariat of the General Agreement on Tariffs and Trade as they are to take on the operator of a local landfill or incinerator. They may also bring to these encounters a cadre of credentialed scientists, skilled lobbyists, and legal eagles—as well as a membership numbering in the tens or hundreds of thousands. And while the environmentalists may lose more battles than they win, their lack of clear-cut victories is irrelevant: Through their actions, they can wield substantial clout in their ability to change public opinion, influence politicians, or simply roil the waters.

One of the biggest differences between today's environmentalists and their forebears is access. No longer relegated to being outside agitators, the national environmental groups have become as much Washington insiders as their counterparts at the American Petroleum Institute and the Chemical Manufacturers Association, particularly with the advent of the Clinton administration. That has a lot to do with the so-called revolving door of politics. Government officials and bureaucrats have long moved from public service into the corporate sector, but in recent years the path from government jobs has also led into the public-interest sector. On the other side of the revolving door, environmental activists have taken positions in government agencies. One of the better known environmentalists to enter government service is William Reilly, who left his job at the World Wildlife Fund to become EPA administrator under George Bush. The same phenomenon takes place at the state level.

The result of the revolving door has been a more experienced caliber of environmentalist, who is likely to possess greater lobbying and negotiation skills than ever before. Ironically, the conciliation and compromise skills some environmentalists bring to the lobbying and regulatory processes have led them to be charged by their colleagues with being too soft on polluters. The biggest critics tend to be grassroots activists, who tend to be more singly focused in their issues, with more to gain or lose in the outcome of their battles, and are often less willing to compromise. As any seasoned Washington insider knows, today's compromise can lead to tomorrow's returned favor. These same insiders also recognize that effective, long-term change is incremental, not revolutionary, a perspective that the more hard-liners perceive as a sign of weakness and disunity.

Also problematic is that some of the groups have become so large that they must rely on contributions from corporations as well as individuals to survive. This also includes money from some of the very corporations they are fighting, which, of course, leads to additional criticism—and the moniker "Environment, Inc." In other cases, environmentalists have been asked to sit on boards of directors of such companies as Dow Chemical, Ashland Oil, and Waste Management Inc. That gives them access, but it also fosters an image of corporate coziness that the more activist groups find unsettling, to say the least.

The environmentalists were the first to borrow techniques from their counterparts—industry lobbyists—by enlisting legions of respected and well-paid scientists and lawyers when needed. But recently, industry has turned to the same citizen organizing techniques pioneered by the environmentalists. Several years ago, when a group of major environmental groups formed the Clean Air Coalition to lobby to strengthen the Clean Air Act, a group of nearly two thousand companies and trade associations countered by forming the similarly named Clean Air Working Group to press their side of the story. And then there's the Superfund Action Coalition, whose name is sufficiently ambiguous to avoid instant identification with industry. Like their environmental counterparts, these industry coalitions claim to be grass-roots organizations speaking for a disaffected constituency. Such efforts can succeed on two fronts: they blur the lines of distinction between the "good guys" and "bad guys," and they can engender unity for the environmentalists' opposition, creating coherence out of disparate voices.

But the power of all these national organizations, lobbyists, and negotiators can pale when compared to a few determined citizens working on the local level, where the interactions among environmentalists, government officials, media, and companies can be far less predictable. Environmental legend is full of heroic efforts of individual activists like Rita Carlson.

Carlson is a Texas City, Texas, homemaker who brought together her neighbors to form the Galveston County Environmental Division. She purposely picked the name because it sounded official, which she believed would give her better access to information from state agencies. Although Carlson's group had only ten active members, they organized a lawsuit on behalf of more than one thousand people who required medical attention after hydrofluoric acid leaked from a Marathon Oil plant in 1987. Her efforts attracted the attention of Marathon Oil workers, who started calling, blowing the whistle on other environmental improprieties going on inside the company's gates.

Or consider the efforts of another small group called the Baytown Citizens Against Pollution. In 1989, the group leaked a memorandum written by the public relations coordinator at an Exxon refinery in

Baytown, Texas, outside Houston. The memo bemoaned the Baytown Citizens' access to information about the plant, noting that members began complaining about specific polluting accidents at the refinery even before news of the event had made its way through Exxon's own internal communications system. "I believe we are entering a significantly changed era with much stronger local environmental activism," the memo stated. In the past, it noted, environmentalists had been less critical of the company "due to the overriding perception of community benefits from the Exxon presence."

That pretty much sums up how things have changed. Where community members once viewed a smokestack's billowing fumes with satisfaction, knowing that it signified good economic times, they no longer take such matters for granted. That smoke, they now realize, could be causing at least as much harm as good.

SHOPPING FOR A BETTER ENVIRONMENT

In some ways, pressures from regulators, environmentalists, accountants, and the financial community pale when compared to that of the ultimate determinant of a company's future: customers. Their "enforcement" of corporate environmental performance may be far more passive and subtle. But by their sheer numbers, the potential power of consumers to affect companies can be considerable.

Sometime around Earth Day 1990, a new realization seemed to strike the collective consciousness of the marketplace like a bolt from the polluted blue: There was money to be made catering to consumers' growing concern about the fate of the earth. This in itself was no revolutionary development. Manufacturers and retailers had long ago proven themselves ready, willing, and able to jump on whatever societal bandwagon happened to be rolling by at any given moment.

But this rush to greenness was different. For one thing, advertising and product label claims transcended traditional feel-good themes— looking good, feeling healthy, being popular, enjoying convenience, and generally embracing highly polluting and resource-depleting life-styles. This time, the ads and labels made a more profound promise: Buy our product and you'll help save the earth.

Who could blame these product purveyors for their ardor? When queried by market researchers, nearly nine out of ten Americans proudly professed their willingness to buy "biodegradable" trash bags and diapers, "ozone-friendly" deodorants, "recyclable" cereal boxes, "natural" cleaners, "recycled" toilet paper, and a plethora of other products claiming to be kinder and gentler to the planet. When pressed further, many of these consumers said they'd even be willing to pay extra for the privilege of doing so. And the parade of products began, neither a trickle nor a torrent, but a steady stream: air fresheners, batteries, coffee filters, detergents, energy-saving devices, furniture, games, hair products, insect repellents, juices, and on down through the alphabet. Only one thing was missing: credibility.

Like so many other environmental matters, the problem of green shopping turned out to be far more complex than anyone expected. First and foremost, there are no perfectly "green" products. Manufacturing, using, and disposing of any product uses resources and creates wastes that must be recycled, incinerated, composted, or otherwise disposed of. Everything is relative and there are few absolutes. There are green products packaged in ungreen ways, ungreen products wrapped in green ways, green products from ungreen companies, and green companies making ungreen products.

Trying to sort out what's what turned out to be akin to trying to throw a rock at a moving target. Simple environmental marketing claims like "recycled" and "biodegradable" turned into hornet's nests of complexities. In their rush to embrace what appeared to be a fast-growing consumer trend, most companies didn't seem to examine their claims for scientific accuracy. The press, the regulators, and the environmental community had a field day. Finally, in 1992, the Federal Trade Commission offered a set of voluntary guidelines covering what marketers should and should not do in making green claims, which became a set of de facto industry standards.

Not that it's been all hype. The green consumer movement has inspired hundreds of companies to examine their products through a green lens, variously reformulating, repackaging, or simply repositioning them to accommodate the new green consciousness. The tuna industry and the fast-food industry represent two of the most publicized examples of companies changing their products or packaging to accommodate a more environmentally conscious world. But there are also many smaller, more incremental changes: companies increasing the amount of recycled content in their packaging; products being made with no or fewer problematic ingredients; and concentrated and refillable products that minimized packaging. Occasionally, one of these developments garners a rash of publicity, such as the 1991 announcement by the L'eggs Products division of Sara Lee Corporation that it would phase out the twenty-year-old hard-plastic egg that had become a trademark in selling its pantyhose and replace it with a container made of recycled paperboard. The story got headlines and air time in the major media. Of course, the change was not without incentives to the manufacturer: the packaging change allowed L'eggs to shoehorn 25 percent more product into the same space on supermarket shelves.

What made manufacturers capitulate to consumer demands? Was it the sheer number of shoppers involved? Hardly. While marketers have had considerable difficulty getting a handle on the scope of the green marketplace—polls measure only what consumers say they do, not what they actually do—few surveys have pegged the most active portion of the green market at more than 10 percent.

Case studies are revealing. McDonald's sales had increased during the twelve months leading up to McDonald's announcement that it was abandoning its polystyrene foam "clamshell" hamburger boxes in favor of paper products. And tuna sales had been relatively flat during the twelve months preceding the announcement by three leading tuna canners that they would stop using tuna caught in ways that harmed dolphins. Indeed, a *New York Times* report pegged the number of individuals actively pressuring tuna companies at less than one million— less than 1 percent of the marketplace. There is no evidence that either McDonald's or the tuna industry's announcement affected sales.

However small in number, the collective voice of green consumers looms large. The combined efforts of consumer and environmental groups, government agencies, schools, and marketers were enhanced by the considerable interest in the subject by national and local media, which spared no effort in bringing this information—and more than a little misinformation—to the public. From local food columnists to network television news shows, reporters and correspondents regularly led readers and viewers down the supermarket aisles, showing them environmental do's and don'ts with nearly every turn of the cart.

Ironically, today's consumers—as well as many reporters and even some environmentalists—still seem as confused as ever. Take aerosols, for example. Until the federal government banned them in

1978, most deodorants, shaving creams, hair sprays, cleaners, and other aerosol products contained ozone-depleting chlorofluorocarbons (CFCs). But only a tiny number of exempted products have contained CFCs since then. Still, a 1992 poll by the Roper Organization found that 55 percent of consumers agreed with the statement that the federal government still allows CFCs in aerosols sold in the United States. Only 14 percent correctly identified the statement as false. Clearly, such persisting misinformation sends the good folks at the Aerosol Council into apoplexy. Ironically, aerosol makers had created their own problems by proclaiming their products' lack of CFCs, slapping such vague terms as "ozone friendly" on product labels. That implied that their competitors' products did contain CFCs, or at least that aerosols were environmentally problem-free. But aerosols do have environmental problems—for example, their hydrocarbon-based propellants can contribute to photochemical smog—and their CFC-free claims caught the attention of regulators, who frowned upon what they viewed as duplicitious statements. That no doubt led to even further consumer confusion.

Besides being confused, consumers are increasingly cynical. The cynicism may be a carryover from the Oat Bran Era—a period in the 1980s when American consumers were all but force-fed a single ingredient, oat bran, that purported to reduce blood cholesterol levels. It didn't take long before consumers had the rug pulled out from under their ardor by subsequent research findings that questioned oat bran's cholesterol-reducing properties. One can be fairly certain that the next time a magic-bullet cholesterol- (or cancer- or hypertension- or whatever-) reducing food or drug is "discovered," consumers will be far less willing to swallow it, literally or figuratively.

So, too, with so-called green products. Having been frustrated with their attempts to purchase allegedly "biodegradable," "ozone-friendly," and "recyclable" products, many seem to have retreated to old brands and habits, waiting until that elusive someday when "they"—an unidentifiable melange of manufacturers, advertisers, regulators, environmentalists, scientists, whomever—get their act together and figure out what really is good for the earth.

This paradoxical state of affairs—with consumers at once demanding greener products and looking askance at anyone making such claims—represents a marketing minefield for manufacturers. What kinds of claims can you safely make? How do you identify your product's environmental benefits?

Carefully, or not at all, is the short answer. Indeed, that seems to be the short-term strategy for many companies, such as Procter & Gamble, which has downplayed environmental benefits of some of its environmentally improved products. For example, P&G's revolutionary Vidal Sassoon Air Spray Hairspray, an aerosol containing no chemical propellants (with an optional refill, further reducing packaging), barely mentions the "E" word on its label or in its ads.

THE GLARING LIGHTS OF DISCLOSURE

Companies had better pay attention to more than just their products, because consumers are increasingly peeking behind product labels to view the companies behind them. And just as Dorothy found that the Wizard behind the curtain wasn't as magical as he appeared, companies' green images aren't always everything they're cracked up to be.

Until fairly recently, information about companies' environmental performance was rather limited. Unless a company was formally charged with an environmental misdeed, or unless a company voluntarily divulged (or was pressured to divulge) facts about its operations and emissions, it was virtually impossible to know who was doing what to the environment.

All that changed with Superfund Amendments and Reauthorization Act, the 1986 law amending Superfund mentioned earlier. Key to that law was the concept of "community right to know"—specifically, about any toxic substances being used or transported by local companies that posed a potential risk to residents of nearby communities. The Bhopal chemical tragedy, as well as another Union Carbide toxic release in Institute, West Virginia, are among the pressures that had increased the demand for such disclosure.

One section of SARA—Title III, the Emergency Planning and Community Right-to-Know Act—set forth an ambitious system to alert communities about dangerous chemicals in their midst and to lay the foundation for an effective emergency response in the event of a chemical accident. Among other things, Title III requires companies to report immediately to authorities certain kinds of releases, make public Material Safety Data Sheets (MSDS) on the chemicals that are used in their plants, establish a chemical inventory reporting system detailing precise information about chemical use in a given facility, and disclose environmental emissions of specified chemicals.

If all that seems a Herculean task, it is. Boiled down to its essence, here are some of the specific provisions of Title III:

- If a "reportable quantity" of a legally defined "extremely hazardous substance" (as well as some other substances) is released into the air, water, or soil, a company must immediately report to community and state officials detailed information about the release, as well as follow-up information regarding how the company responded to control the release and any known or anticipated health effects of the release.
- Companies must annually report to local and state authorities the exact amount of hazardous chemicals stored at every U.S. facility, as well as the method of storage and the location within the facility of the chemical. This information must be provided to the public in writing upon request, except for information deemed to be trade secrets.
- Companies must annually report the exact amounts of more than three hundred toxic chemicals present at the facility at any time during the previous year, and the amount of those chemicals released into the air, water, or soil by each U.S. facility. (Facilities using only small quantities of toxic chemicals are exempted from this.) This information is collected and made available to the public as a data base known as the Toxics Release Inventory, or TRI.

For some companies, the letters "T-R-I" have become almost as feared as the letters "I-R-S." Thanks to this national data base, environmentalists, reporters, regulators, community groups, and concerned individuals can now learn the dirty secrets of nearly any factory's environmental performance (at least those factories located within U.S. borders). And that information can be amassed and massaged—plant by plant, company by company, sector by sector, year by year—to tell the bigger tale about which companies in which areas contribute the greatest (or least) amounts of which pollutants. Raw TRI data are available in a variety of formats. There's the traditional paper hard copy, of course, published annually by the EPA. More accessible, however, are several on-line computer services, offered by private and public-interest groups, as well as the EPA itself.

The Council on Economic Priorities has been collecting information about companies' social responsibility since 1969, some of which it publishes in its annual *Shopping for a Better World,* described in chapter 2. The effort is somewhat less than perfect, especially when it comes to the environment. For example, readers of the 1992 edition would find that Pampers disposable diapers were given a "top rating" on the environment—not because the product is especially earth-friendly, but because Procter & Gamble, its manufacturer, was said to have a progressive record on the environment. (A disclaimer in the back of the book notes that "our ratings apply to the company as a whole and do not purport to rate individual products.") But such details haven't detracted much from the success of *Shopping for a Better World.* In fact, the guide has helped whet the appetites of Americans for even more information about companies' records, with the environment being at the top of their wish list.

But data for their own sake are of limited value, which led the council to launch its Corporate Environmental Data Clearinghouse (CEDC) in 1991. The product of that effort is not a book—at least not yet—but a series of detailed reports on several aspects of a company's environmental record. A typical CEDC report covers a wide range of information, including TRI data for the latest reporting period. If the company has a published environmental policy, it is reprinted, along with descriptions of its lobbying and political issues, products and technologies, waste management practices, pending litigation, health and regulatory concerns, and the known environmental impact of its operations. There is also information about any awards or citations given for environmental performance, as well as contributions made to environmental causes. CEDC compiles its information from government agencies, environmental groups, media reports, and questionnaires sent directly to companies. Companies are given draft copies of the reports for review before being finalized and published. The entire collection of reports is made available by subscription, or singly at a sliding fee; reporters can often obtain reports at no charge.

A SNAPSHOT OF KODAK

Consider a typical report—this one published in 1992 and focusing on Eastman Kodak Company, the world's largest and oldest manufacturer of photographic film and related products. CEDC's profile of Kodak stretches to thirty pages, beginning with an executive summary highlighting the key findings of the report. Included are details of Kodak's toxic chemical releases as the company reported through the Toxics Release Inventory process. CEDC then ranks the releases—in volume as well as tons per $1,000 in sales—among Fortune 500 companies and among the seventeen companies within the scientific and photographic equipment industry. In this case, Kodak's TRI emissions rank thirteenth among the Fortune 500, and second within its industry. The report's authors make no value judgment on this; they simply report the facts.

Then there is a description of Kodak's business operations, facilities, and territories, a recitation of its written environmental policy, and an explanation of how environmental policy is implemented through the chain of command. In Kodak's case, direction comes from the company's Management Committee on Environmental Responsibility, headed by the CEO and monitored by the board of directors' Public Policy Committee. A Health, Safety, and Environmental Coordinating Committee implements company environmental policies and the company's Health and Environmental Laboratories have research staff who review and recommend environmental policies and actions.

The profile goes on to report the most recent figures on Kodak expenditures for pollution prevention and waste treatment, as well as capital expenditures related to environmental control. Despite a stated goal of recycling over 99 percent of methylene chloride by 1995, says the report, "Kodak facilities still emit the largest amount of methylene chloride of any company in the country."

On the plus side, there is a description of Kodak's Community Advisory Council, made up of community leaders of neighborhoods around Kodak's Rochester, New York, plant. Part of the council's role is to convey to the company the environmental and health concerns of residents.

So far, we have covered barely one-fifth of the report.

On page 7 is a description of Kodak's products and related environmental issues. The discussion here focuses on the company's "much-criticized" disposable cameras, which Kodak is attempting to recycle through its network of photofinishers. Following that are four pages detailing Kodak's environmental impact—its waste-management and energy-conservation efforts, more on its toxic releases, and a description of four spills of toxic materials that occurred at the company's Rochester facility during 1988. Among the issues discussed in this section is the research on plastics recycling funded by Eastman Chemical Company, a Kodak unit, which is the world's largest producer of polyethylene terephthalate for plastic bottle manufacture. There is also a description of Kodak's efforts to reduce the packaging of several of its products.

Next come legal and regulatory issues, including a state-by-state analysis of environmental violations and legal entanglements involving Kodak's U.S. plants. Among other things, the company is a potentially responsible party at nine Superfund sites and the EPA has proposed multimillion-dollar fines against the company for violations of the Toxic Substances Control Act. There is also information about a suit against Kodak by the Natural Resources Defense Council, alleging illegal waste discharges resulting in eighty-eight violations of the Clean Water Act.

The final part of the report includes footnotes as well as boilerplate information about several key corporate environmental issues, including TRI, chlorofluorocarbons, hazardous-waste incineration, Superfund, and the Ceres (or Valdez) Principles, a set of ten environmental standards that companies are being asked to sign by a coalition of environmental and investment organizations. (Kodak has not yet signed.)

The sum total of Kodak's profile—fairly typical among CEDC's offerings—is a reasonably thorough snapshot of the company's environmental record and commitment. Although the reports can become outdated rather quickly, as new environmental initiatives are launched or new problems surface, they provide easy access to a great deal of information that could be used by a wide range of interested parties.

The Corporate Environmental Data Clearinghouse isn't the only effort to compile data on companies' environmental performance. Another is the Environmental Information Service of the Investor Responsibility Research Center (IRRC), a nonprofit research organization funded by large institutional investors—university endowments, insurance companies, pension funds, banks, and foundations, among others charged with investment responsibility over large sums of money. Institutional investors' clout over corporate governance has grown in recent years, particularly in light of a set of rules issued in 1992 by the Securities and Exchange Commission, which for the first time allow big shareholders to gather to discuss how to pressure company management. Previously, such groups had to spend millions of dollars to contact every shareholder.

A growing number of these organizations have set up social "screens" through which investments must pass before being deemed acceptable. Much like the Council on Economic Priorities' criteria for rating products, investment screens may look at any number of aspects of company operations, depending on investors' interests and concerns. During much of the 1980s, for example, many university endowments, under pressure from students, refused to invest in companies that conducted business in South Africa, in reaction to that country's policies of racial apartheid.

Now, with apartheid on the wane, at least from the perspective of investor concern, the environment has taken center stage. All investors, especially big ones, are concerned about being caught off guard. That means that companies must be able to thoroughly explain their environmental positions and performance through audits, raw data, and financial reports.

IRRC's Environmental Information Service has become a part of that process. Launched in 1992, it offers analyses of companies' environmental performance, including "key environmental challenges and opportunities," according to its mission statement. Among other things, IRRC published a comprehensive *Corporate Environmental Profiles Directory*, containing a vast amount of complex information about the environmental performance of each of the Standard & Poor's 500 U.S. companies. Subscribers to the service receive a history of each company's compliance record, a thorough description of its environmental liabilities and cleanup responsibilities, the number and value of penalties and consent decrees, and descriptions of a company's environmental policies and programs.

What's most perplexing to some companies about all this disclosure is its accuracy, or lack thereof. By and large, most admit that the coverage in the reports and corporate profiles is fair. But that doesn't mean everything is always correct. Consider Chevron Corporation, whose CEDC report contained some very critical information; it also received a low rating in *Shopping for a Better World*.

David Sander, Chevron's senior environmental representative, says that in retrospect, his company didn't comment adequately on the draft CEDC report. "I don't think the people here that were working on it realized the seriousness of the information that was being collected. With everything else that is going on in a large corporation," he says, Chevron didn't pull its facts together fast enough. "It's probably our fault." Sander was also displeased about several points in the CEP shopping guide that did not adequately tell Chevron's side of the story. For example, it reported that Chevron was cited for 880 Clean Water Act violations at one California refinery in 1986; Sander says Chevron was in compliance by then. Another complaint has to do with the number of Superfund cases in which Chevron has been named a potentially responsible party.

Overall, says Sander, "The report was balanced. You had the good, the bad, and the ugly. I guess you could say it had an apparent bias toward the environmentalists' point of view. While there were errors and incorrect information, the majority of the information was correct."

Sander offers this counsel in working with groups seeking data or comment on company operations: "Cooperate, but be aware that any information you submit could be presented in an unbalanced light. CEP had information and facts that were very much one-sided from environmental groups. There was no opportunity for us to respond to that." Moreover, he offers, "Have a formal process within the company to sign off on the report." He also suggests reviewing the group's reports on other companies to get an idea of what to expect.

Investors and environmentalists aren't the only ones interested in all this information. Customers—both individual consumers and corporate clients—are following and sometimes heeding this information, too. Among the growing pressures on firms by customers and stockholders is to avoid doing business with companies that have undesirable environmental records. Companies with clout are beginning to hold contracts hostage until other companies disclose information about environmental performance; and they'll cancel those contracts with companies that don't measure up—or who simply won't disclose their policies and records. More on this in chapter 5.

All of this could be fairly straightforward if customers, investors, and other interested parties all used a standardized set of criteria for judging companies on the environment. But that's far from the case.

Says Melisa K. Huhn, whose firm, Scudder, Stevens & Clark, manages $50 billion in institutional assets: "We don't have two clients who screen investments the same way, or who agree on what environmental responsibility means."

That puts the burden of proof squarely on companies that may need to demonstrate—over and over, and from a never-ending parade of inquisitors—anything from their simple environmental compliance to their proactive commitment and leadership position on environmental issues. Even for companies with nothing to hide, the time and expense needed to respond to questioners (and their questionnaires) can detract from dealing with the other important issues of the day. One corporate environmental vice president who requested anonymity bemoans: "My small staff is knee-deep in ten- or twenty-page forms that must be filled out. Sometimes, they ask reasonable things. But a lot of them are asking things that are none of their business. And yet they're judging us by the answers, and presumably making decisions that will affect their relationships with us. Ironically, all these forms are keeping us from taking on the many things that need to be done here to improve our environmental record."

However unfair this may seem, there's no turning back. In chapter 5, we'll delve more deeply into how companies can successfully communicate their stands on the environment to suppliers, investors, and other stakeholders. For now, suffice to say that there are precious few places for companies to hide these days. The klieg lights of disclosure seem to shine increasingly brighter every month, as regulators, suppliers, customers, and neighbors require new types of information. And companies are finding that there is little they can do but squint, respond—and forge ahead.

empowerment

CREATING GREEN LEADERS FROM TOP TO BOTTOM

IF YOU UNDERSTAND nothing else about the potential of the people in your organization to effect environmental change, know this: A growing number of them are recycling, insulating, and otherwise greening their personal lives, either because they want to or because they are being required to by state and local laws. And, with the possible exception of a recently converted nonsmoker, no one is more self-righteous than a recently converted environmentalist. They take pride in their deeds and the part they are playing in the future of their community, their nation, and their planet.

But then they go to work, where they see tremendous waste and inefficiency—in the front office, on the factory floor, in the supply room, and just about elsewhere else. The trash accumulated by a handful of coworkers each day dwarfs that modest pile of newspapers they put out on the curb at home for pickup each week. The pollution prevented by the energy-efficient light bulbs they installed around the house may seem obliterated by the harsh glare of the endless banks of fluorescent lights at work, burning long after most people have gone home, controllable only by an inaccessible computer in the basement. It doesn't take a degree in the behavioral sciences to recognize the frustration and cynicism that can result. And those bad feelings can affect performance, commitment, quality, and pride.

The flip side, of course, is that when companies commit to some of these same goals—when they give their employees permission and encouragement to think and act environmentally—their efforts are often enthusiastically embraced. In many companies, environmental initiatives actually begin with line employees, bubbling up through the ranks until top management, like any astute leader, signs on to the program.

Consider the story of Heather Bell, an American Airlines flight attendant. In 1989, after just two years on the job, she got fed up with the waste onboard aircraft. "When you become a flight attendant, I think the first thing you noticed at that time was the amount of food and material that comes onboard the aircraft and the amount that ends up in garbage cans," she explains. "We have very small garbage cans, so you're very aware of what you're trying to jam in there. It became very obvious to me that something should be done."

Starting with a small-scale project at her home base at San Jose International Airport, and with the approval of airport management, Bell enlisted others' help to collect aluminum cans. "I asked the flight attendants to take the cans and bag them separately. I asked cabin service personnel to help by taking them off the aircraft and to the recycling bin. And I asked a recycling company to come and pick it up." Then she sent out messages via electronic mail to American's other seventeen thousand or so flight attendants. "I spent a lot of time at the airport running up to planes and talking to the flight attendants: 'Have you heard about our recycling program? Did you recycle anything for us?' "

The program spread quickly to airports in San Francisco and Los Angeles. "I started getting calls from flight attendants all around the system, asking, 'How do we get this started at our airport?' Which is exactly what I wanted to hear." An L.A.-based colleague, Jacki Graham, was the first to join in. By Earth Day 1990, thirteen American Airlines facilities across the country had joined the effort.

Just before Earth Day, Bell wrote American Airlines CEO Robert L. Crandall to tell him about the program. "I wanted him to know we were very proud of it, that although the program had been running just six months, we had already received one award"—the Mayor's Award from the city of San Jose. "I received a very nice letter back saying 'This was great, I didn't even know this was happening, and what can we do to help?' " That was the point when the program could be deemed a success.

The story goes on from there: Now chaired by Graham and fully supported by the company, the program has distributed $80,000 from selling recyclables to a long list of environmental and social-service charities. It has received extensive media coverage and awards from federal and state government agencies, as well as Bell's Recycler of the Year award from the Keep America Beautiful Foundation. The flight attendants also handed a $200,000 check in 1992 to the Nature Conservancy to purchase environmentally endangered acreage within the cedar glades of middle Tennessee—not far from the Nashville airport. The area hosts the world's largest known colony of *Echinacea tennesseensis*, the Tennessee coneflower. The daisylike, purple flower has been found in only five places, all within fifteen miles of Nashville.

Bell makes all this sound so easy. "I just took the approach that we would show them that we could do it, that the employees really were there behind it. And they would make the extra effort." And they did.

The message is implicit, if not explicit: The most environmentally successful companies work hard to create and support green leaders throughout the company.

Hardly anyone in business today will argue against the importance of leadership and the impact it can have on an entire organization's motivation toward quality and excellence. The business jargon of the 1990s is filled with references to ways to stimulate individuals to act like leaders, perhaps even like owners. "Flexible organizational networks." "Top-down, bottom-up leadership." "Holistic thinking." "Cross-functional teams." These are among the many buzzwords filtering through companies these days. And while management trends on which they travel may come and go every few months or years, the essential principle remains rock-solid: Companies in which leadership and authority are spread throughout the work force are the most committed and productive.

This principle is an essential—some would say *the* essential—component of total quality management (TQM) programs. The TQM literature usually begins and ends with the importance of leadership, and the role it plays in fomenting corporate excellence. W. Edwards Deming, one of a handful of TQM gurus, underscores this in several of the fourteen points he offers up as key to quality-based companies. For example, Deming's point number eight is that managers should "drive out fear" by creating an environment in which employees are not afraid to ask questions, even when they do not understand their jobs or the right ways to do things. Point number nine tells managers to break down barriers between staff areas, replacing departmental competition with cooperation. And point fourteen encourages companies to form a special top-management team to carry out the quality mission. Neither workers nor managers can do it by themselves, he says.

To underscore his belief in leadership commitment to major change, Deming has been known to walk out of his first meeting with a company if the CEO isn't present. He believes that without top-level commitment, he's wasting his time.

Perhaps. But without employees like Heather Bell, it's awfully lonely at the top.

A NEW KIND OF LEADERSHIP

Leadership seems to be on everyone's agenda these days. In the published requirements for the coveted Malcolm Baldrige National Quality Award—given out each year by the Commerce Department to a handful of companies that meet standards of overall excellence—leadership qualities constitute a significant portion of the criteria on which applicants are judged. The Baldrige judges examine senior executives' personal leadership and direct involvement "in creating and sustaining a customer focus and clear and visible quality values." Also examined is how these ideas are integrated into the company's management system "and reflected in the manner in which the company addresses its public responsibilities." When you combine this with several aspects of effective leadership, such as employee involvement, recognition, and morale, nearly a fourth of the Baldrige Award's criteria have to do with the ability of companies to create leaders at every level of the organizational ladder.

Top management's genuine commitment is key. Employees can see right through a program that lacks it. "Most people in business today are scary-smart, just like kids are scary-smart," says Jeff Hoye, president of Strategic Intent, a Boulder, Colorado, management consulting firm.

"You can tell a kid certain things, but they watch you. Just watch a kid at the dinner table. He's watching Mom and Dad and the guests, and they just know. They can sift through the words and pretty much see where you fall on different issues.

"The same happens with employees. They're just as scary-smart. When a program is rolled out, usually people look to the parent—the senior executives, the powers that be—and they watch. And they can tell if this is a real deal or 'just another one of those.' And if it's 'another one of those,' then everyone takes a this-shall-pass attitude: 'We've competed with the Japanese, we've searched for excellence, and now we're going to save the environment.' The program may be good on paper. The corner office blesses it, but they don't really walk their talk. People see that, so they don't invest their energy into it. And the next thing you know, it's gone."

None of this emphasis on leadership is particularly new at Herman Miller, the Zeeland, Michigan, furniture maker. For decades, its corporate culture, born of seven decades of family ownership, has emphasized the role of employee involvement in company strategy and decisions. Max DePree, whose father started the company in 1923, and who himself was CEO from 1980 to 1987, preached the leadership gospel constantly. In addressing management meetings, words like *assets* and *profits* rarely graced his lips. Instead, he talked of "being open," of "covenantal relationships," and of "meeting personal goals." "We're going to inhibit our own growth if we don't help everybody gain a good knowledge of the value system and the culture of this organization," was a typical DePree pronouncement. His convictions stem from his Dutch Reform background, which emphasized hard work, fairness, and the belief that individuals need to reach their highest potential. At Herman Miller, those beliefs came together in "participatory management," now a forty-year company tradition, with all employees owning stock and having a say in how the business operates. Almost from the beginning, such policies and beliefs have dominated the company's operating credos.

Those credos have also found made their way into environmental policy as well, starting with a company policy that at least one-fourth of all company facilities must be green space—lawns, gardens, pastures, forests, and the like. (The 800,000-square-foot Zeeland headquarters alone boasts more than thirty acres of wildlife sanctuaries.) The company's environmental policies and practices extend to recycling, waste reduction, pollution prevention, and all the other components of good corporate environmental stewardship. On an operational level, such policies aren't necessarily mandated from the top, but instead are ideas and innovations that originate throughout the organization.

Sometimes, the ideas are radical. For example, in 1990, research director Bill Foley noted the amount of tropical hardwood Herman Miller was consuming for some of its top-of-the-line furniture, including its $2,300 Eames lounge chair, a 1956 design that sells steadily and is in the permanent collection of New York's Museum of Modern Art. Foley recognized that the rosewood and Honduran mahogany used for the chair were playing a role in destroying tropical rain forests. After considerable debate among everyone from line employees to senior executives, the company decided to replace the woods with walnut and cherry.

That move startled many outsiders, who questioned Herman Miller's tinkering with one of its most highly regarded products. But it didn't surprise many inside the company, for whom it was just another day of debates and decisions. Herman Miller employees embrace the decision-making process, a reflection of DePree's emphasis on individualism and self-determination. And the process hasn't exactly hurt profits. During the 1980s, investors enjoyed a 27 percent annual return. That's one reason *Fortune* magazine has long ranked Herman Miller as one of "America's most admired corporations." The company has received other plaudits, including a Corporate Conscience Award in 1991 from the public-interest Council on Economic Priorities, and the President's Environment and Conservation Challenge Award "for excellence in developing innovative solutions to the nation's environmental challenges."

Herman Miller's unique leadership—and its environmental success—didn't happen overnight. It can take years to establish the proper level and style of leadership in any organization, especially when it comes to the environment. Few individuals or companies move from "ungreen" to "green" overnight. Rather, it is a slow, deliberate, and ongoing process, traversing a continuum that looks something like the graphic at the top of the next page.

Fortunately, the **Denial** stage is fading fast among U.S. companies. Relatively few would admit publicly to such an attitude these days. Companies face too many pressures to simply keep their heads in the sand on this subject. Most manufacturing companies have experienced some kind of chemical spill or run-in with environmental regula-

The Leadership Continuum

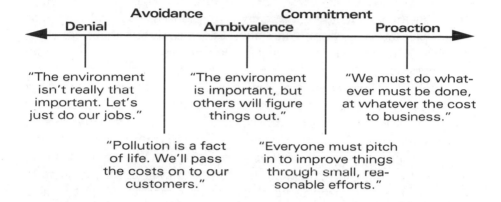

tors or environmentalists. Companies still in the Denial stage are more likely found in other industries—retail, for example, or banking or insurance. These are firms that run relatively clean operations and for whom the environment remains the concern of "others."

• The **Avoidance** attitude is traditionally the most prevalent, because it is a way companies ignore their own wastes and emissions. Companies in this stage feel that if they spend their money on environmental matters, little will be left for profits. These shortsighted companies are often the ones teetering on the edge of insolvency anyway. Though they acknowledge their pollution, they fail to take responsibility for it, a factor that may well have contributed to their precarious financial straits. It is likely that there is a strong link between their polluting processes and their cash crisis, as both point to inefficiencies within their operations. This attitude also affects companies in less dire straits, concerned more with short-term cash flow than long-term competitiveness. Obviously, this is shortsighted. For one thing, their competitors will likely be "greening" their operations, becoming more cost effective through lower manufacturing and overhead costs.

• The **Ambivalence** stage is the first step toward environmental responsibility. These companies are aware of the problem—an important move in the right direction—but they have a poor understanding of solutions. Companies at this stage are likely to have created some kind of environmental department or operation, though it is probably more reactive than proactive, dealing principally with regulatory compliance or potential liability. These companies have usually encountered some bad press recently or experienced a run-in with environmentalists; now they are flailing about internally trying to keep the tarnish of their image, sales, and stock to a minimum. Everyone *knows* that something must be done, but that "something" remains elusive, as is the leadership needed to pull it off.

• **Commitment** represents the goal for the majority of companies seeking to "go green." Getting everyone on board, hunkering down for the long term, tackling issues throughout the company, seeking incremental change—all are signs that the environment is becoming a serious business issue. These companies have established environmental departments, whether large or small, and have found better ways to do lots of things in order to minimize pollution and waste. But dealing with the environment remains a necessary evil for them; they have not begun integrating environmental thinking into such areas as strategic planning, accounting, and compensation.

• **Proactivists** see the environment as a top priority—on a level with strategy, stock price, and sales. Their environmental efforts are driven by a top-level executive, most likely reporting directly to the CEO or board of directors. Indeed, the environment has become woven into their cultural fabric, with employees at all levels actively involved with reducing pollution and waste. These companies have probably reached out to other constituencies—customers, suppliers, neighbors, even competitors—to educate, learn, and share knowledge on environmental topics. They aren't necessarily doing everything right; they likely have not yet reduced emissions and waste to ideal levels, for example. But they are actively involved at all levels in the pursuit of environmental excellence.

These classifications are admittedly simplistic, and it's quite possible for companies to be at several different stages at once. For example, a company could be ambivalent about air pollution but proactive on solid waste. And some companies are proactive on some topics, while denying that other problems even exist. The same differences could exist for divisions or even product lines within companies. Many will regard the far right of the continuum, "Proaction," as more like "Overreaction," especially when it comes to the "at whatever cost to business" part. For them, "Commitment" may be sufficient. As with any range of attitudes, most companies are somewhere in the middle.

MOVING TOWARD PROACTION

No matter where your company sits on the spectrum, what's important is to get everyone at all levels involved in the greening process. Of course, that's easier said than done, and the process of incorporating environmental thinking throughout an organization differs for nearly every company. The most successful companies have at least three things in common:

- They designated someone high up to be in charge of the company's environmental performance, which indicates that this is a priority of top management.
- They issued a policy statement detailing the company's environmental commitment and goals.
- They charged everyone within the company with adhering to the policy and meeting the established goals.

The order and style in which these things were done differ widely based on corporate cultures. All of them can be done at once, or a few tentative steps can be taken at a time. Some companies pull out all the stops, launching elaborate and expensive campaigns complete with a clever title, slogans, imprinted coffee mugs (among many other giveaways), a press release, and an employee rally. Others do things more quietly or less formally, issuing a simple memo or announcing a new initiative during a company meeting. Don't be fooled by extravagance: It often indicates a program that contains more style than substance. And a quiet, relatively informal effort can be just as productive, if it is backed by genuine commitment. Whatever the style, whatever the process, whatever the number of frills, the goal is to get everyone to make environmental thinking a daily part of business life.

Let's start with the idea of placing the environment at the top of your company's agenda. There's plenty of evidence that this issue is becoming a growth industry for management, moving up the corporate ladder in importance, particularly inside larger companies. The international consulting firm Booz-Allen & Hamilton shone some light on the topic with its 1991 survey of more than two hundred executives in fifteen industries. About nine in ten of the surveyed executives worked for companies with sales over $500 million, with more than a third of the firms exceeding $5 billion. Based on their findings, Booz-Allen divided the respondents into "Leaders" and "Non-leaders" in addressing environmental matters.

The survey found that "many corporate environmental efforts are still premature": A fourth of the companies didn't even have a published environmental policy. Of those that did, half had been established since 1989. Another principal finding was that the existing programs tended to be far more reactive than proactive, driven more by concerns about fines, lawsuits, and negative publicity than by opportunities to turn the environment into a competitive advantage. Only one in ten respondents believed their companies to be innovators in their environmental programs.

Still, Booz-Allen's researchers found an increase in attention to environmental issues across functions—in decisions about strategic planning, research and development, public relations, risk management, marketing, and diversification. But there were significant differences between the Leaders and Non-leaders. Booz-Allen concluded: "The Leaders recognize that environmental issues must be coordinated in a systematic and proactive manner, by developing formal mechanisms to consider environmental impacts. Such cross-functional integration of environmental concerns anticipates problems at the earliest stages to minimize risk and recognize opportunity." They went on: "Because environmental concerns affect so many corporate functions and levels of decision-making, the amount of leadership from top management largely determines the success of environmental programs. High-level leadership of environmental issues sends a strong message to middle management and staff, and should be expected to yield more successful programs."

The Booz-Allen findings were echoed in a 1992 study conducted by Abt Associates, a Cambridge, Massachusetts, consulting firm. Abt's Richard Wells and Tony Lent surveyed forty-two companies representing all major industry sectors and found that corporate environmental management "is an area of rapid and exciting changes." But: "Systems to manage and measure the success of these new programs lag behind corporate recognition of their strategic importance."

Wells and Lent found that the expansion of corporate environmental programs and responsibilities "closely mirrors our expanding recognition as a society of the central role of the environment in our lives." What once was an isolated corporate function concerned solely with environmental compliance now pervades all corporate functions. "We received almost as many mentions of new responsibilities—such as marketing, product development, and research and development—as traditional ones—such as compliance and plant-level performance," according to Wells.

Another revelation came when they asked how frequently executives *outside* of environmental affairs had a role in environmental decision making. Executives reported that some areas that previously did not have an environmental component now regularly integrate staff into those functions to evaluate the environmental implications of their policies. This was most common in product development, R&D, and marketing.

The study found that most companies had one or more new areas in which environmental programs were being planned. Most frequently named were environmental marketing, designing products with environmental considerations, and improved measurements of environmental performance. All are consistent with companies' increased use of TQM programs, which stress improving product and service quality as well as methods for gauging success.

Equally telling were the areas not yet being addressed. For instance, few companies track their customers' satisfaction with their environmental performance, and fewer still try to measure the effect of their environmental performance on sales of their products.

In the end, both Booz-Allen and Abt found the environment gaining importance in companies, and becoming more pervasive within company operations. Clearly, that's good news. But it presents as many challenges as opportunities. Among the biggest challenges is the need for top-level coordination of environmental efforts to ensure proper direction and authority. Booz-Allen's study found that respondents were "most comfortable with their environmental policies when corporate leadership is established high in the organization."

A third study of environmental managers was released in 1991 by Coopers & Lybrand, the accounting firm. Based on a survey of 500 managers, members of the National Association for Environmental Management, as well as conversations with nearly 150 of them, the study looked at the duties, background, and training of those in the profession. As might be expected in this emerging professional universe, the study revealed a wide range of titles, salaries, educational backgrounds, and reporting relationships within their companies. Overall, environmental managers tend to be a highly educated group, with more than a third holding advanced degrees; fewer than one in ten hadn't graduated college. Compensation ranged from under $30,000 a year to more than $100,000. Most managers reported through the operations organization, though others reported to the general counsel, facilities/maintenance, financial/risk management, engineering, human resources, administration, or safety and health departments. Fewer than one in ten reported directly to the president.

While the Coopers & Lybrand study didn't purport to be definitive—participants had volunteered to be surveyed—it did provide a snapshot of this emerging profession. "Lack of management support for environmental priorities was a recurring theme, no doubt adding to the perception of organizational isolation," reported Coopers & Lybrand's Michael Gilboy and Rolf Grun in the study's summary. "However, we did find that more and more companies are beginning to take a proactive approach to environmental concerns in the belief that good environmentalism means good business."

They concluded: "Virtually all of the nearly 150 professionals with whom we spoke expressed an urgent need to advance their own perceived professionalism, both among their peers and, perhaps more importantly, among the general business and regulatory communities."

BEYOND FANCY TITLES

As Booz-Allen, Coopers & Lybrand, and others point out, even having a top-management environmental leader—a vice president for the environment, or some other senior executive position—is spreading among companies. While high-level environmental decision making is not new—the Conference Board reported in 1974 that almost 90 percent of 516 responding companies made environmental policy decisions at the vice-president level or higher—the idea of having a senior executive devoted exclusively to environmental (and sometimes health and safety) issues only became widespread in recent years. Arthur D. Little reported that nearly half of the Fortune 100 companies had a vice president in charge of environmental affairs in 1991, compared with 38 percent in 1990. Among the Fortune 50, 62 percent had executives directly responsible for environmental affairs. Previously, these responsibilities were typically handled by a chief safety officer, a plant manager, or even a legal or public affairs manager, who helped keep companies out of environmental trouble by monitoring compliance with federal, state, and local laws.

The phenomenon can be seen at relatively smaller firms, too. For example, Glenda Goehrs serves as vice president for environmental affairs for GSD&M, a two-hundred-person, $150 million-a-year advertising agency based in Austin, Texas. This is the first such position in the advertising industry. And the Walt Disney Company has a vice president for environmental policy—with a campaign featuring Jiminy Cricket preaching "environmentality"—making sure that Mickey, Minnie, and friends maintain a squeaky-clean operation.

Things are somewhat further along in Germany, where a law that took effect in 1992 requires most companies to name top managers who are responsible for complying with environmental laws and for presenting compliance plans to the government. These so-called eco-managers put Germany at the cutting edge of corporate environmentalism, forcing businesses to view compliance as a strategic issue as much as a technical one. That means companies like Bayer AG and Henkel KGaA are now preaching environmental consciousness to employees. Bayer, for one, has given a member of its managing board responsibility for 1,100 employees with environmentally related jobs across a variety of disciplines.

Germany's experience is unique. In the rest of the world, eco-managers are still trying to fit into corporate cultures that don't necessarily embrace their missions. As a result, many green executives are given conflicting signals.

Consider the case of someone we'll call Martha, senior vice president for environmental affairs for a brand-name retailer. (She asked that her real name and company not be mentioned.) "The president has given me the responsibility of getting our company's environmental act together," says Martha. "But they haven't exactly made it easy. For one thing, I've got a staff of three. When you consider that we've got more than 650 stores, as well as warehouse and distribution centers, that level of staffing doesn't go very far. I'm being asked to oversee our compliance efforts, coordinate communication among store managers and department and facility heads, and think up promotional opportunities using environmental themes. Oh, yes—I'm also supposed to be setting up a paper recycling program here at headquarters."

Martha's plight mirrors that of other senior environmental officers who complain that they are not being given the authority or the tools to do their jobs. In most cases, top management is simply not looking at the big picture. Their principal concern is keeping the company in compliance and out of trouble with regulators. Obviously that's important, but it's not everything about the environment that should be addressed.

Of course, it's not enough to give someone high up a fancy title with the word "environment" in it. Titles are cheap. In fact, most large organizations suffer from title inflation, with a plethora of assistant vice presidents, vice presidents, senior vice presidents, executive vice presidents, and further still up the ladder—always a step or three away from the top. And, as everyone knows, not everyone with a fancy title has the ability to get things done—at least not to the same degree. Aside from differences in personal capabilities, a great deal depends on how much responsibility, authority, and funding each executive is given to do his or her task.

"The environment has always been sort of off to the side," says Richard Toftner, a former EPA official who has spent most of the last twenty years consulting to companies. "The guys that show up for seminars around the country are guys who were plant managers or had some other job, and all of a sudden the boss says, 'Now you're in charge of environment, health, and safety.' And they're trying to get a crash course in the subject. The companies that do that are really short-changing themselves." Moreover, says Toftner, "A lot of these guys don't have access. They report through the vice president for engineering who really couldn't care less."

IRRC's survey of Standard & Poor's 500 companies found that 44 percent of those responding to its survey said that the senior person charged with overseeing environmental affairs was a vice president; at 22 percent, an executive or senior vice president held this responsibility, and at another 22 percent of companies environmental matters were handled by someone with the title of director.

But these statistics don't tell the whole story. Dr. Bruce W.

Piasecki, director of environmental management programs at Rensselaer Polytechnic Institute's Center for Science and Technology Policy, talks about the problem in terms of staff, title, and function. "It doesn't matter if you have one vice president of environmental safety and health if you haven't formally, according to the normal practice of corporate structure, isolated staff, title, and functions properly to assist that so-called leader's role." Piasecki has studied extensively the jobs of hundreds of U.S. environmental executives. He found big differences among the job descriptions and support given to top environmental officials.

"Some companies claim that their executive is an environmental executive, but when you analyze staff, title, and function—what they're actually in charge of—you find this isn't the case," says Piasecki. He points to his own research, which found that "86 percent of the environmental professionals and managers work at the facility-compliance level, which means that they're very removed from the power and the true heart of a corporation—the people who do strategy, finance, and accounting." As a result, he says, "only 14 percent of the multinationals' environmental managers have high enough staff, title, and function status to really get anything done to truly be proactive."

Not everyone agrees with this analysis. "It's only reasonable that the vast majority of environmental professionals and managers work at the facility level," says J. Ladd Greeno, managing director of Arthur D. Little's environment, health, and safety practice. "Most companies are quite decentralized today and it would be a big mistake to assume that just because environmental staff focus on plant-level, site-specific issues, they can't get anything done. As a comparison, most plants have controllers and purchasing agents, among other managers. It does not follow that they can't get anything done because they are at the plant. In fact, they are at the plants because that is precisely where the work is to be done."

This trend toward decentralization may at first seem to fly in the face of the company's efforts to provide across-the-board environmental leadership. But as Greeno points out, decentralization may work toward instilling environmental responsibility at the plant level on a day-to-day basis, with each manager finding ways to seek environmental excellence. But that by no means absolves headquarters' own responsibility to meet and beat companywide environmental goals. And considering the legal climate, in which company executives can be held personally liable for nearly every environmental action taken by every employee, even the most well-designed decentralized management must still be watched closely from the top.

According to Piasecki, any corporate environmental leadership program must address and balance three essential components:

● **Containment**—the need to limit a company's liability to pay for serious environmental problems

● **Regulatory compliance**—the need to stay within established federal, state, and local requirements

● **Moneymaking**—the need to stay in business and make a reasonable profit

Any attempt at leadership that doesn't embrace all three of these goals is doomed to fail. "It is profoundly deceptive to simply promote someone to a vice-president role and not give them any functional ability to synthesize liability containment, regulatory compliance, and moneymaking," says Piasecki. "In other words, if all you have is a vice president of environment, safety, and health, and that person can only use his or her staff to deal with regulatory compliance, then they are not ever able to be proactive. They are fundamentally responding to a thin sheet of ice, and they're skating on top of it. I think the problem with environmental management today is that we've had twenty-two years of thinking about it as a regulatory compliance function only."

THE GREENING OF THE BOARD

By now it should be clear that any commitment to environmental excellence must begin at the top if it is to permeate the company. That means leadership from the board of directors. "Environmentally sound business practices do not come about by assigning staff to a series of discrete and unrelated technical problems," says Dr. Pieter Winsemius, a partner in McKinsey & Co. and coleader of McKinsey's worldwide environmental practice. "Where ecology is concerned, everything is related. The horizon of considerations should therefore be extended as far as possible. Environmental awareness has to go beyond mere problem solving and become a constant business priority at a very high level."

According to a 1991 McKinsey survey of 403 CEOs and senior executives worldwide, only half have a board member with specific environmental responsibility. That concurs with a 1991 survey conducted by Touche Ross & Co. of 250 companies in sixteen European countries including most European Community members, as well as Sweden, Switzerland, Turkey, Poland, and Hungary. The survey revealed that 55 percent of European companies have board members directly responsible for environmental issues. However, few directors were found to be responsible solely for environmental affairs; the responsibility was usually assigned to directors who manage technical issues. A 1992 survey by the Investor Responsibility Research Center found that among the Standard & Poor's 500 companies, sixty-six had at least one board-level committee dealing with the environment.

A small number of forward-thinking companies have put an environmentalist on their board of directors, moving the environment from the backyard to the boardroom. Although the notion of "green" board members was first viewed as a handy way for companies to co-opt environmental critics, the practice is gaining acceptance as an effective means of bringing environmental expertise into the company in a meaningful yet confidential way. Since 1988, seventeen U.S. companies have put environmentalists on their boards, according to *Directorship*, a respected newsletter that tracks publicly traded companies. Among them are Ashland Oil, Atlantic Richfield, Exxon, ITT, Pacific Gas & Electric, and Waste Management Inc. "The companies do seem to be very interested in the subject and are looking for more concerned people in this area," says Elsa Nad, editor of *Directorship*. "The directors seem to be trying to educate themselves as to the results of much of what they do. There comes a point where public opinion, even if it is not by people who are directly affected—shareholders—does enter the boardroom. After all, these people read the papers and they do know what goes on in the world. They're human beings, too. They want to breathe fresh air and drink clean water."

Do environmentalist board members make a difference? John Sawhill, a former Secretary of Energy and now president and CEO of the Nature Conservancy who sits on the board of Pacific Gas & Electric, thinks so. "An environmentalist does have influence when he or she sits on a board because just by being there people tend to discuss the issue in different terms," he says. "Other board members reach out and look at environmental options that they might not otherwise look at just because they are reminded constantly of the fact that there is an environmental component in many of their decisions. So, it's almost the Woody Allen story: 90 percent of success is just being there. I do think that environmentalists that are working every day with issues like clean air and clean water and endangered species are so knowledgeable about these things that they can comment intelligently about the impacts of decisions and what government regulations really are and mean, and what new trends are likely to be emerging. And that can all be really useful."

But at least one environmentalist, S. Bruce Smart, Jr., senior counselor at the World Resources Institute and a director of Chevron Corp., thinks this approach may be unnecessary, perhaps even counterproductive. "I am not much of a believer in the concept of the special interest director, the school of thought that says 'put an environmentalist on the board so he or she can be a watchdog,'" he says. "Boards don't work well if they are made up of a collection of special interest representatives. It is far better to have a group of independent and competent individuals, diverse in background but dedicated to improving the total performance of the corporation, not just one element of it. That means, as far as the environment is concerned, that each director needs to bring him- or herself up to speed on what is happening, what is fact and what is only conjecture, in order to be able to give helpful counsel to senior management on environmentally related subjects." Concludes Smart: "Like it or not, the effective director has little choice but to become a practicing environmentalist."

Of course, that's true not just for board members, but for all senior executives. "Leaders create the future by emphasizing what the company's people must learn, not by reinforcing what they already know," says Rosabeth Moss Kanter, editor of the *Harvard Business Review*. "What CEOs choose to learn themselves, on their own, sends a powerful signal about the skills others should acquire."

Sawhill offers this counsel for companies that are thinking about adding an environmentalist on their board: "Try to find someone who has done a variety of things, so he or she can bring a broader perspective to this issue. I may be a good example of that. I was a university president, a business executive, a consultant, and a government executive. The mistake would be to pick someone who joined an environmental organization when they got out of school and done nothing else. They wouldn't have a broad enough view of how environmental issues fit into a broader group of economic and social issues."

A MATTER OF PRINCIPLES

Beyond leadership, of course, is a set of principles for the company to follow. While the majority of large corporations now have some kind of written environmental policy statement, they vary widely in vision and scope. At one end is a major U.S. pharmaceutical company, whose policy reads, "All employees of the Company, and all of its facilities and operations, shall comply with all applicable environmental laws, rules, and regulations, including those dealing with emissions to the atmosphere, discharges to surface waters or publicly owned treatment works, drinking water supplies, solid hazardous waste management, releases of hazardous substances, community emergency response planning, and toxic substance control."

"Shall comply" isn't a particularly proactive policy. It says, in effect, "We won't break the law." And while that's certainly a worthy goal, it's not enough if other companies are moving forward, getting ahead of the regulatory curve, leaving the merely compliant companies in the dust. And when you just keep up with regulations you make government one of your principal partners, which is a relationship few companies cherish. Being out in front lets you do business without that extra burden.

At the other end of the spectrum are companies that have set fairly specific environmental policies for themselves, committing to do such things as minimize environmental risks; prevent pollution rather than control it; conduct and support research into new technologies that will reduce the environmental impact of company operations; and constructively work with other companies and government agencies to solve environmental problems. This type of do-no-harm approach to policy-making is in sharp contrast to the break-no-law variety.

Not only are individual firms establishing their own policies, but so are a number of industries and business groups. For example, there's Responsible Care, a code of ethics for the chemical industry that consists of ten general principles as well as guidelines on management practices for process safety, pollution prevention, product distribution, and community awareness and emergency response. Under Responsible Care, companies evaluate their own environmental performance. In 1988, the Chemical Manufacturers Association (CMA) made Responsible Care a central program, eventually making participation mandatory for membership in the association. If a member company consistently fails to live up to the program's standards, its membership in CMA could be revoked. So far, that hasn't happened.

The idea of Responsible Care is to instill public and government trust in the chemical industry. That trust had been sorely lacking in recent years. In fact, surveys revealed that only 37 percent of Americans thought the chemical industry was essential. It ranked the industry next to the bottom in public credibility. Only the tobacco industry was lower on the list; even the nuclear power industry was higher. Responsible Care's unofficial motto—"Don't trust us. Track us."—acknowledges the industry's lack of credibility. In attempting to build public trust, Responsible Care's founders also created a public advisory panel, which meets five times a year, and a system of community advisory panels at the local level. The fifteen-member public advisory panel is composed of people from outside the industry.

The program is not without its critics, but it has received wide recognition and praise from various sources, including the Environmental Protection Agency. Indeed, EPA administrator William Reilly said in 1991 that his inspiration for EPA's voluntary toxic-emissions reduction program came from Responsible Care.

Not everyone is so laudatory, however. In 1992, the U.S. Public Interest Research Group (PIRG) took the CMA up on its unofficial motto, and tracked the industry to see how well it was complying with its own guidelines. The study revealed that despite the industry's enthusiastic endorsement of Responsible Care, the program had not fully made its way inside the gates of U.S. chemical plants. The project focused specifically on Responsible Care's tenet "to recognize and respond to community concerns about chemicals and our operations."

In the study, PIRG personnel called 192 CMA member facilities in twenty-eight states and asked nine basic questions about toxic chemical use and accident prevention. At 81 of the facilities—42 percent—callers could not reach anyone to answer their questions, "despite repeated attempts." Where callers were able to reach a company spokesperson, 58 companies, over half, "couldn't or wouldn't even answer half of the questions." And 27 percent of the companies did not answer any questions. Says Carolyn Hartmann, U.S. PIRG's staff attorney and author of the report: "The survey indicates that the vast majority of the companies are still operating under the motto of, 'Trust us. Don't track us.' "

Robert D. Kennedy, chairman and CEO of Union Carbide, a CMA member, views such criticism as growing pains, bumps on the road to an improved environmental future for the chemical industry. And he lays the burden firmly at the feet of top management to make things work. "Unless we CEOs and senior management personally commit ourselves to environmental action and leadership, the rest of the organization won't take the company's environmental goals seriously," he says. "The work load for managers these days is very, very heavy. They don't have the time to do everything they're asked. So they learn to read the signals: Which directives require action and commitment, which are simply for the record. Every manager and employee knows that, and knows which signs to follow."

It remains unclear whether Responsible Care will gain Americans' trust of the chemical industry. Clearly, it will be an uphill battle. The industry's record on toxic emissions remains unenviable, and despite improvements it still leads all other industries in volume of emissions. The environmental community hasn't let up in its criticisms of the industry, nor should it. And although Kennedy, for one, preaches the Responsible Care gospel tirelessly in speeches and presentations, he recognizes that it will take more actions than words to get the job done. "We will not tell the public what fine people we are," he tells audiences. "We won't tell them how important chemistry really is in their lives. We won't even claim to be responsible. We will let the public know we expect to be held responsible for our commitments. We will explain our goals up front and our commitment to continuous improvement. We will tell people that we have very little progress to report so far—we've just started. We don't expect them to trust us. We ask them to track us. And if we continue to make progress as they track us, we believe we can earn their trust."

The Responsible Care initiative isn't the only industry program aimed at establishing corporate commitment to the environment. In 1990, the International Chamber of Commerce (ICC) drafted a sixteen-point "Business Charter for Sustainable Development," which said that companies around the world would commit themselves to improving their environmental performance by adhering to the Charter's principles, including environmental management practices, measurement techniques, and internal and external disclosure requirements. More than six hundred companies worldwide have signed on.

In the United States, the ICC's charter has been championed by the Global Environmental Management Initiative, or GEMI, which encourages companies to endorse the sixteen points. Meanwhile, a coalition of socially responsible companies, investment firms, and environmental groups calling itself the Coalition for Environmentally Responsible Economies (Ceres) is asking companies to commit to *its* initiative, called the Ceres Principles (originally named the Valdez Principles).

Let's take a look at each.

Ceres' investment firms include the members of several pension funds, most notably those of New York City, the state of California, the Industrial Union Department of the AFL-CIO, and the Presbyterian Church. In total, Ceres member firms claim to control $150 billion in pension and mutual funds.

Ceres asks companies to endorse the ten Ceres Principles, a code of environmental ethics that ensures that companies are doing all they can to protect the earth, minimize waste, use resources and energy wisely, reduce risks, develop safe products, and generally behave in an environmentally responsible manner. According to Ceres cochair Joan Bavaria, the principles weren't designed to fit every industry's specific needs. Their primary purpose, she says, is "to inject the earth ethic into corporate management." More significant, the principles ask endorsing companies to pay for any environmental damage they cause, compensate the people affected, create a group within the board of directors in charge of the company's environmental behavior, and conduct an annual evaluation of the company's environmental performance.

Ceres endorsers also promise to make public potential hazards and incidents that cause environmental harm or pose health and safety hazards. Moreover, it commits firms to make a yearly audit of their environmental performance by an independent auditor, and to make the results public. Clearly, such provisions have raised more than a little concern among corporate counsel, because they could increase a company's exposure to lawsuits.

"It was never the intent of the drafters of the Ceres Principles to change the legal rights of companies," says Ceres cochair Denis Hayes. He admits the principles may be a tad stringent. Among the firms that were reluctant to endorse them had been Ben & Jerry's and Patagonia, two firms with strong records of social activism; Ben & Jerry's eventually signed on. As of mid-1992, the Vermont ice cream maker was among forty-eight companies that had endorsed Ceres. A third are social investment or other service firms. The others are both for-profit and nonprofit, with sales and income ranging from a few million to $800 million. Among the organizations represented are Domino's Pizza Distribution Corporation and the Metropolitan Sewer District of Louisville, Kentucky.

Ceres' main strategy is to use shareholder pressure to persuade additional companies to endorse the principles. In 1992, Ceres put the principles on the agenda at shareholder meetings of sixty-seven large companies. None of the initiatives passed. But that didn't translate into total failure. Ceres—along with the Interfaith Center for Corporate Responsibility, another group pressing for disclosure—negotiated some "settlements" with several companies. In exchange for withdrawing the resolution to endorse the Ceres Principles, companies agreed to issue annual environmental reports. Amoco, AT&T, Chevron, Browning-Ferris Industries, Gannett, Monsanto, Occidental Petroleum, Polaroid, and Waste Management Inc. are among the companies that agreed to do this.

GEMI's strategy is to lobby other businesses on the benefits of environmental management. Chairman George Carpenter says "GEMI is not a P.R. exercise. The subject of our advocacy is other business." He says GEMI started when the Business Roundtable created a work group to examine "the whole subject of environmental and safety principles which were coming forward at that time. And we said, 'Where should the business community be on the subject of codes of ethics?' " One conclusion was that this was a ripe area for self-regulation. "We said that if business does not step forward in this area, then others will do it for us"—namely, regulators or environmentalists.

The sixteen ICC principles championed by GEMI cover some of the same turf as Ceres. Among other things, they asks companies to make the environment a priority; to integrate green thinking throughout the company; to develop products, processes, and operations that do minimal harm; and to encourage contractors and vendors to have similar care for the environment. The final provision asks companies to conduct regular environmental audits and compliance assessments. The biggest difference between GEMI and Ceres involves the matter of public disclosure. While GEMI encourages openness and dialogue with employees and the public, it does not require members to open their books to either party.

Compared with Ceres' smaller-sized endorsers, the nineteen company members of GEMI are big outfits. They include Allied-Signal, Amoco, Apple, AT&T, Boeing, Browning-Ferris Industries, Digital Equipment Corporation, Dow Chemical, DuPont, Eastman Kodak, Merck & Company, Procter & Gamble, Union Carbide, and W. R. Grace.

Ceres, GEMI, and Responsible Care are just three of the better-known environmental codes. All told, IRRC counted more than twenty-five voluntary codes of conduct in 1992, most developed by trade associations and other business groups, such as the American Petroleum Institute and the American Paper Institute. And then there are the many codes established by individual companies. Of the Standard & Poor's 500 companies, 37 percent said they subscribe to a code.

Of course, signing any set of principles is less important than what you do with them. Does anyone know about them? Are the goals tangible? Should they be reviewed and upgraded from time to time? How are the goals measured? Are managers rewarded for meeting them? Should they be? If they are largely a P.R. exercise, they will be of limited value. Ultimately, such principles amount to a double-edged sword: They give company officials something to point to when asked about environmental commitment. But they also beg the follow-up question, "So what have you done to live up to them?"

What's more important is to put the principles to work. Use them as the basis for your strategic plan. Link the goals to managers' and executives' promotion or pay. Translate them on a day-to-day level for each division, department, unit, and individual. To the extent that they force a reevaluation of company policy and philosophy, either Ceres or GEMI can be a valuable management tool.

Consider Kevin Sweeney, director of public affairs for Patagonia. He says his company hopes to sign the Ceres Principles. In the meantime, the principles already have had an impact. "They exact an incredibly high standard, and we're not able to meet it," he says. "Having these things down on paper has forced us to ask, 'Do we live up to that standard?' " Sweeney says one problem is how to apply the principles to company operations: "We design and distribute clothes. We're like a law firm—we don't produce anything. For us the issue is, where does the responsibility lie? Are we responsible for the pollution of our goods? On a legal level, no. On another level, sure. We need to make every effort to make sure that we live up to the full spirit of the principles."

GETTING EVERYONE ON BOARD

Establishing a set of principles to live by is one thing. Getting everyone in the company to embrace them on a daily basis is another. The big challenge for any firm today is the quest for total employee involvement. Every organization is filled with naysayers, those who will take issue with just about any new program that comes down the pike. Their opposition may have little to do with the actual program as much as with fear—of change, loss of authority, failure, or whatever. And this is just as true when instigating environmental programs.

One reason for employee fear may have to do with company leaders' failure to articulate the company's environmental commitment, and then translate that commitment into specific goals. That leaves employees foundering. They've heard top management's proclamations about the environment, and may well agree heartily with them. But that may not be enough to help them translate that commitment into their own jobs.

For many companies, the problem has to do with some challenges traditionally faced with goal setting—the process of establishing specific targets for individuals, departments, and the company as a whole. The goal-setting process is changing in many companies, from a top-down approach, in which those at the top set goals and those at the bottom put them to work, to a more participative approach, where goals are established as close as possible to those who must meet them. In reality, both types of goal setting are needed. an overall vision from the top, fleshed out by those at lower levels.

Wherever the goal-setting process takes place, it is important to understand that not everyone in an organization approaches new concepts and projects in the same way. "For some people, goal setting takes the form of establishing formal objectives, mission statements, PERT charts, and the like," says Otto Kroeger, who heads a psychological management consulting firm based in Fairfax, Virginia. For them, a goal might be, "Let's reduce our solid waste disposal by 50 percent by the end of next year, and increase our use of recycled content by 35 percent this year and 40 next year." Such a pronouncement might be followed by an in-depth analysis of solid waste sources, complete with bar charts and tables indicating the potential improvement for each material, by department, by facility. Each department head would then be asked to come up with a detailed plan of how his or her department or facility will meet those goals, including interim goals and deadlines.

For others in the organization, such structure means only one thing: confinement. Says Kroeger: "These individuals are not as bound by time, preferring to respond according to when and how the spirit moves them. They tend to think of goals more in general terms than in specifics and as a result are less concerned about specific deadlines so long as the overall project is in the ballpark. Such individuals can find having to march in step a setup for tripping and stumbling." These people might find it easier to meet the company targets through a trial-and-error method, experimenting with what works best for each department or facility, and fine-tuning the process as they go along. When they don't have targets and deadlines, it's just as likely that such individuals would exceed the goals ahead of schedule as it is that they would miss them altogether.

Kroeger emphasizes that both goal-setting styles are equally valid. Indeed, he says, "We need both types of individuals to make the process work. The more rigid types, although it might appear on the surface that they have their act together, can waste time forging ahead with plans that aren't well designed. They need the less-structured types to instill the flexibility that may be necessary for success. And, of course, the less-structured types need the more rigid ones to bring some semblance of order to the process."

What's important, then, aren't so much the specific goals as the ability of everyone in the organization to buy into them.

That requires empowerment—the ability of employees at the lowest possible level to have a part in goal setting, and to organizational systems that turn pyramids, ladders, totem poles into a polyphony of ideas, and visions into action.

Heather Bell and her colleagues at American Airlines represent a classic case study in setting a goal and putting it into action, without necessarily having top-level support. Although she was far down the company's hierarchy, she managed to create a program that eventually percolated up through the system, and was ultimately embraced by the chief executive officer. It takes a rare breed of employee to tackle the entire system on his or her own, and an even rarer breed of company to permit such bottom-up leadership to take place.

Other companies are learning how to nurture this kind of working environment. For example, Larry Quadracci, president of Quad/Graphics, the Wisconsin-based printer, has helped turn his more than five thousand employees into active environmentalists both at work and at home. But Quadracci doesn't take much credit. "Frankly, I don't know if I led or whether I followed. I think that taking better care of ourself and our world is good business. I think it is all a matter of establishing values. You can decide which way you're going to run your business. But beyond that I would suspect that I more followed than led."

Quadracci's employees credit him with creating an atmosphere in which employees feel free to make suggestions and implement their ideas. "It's important that you have reinforcement from the top," says John Imes, Quad's environmental manager. "In some companies it's critical that you have someone say, 'We must do this by this day, etc.' In our company, Larry doesn't do that. He leads by example. He reinforces our commitment in his speeches and publications and his day-to-day interaction with employees."

Quadracci doesn't do it alone. He has help—from a goat. Specifically, a *Capra domesticus*, a ninety-pound Angora named Gruff that lives at Quadracci's house, grazing on his acreage. An employee suggested that Gruff get involved with environmental activities by becoming a mascot for recycling—which is a large part of what goats do all day. The employees came up with a slogan—"Be a Gruff . . . Recycle Stuff"—with the goat's image emblazoned on mugs, posters, and brochures. Gruff has his own electronic-mail address, and employees send questions and comments about recycling and the environment. These "letters" are copied into Quadracci's own mailbox, and personally answered by a Gruff ghostwriter. Gruff also makes frequent appearances—at the plants, at Quad family events, and at community events.

Gruff's role as a conduit for employee participation is just one part of environmental efforts that have made Quad/Graphics a leader in the printing industry. It is also one of the most profitable printing companies in the nation, with an annual rate of growth that has averaged over 40 percent since 1980. The company's environmental performance and innovative style have attracted the business of many environmental and outdoor magazines such as *Audubon*, *Sierra*, *Outside*, and publications of the Cousteau Society and the National Wildlife Federation, among other environmental groups. They join *Time*, *Newsweek*, *U.S. News & World Report*, *Playboy*, *Mother Jones*, *The Atlantic*, *Harper's*, and some ninety other magazines as Quad customers.

GREEN TEAMS

You don't need an advanced degree in management to know how hard it is to get a lot of people to move in the same direction at the same time. Each of us requires different amounts of information, motivation, and inspiration to get going. This is especially true if "getting going" involves doing something new or different from the way we are used to. That's certainly the case when motivating employees about being environmentally responsible at work. There are a host of natural barriers to change, from ingrained habits to inadequate education to good old bureaucratic inertia.

The traditional relationships among workers, managers, and executives can be another formidable barrier. "Though companies may like to think of themselves as one big, happy family, in reality, many operate like dysfunctional families, with individual members each suffering from an arrested development," says psychologist Robert H. Rosen, author of *The Healthy Company.* As he looks at companies, he sees a family consisting of "adolescent employees," who wrestle with identity crises, never sure from moment to moment how much responsibility they want or can handle; managers who are "malfunctioning parents" who refuse to give their "kids" any freedom or responsibility, or who throw up their hands in helplessness and declare that they cannot control them; and companies that act like "manipulative grandparents" by perpetuating the long-standing paternalistic assumption that a select few in a company know what is best for all employees. The sum total, says Rosen, is "a small-minded company that does not get the best work out of its employees."

Companies that are breaking through those barriers are those that are infusing the entire organization with power—the authority and responsibility to do what's best for the company. That's not always easy to do. As Rosen points out, "Empowerment skills do not come naturally for many employees, and people do not become believers overnight." But when they do, they can become a powerful agent for change within an organization.

And that power can be put to no better use than when employees are charged with implementing positive environmental change. Employees often embrace this task with missionary zeal. Indeed, they may have been frustrated by the lack of environmental commitment previously shown by their employer.

Tips for Motivating Employees

n Set realistic goals. If your plans are too grandiose—"Let's make our company the most environmentally responsible in the industry"—you'll set everyone up for disappointment and failure. Instead, begin with something specific and relatively simple—a paper recycling program, a campaign to buy more products with recycled content, or a companywide effort to reduce packaging waste.

n Try to elicit grass-roots support before you officially launch a program. You'll increase your chances for success if you know your program will be supported by those who have to implement it. Get as much feedback as possible early on.

n Try to get management support. But if you can't, don't abandon the whole idea. Do what you can without the boss's blessing. If it becomes evident that employee efforts are cutting waste, saving money, improving the company image, or increasing employee motivation, management will eventually get on board.

n Seek out committed individuals within your company to join in your efforts. They may not always be department heads or otherwise obvious candidates, but their enthusiasm and prior knowledge about environmental topics can make them significant contributors.

n Most important, create a mechanism for free-flowing communication among everyone in the company about environmental initiatives. Set up a forum for exchanging ideas and information. Use bulletin boards, newsletters, memos, meetings, electronic mail, paycheck stuffers, and any other means of getting the word out. The more interactive the communication, the better.

The question, then, is how to turn this natural enthusiasm—and all the benefits it can bring to company operations, productivity, and morale—into good, green company projects, processes, and policies. One answer: Form a green team.

Simply put, a green team is a group of individuals representing different parts of your company—different offices, floors, departments, or facilities, for example. The members of the team link the company's environmental goals with the rest of the organization—the people who will have to realize that goal.

Although they are known by a variety of names, a growing number of firms are setting up some kind of green team. They vary widely in size, clout, organization, and operation, among other things, but each is charged with essentially the same mission: to help set up good, green programs and to make sure they succeed. Another thing that varies from company to company is how green teams get started. It can begin with top management, lower-level employees, or somewhere in between. It can begin as an informal, voluntary effort or as a formal CEO-mandated policy. At Goldman Sachs, the Wall Street investment firm, the green team originated as a management-appointed committee looking for ways to cut costs. According to Maria Byrne, a company librarian and the team's cochair, the group soon recognized that "it all comes back to waste and the environment. Everything is tied together, so maybe we should have some kind of awareness program."

At Ace Hardware's home office in Oak Brook, Illinois, "It was a management decision," says Linda Baechtold, Ace's advertising coordinator. "The officers here are very supportive of the environment and they feel that it's a growing concern that we should be involved in. So it was at their direction that a green team was formed."

At the Kodak Colorado Division of Eastman Kodak Company, the team began as a grass-roots effort by employees and was later embraced by management. A similar evolution took place at supercomputer maker Cray Research Inc. in Minneapolis. There, the team began as an ad hoc employee group, says Cray's Joanne Whiterabbit. When the group realized it needed management support to get anything done, she says, "We did a formal presentation to senior management. They gave us their blessing and said, 'Go do what you need to do.' Since that time we have established a formal group."

The people at Apple Computer in Cupertino, California, tell a slightly different story. David Skinner, manager of Apple Recycles, which is responsible for waste reduction and water and energy conservation at the company, says it all started when one employee's thoughts were stimulated by *Time* magazine's selection of Earth as "Planet of the Year" in 1989. The employee decided, " 'Maybe we need to do something for the planet,' and at the same time, 'Why can't Apple be doing more?' " says Skinner. "So they got on our electronic mail system and started an employee discussion about Apple and the environment. Out of that came a group of fourteen employees that started brainstorming ideas for things they could do that could have an impact."

They began with an experimental white-paper recycling project. In the process, the group learned that Apple employees were indeed willing to participate in environmental programs, and that the company might see some cost benefits in the process. The group proposed to the Apple executive committee in 1989 that the company begin full-scale paper recycling. By the end of the first year, the group amassed more than forty tons of paper; today, the company recycles an average of seventy-one tons a month, along with four and a half tons of glass, a half ton of aluminum, hundreds of laser printer cartridges, and other surplus or waste materials.

All of these efforts have been consolidated into Apple Recycles, a department headed by Skinner that includes ten employees. To make the program work on Apple's sprawling Cupertino "campus," Skinner has organized a network of "building champions." Says Skinner: "They act as resources to the greater population in terms of questions about if some plastic piece that they've come across or if something they've received can be recycled. They also help to act as eyes and ears and field questions or problems that come up with the program."

Acting as "eyes and ears" may be one of green teams' greatest values. While the act of recycling may seem pretty straightforward to some, others can quickly become confused, frustrated, and discouraged by problems unforeseen by the program's organizers. What works in purchasing may be totally inappropriate to personnel or public relations, not to mention manufacturing and maintenance.

Green teams can help head off problems by creating two-way communication. Questions and concerns can be efficiently routed through team members, resulting in quick answers or resolution. The tricks of the trade learned in one part of the company can be spread to other parts through team members. And the team can help pass along news of company successes: "We saved three tons of paper from going into landfills last month!"

Teams also vary in size and makeup. Group dynamics limit the effective size of a team to about ten or twelve people, according to David Gershon, who has implemented his Corporate Environmental Leadership Program at several companies. But larger groups can work, too. Ace Hardware's team has fourteen people; Goldman Sachs' has thirty. The exact number doesn't really matter. What's more important is that the group represents some kind of cross section of the organization—or at least has access to as many people as possible. Depending on a company's size and structure, representation could be by department, floor, building, or office. (Organizing by job title or description isn't recommended because it can create unhealthy competition among groups that should be cooperating.) Ideally, the team should include at least one representative from top management, perhaps even the chief operating officer.

Management support is crucial. For the green team to be effective, every employee must know there is a mandate from the top, lest the group's programs and proposals be viewed as one department's or divison's agenda, and get mired in turf wars and company politics. Even with the boss's okay, there can be resistance, perhaps even hostility, to proposed changes.

Just about everything else—the group's structure, leadership, meeting frequency, and so on—is at each company's discretion. There are few rules, or even tried-and-true formulas, on which to rely.

What about costs? Most teams will cost something, if only because meetings are typically held on company time. Managing the group's efforts may cost, too. "Obviously there's a cost in everything," says Ace's Linda Baechtold. "My time is worth something. Their time is worth something. The money for different things we have done or tried to do had to come out of somewhere. Working for the environment unfortunately is not free."

Still, those investments are often offset by savings. Consider some of the waste reduction realized by the Butterworth Environmental Action Team, at Butterworth Hospital in Grand Rapids, Michigan. In looking for ways to cut waste, the group saved thousands of dollars at the 529-bed hospital, and sees potential to save thousands more. Example: purchasing five thousand reusable bed pads kept thirty thousand disposable pads out of the dumpster, resulting in savings of more than

$15,000 a year. And the team learned that its neonatal intensive care unit had been tossing out thirty tons a year of four-ounce glass formula bottles; they're now being recycled.

One could fill chapters just with green-team success stories. Apple's efforts alone could fill a small book. Once that company's green team got off the ground, it seemed to realize that there's almost no limit to what it can do. Apple employees are now recycling just about everything. And what they can't recycle, they give away. In 1991, says Skinner, the company gave away nine pallets of binders, seven pallets of video cases, three pallets of office supplies, and thousands of diskettes, audiocassettes, and other items. In Apple's marketing department, old computers are repaired or upgraded and sold or loaned. The group has begun recycling spent rechargeable batteries from portable computers.

"Our efforts are spread across the board," says Skinner. "A lot of what we have done has been from the ground up. It's becoming an ever greater part of our culture. The issues are becoming a part of how we do business."

In the end, the biggest benefits of green teams may not be in saving cash and trash, but in empowering and motivating employees. They can give employees a vision that's larger than just making money or moving up the promotional ladder. They can instill employees with a sense that their company is making a difference. They can be as beneficial to morale and loyalty as they are to reducing pollution and waste.

e d u c a t i o n

THE PERSUASIVE POWER OF DIALOGUE AND DISCLOSURE

IN 1990, AMOCO Corporation realized it had a problem. Ground-water tests indicated that a large body of hydrocarbons that had amassed under its Whiting, Indiana, refinery might have "migrated" off the property into the surrounding community. This was no small finding. For one thing, the contamination—nearly seventeen million gallons of crude oil, intermediate stocks, and refined gasoline, according to company estimates—was about one and a half times the size of the Exxon *Valdez* oil spill. Moreover, the refinery bordered parts of the northwest Indiana communities of Hammond, Whiting, and East Chicago; hundreds of homes were within a few blocks of the plant.

The company needed to act, and fast.

The situation Amoco faced and the way the company responded shows why it has become increasingly necessary for companies to communicate their environmental policies and performance to a wide range of individuals and organizations. In this era of heightened environmental concern, your company's ability to interact effectively with customers, neighbors, employees, suppliers, regulators, stockholders, media, environmentalists, even competitors depends substantially on how these sectors view your record on the environment. That, in turn, may determine the success or failure of your relationships with some of these key players.

Besides being the Decade of the Environment, the 1990s also represent the maturing of the Information Age, in which data—everything from raw statistics to media reports to baseless rumors—travel far faster than ever before. The collision of these two forces means that environmental information—and rumors—travel fast and furious, too, often blurring the distinction between perception and reality. The wood you use in your product may be an unthreatened species from an unthreatened domestic forest, but the public may still believe that your company destroys tropical rain forests. You may have installed the latest in pollution-prevention technology, but local reporters may still link your company with others in the area that have abysmal environmental records. And the white clouds bellowing from your smokestacks may be water vapor, but those who see it are likely to think it is a noxious chemical that is increasing the area's cancer rate. The perception in these cases may simply overwhelm the rational facts.

People naturally fear what they don't know, especially when it concerns their health and safety. The public also doesn't trust corporations to tell the truth. And when people are scared and distrustful, they tend not to pay attention to the facts of a situation, to say the least. Companies, therefore, must work harder than ever to educate their many "publics" about their environmental performance—before, during, and after problems occur. Even if your industry isn't known for emitting noxious chemicals or creating toxic wastes, it may still be judged by a variety of groups, who may base their purchase, investment, enforcement, or other actions on your firm's environmental performance.

Amoco's need to carefully but thoroughly disclose information about the leaked hydrocarbons presented an immense and delicate challenge. The 350,000-barrel-a-day Whiting refinery, built in 1889, is one of the oldest and largest in the United States and a key source of refined petroleum products for both Amoco and for the Midwest region, where the company is a leading marketer of gasoline. The town of Whiting's history is closely intertwined with the refinery. Around the turn of the century, Whiting was a quintessential company town, and over the years it grew up with the refinery. In the early days, the refinery owners constructed homes for employees in the community. It also built the town's community center, which it turned over to the public in the 1950s. In more recent times, Amoco and the town loosened their links, as other industries moved in and a large percentage of Amoco workers left Whiting, moving farther out to such suburbs as Merriville and Crown Point.

Long before the underground contamination was discovered, the refinery's management knew it needed more community involvement in order to regain some of the close links it had lost over the years. In 1989, the company surveyed the community to determine its views about the refinery as well as other local institutions and issues.

The results, which came back in September 1990, revealed that Amoco was well known in the community, as much for its retail operations as for the presence of its refinery. Generally, local residents gave the company broad approval—almost two-thirds said that Amoco was good for the community—though the public was concerned about Amoco's efforts to protect the environment and the safety of the Whiting plant. Amoco's communication efforts were rated as good, too. More than half the respondents said Amoco was a highly or generally believable source of information. Residents expressed interest in building a better relationship with the company. They wanted Amoco to support education programs in the schools, offer more plant tours, speak more often to community groups, and run more informational ads in newspapers. On the list of public concerns, air and water quality topped the list, scoring even higher than such traditional community issues as education and crime. This wasn't surprising. In recent years, a number of industries had gone out of business or moved out of the region, leaving behind a number of serious environmental problems. This caused citizens to be concerned about the pollution emanating from steel mills, chemical plants, and other heavy manufacturing facilities that remained.

Amoco officials had actually been aware of the groundwater contamination for several years. The company had drilled more than three hundred wells on company property to test and monitor the contamination, and had installed several systems and monitoring devices, which seemed to be working to contain the flow the hydrocarbons. Periodic health screenings of employees had revealed no signs of health problems for those working above the contaminated area. Still, in 1989 Amoco officials conducted comprehensive tests to determine where the underground hydrocarbons had accumulated in order to better engineer their containment systems and, following that, begin remediation efforts.

The refinery's remediation services department, which had been conducting the tests, informed refinery management in late 1990 that the contamination might have spread. Amoco officials realized that they needed to conduct tests outside refinery property, which would require permits, and in turn public disclosure. Suddenly, this was no longer just an in-house concern; it was the community's, the media's, and the regulators' as well. Several staff people were gathered to form an internal task force, which would determine how and when to make the information public.

"We knew it was important that residents be told, especially those living in close proximity to the plant, as quickly and as responsibly as possible, about the potential of hydrocarbons leaving the property," recalls Patricia Wright, now Amoco Corporation's director of corporate media relations. "We knew we had to have complete materials and information available so that residents and a number of other publics could have as many of their questions answered as possible."

Wright continues the story: "The task force made some decisions early on and quickly put together an approach and took it to the management of Amoco Oil Company, the subsidiary that operated the refinery. The group briefed the management committee, and they gave us their full support." One of the first key decisions was to conduct groundwater tests off Amoco property.

The group recognized that the way it notified the public would be critical to gaining community support and minimizing panic. "We knew we would have to answer the question, and very quickly, 'What impact does this have on me?' from the personal point of view of the citizens of the area," says Wright. "As soon as we told people there was a potential that hydrocarbons were underground off of our property, the first thing they would want to know is, 'What are the health effects? Am I endangered?'

"The decision was made that we would announce in a totally upfront manner to everybody we could think of that was personally involved or had a need to know or a right to know exactly what we knew and what we were going to do about it. We would do it in a manner of candor. We would tell them everything that we knew. We felt that was the only way that we could get understanding. That meant putting together a communications approach that could reach the people with the information they needed to have. We were also very conscious of the fact that this concern about personal health probably would be overwhelming. And in order to be able to allay the fears and concerns about human health risks, we decided we would have to do residential air monitoring, with results given back to residents within a few days. We felt that was the only way we could sufficiently answer that question, 'Am I at risk?' "

The group developed some objectives for its communications efforts. One priority was that citizens and regulators hear the news directly from the company, not filtered through the media or the rumor mill. "We didn't want them to hear it from anybody else," says Wright. "We felt we owed that to all the people involved. We wanted them to understand what steps we would be taking to determine if hydrocarbons had moved off our property underground. We wanted to prevent any community panic or fear by providing materials and personnel who could adequately address questions the community might have. We also wanted to provide ongoing communication to keep them informed and effectively deal with rumors. Finally, we wanted to develop contingency plans to provide emergency housing in the event that any members of the community wanted to move temporarily from the area. We felt that was probably not likely, but we wanted to be prepared."

The group set January 23, 1991, as Announcement Day. On that day, Amoco officials sent seven teams to visit with more than a hundred key individuals to inform them of the situation. Among those visited were mayors, fire chiefs, and city leaders in Whiting, Hammond, and East Chicago; representatives of the Indiana Department of Environmental Management; the state and county health departments; the governor's office; the state legislature; the federal EPA; local environmental groups; union officials; and local congressional delegations. The group also held a briefing for local media. Another group contacted was Amoco's own plant management council, because the story wasn't widely known throughout the refinery. Says Wright: "We put together an information kit, and each individual who was contacted received four fact sheets on various aspects of the investigation. There was also a letter in the packet from the refinery manager and a map of the refinery showing the area of concern. The area of concern was very conservative—that is, much larger than it probably needed to be."

"Every individual and business in that area was hand-delivered a packet of information on January 23. We also posted bulletins in our refinery for our employees to read. Letters were mailed to each of our sixteen hundred employees' homes and to retired employees, because they are a big part of that community and have a very active retirees' club in Whiting. All correspondence showed a toll-free '800' number that people could call and leave a message and somebody would get back to them. We had toxicologists from Amoco standing by to answer questions, or we could refer people to the state health department."

All of that happened on Announcement Day.

Even though the story didn't get a lot of attention in the nearby Chicago media—mostly because it hit amid the fighting of the Gulf War—local media was heavy and, in some cases, sensationalistic. Papers in Hammond, Gary, Whiting, and other towns played it big. Some reporters and editors blew things out of proportion. MASSIVE OIL LEAK SLOWLY SPREADS FROM WHITING, the headline of the *Hammond Times* screamed.

The day after the announcement, Amoco began three types of monitoring. First came a combustibility test to determine whether there were explosive concentrations of vapors in the air. The company didn't believe this was necessary, but they did it anyway, hoping it would answer the immediate question of "Is there any possibility that my house will explode?" Also, the results from the combustibility test were available instantaneously. Next came grab-bag air monitoring, which tested for benzene concentrations. Benzene, one of three principal hydrocarbons in petroleum—the others are xylene and toluene—is a known carcinogen, causing leukemia and blood disorders. Amoco hired an outside contractor, who brought a sophisticated on-site laboratory to each home visited. Those tests results were available within about forty-eight hours. The third test involved benzene patches, which are left on walls in strategic places, usually for about two weeks. They measured the amount of benzene in a home over an extended period of time. Each contractor was accompanied by an Amoco representative, who could answer questions on the spot. "Sending the Amoco representative as part of the team was beneficial," says Wright. "It gave us the opportunity to hear their concerns and answer questions from them directly."

The air monitoring programs continued over the next few weeks, along with a focus on one-to-one contact with local residents. All five hundred homes in the affected area were given the opportunity to have an industrial hygienist and an Amoco representative visit them. The two-person teams brought a survey form to be filled out, and were also to conduct all three types of air monitoring.

Amoco's communication efforts continued unabated. The company began distributing *The Communicator,* a two-page newsletter, to all area residents. The newsletter provided up-to-date information on investigations and cleanup efforts. There was also a second toll-free number, which gave a recorded update on the monitoring. Amoco officials participated in a town meeting held by the mayor of Whiting and the company set up a citizen's advisory committee from the local community, which met on a monthly basis. In addition, Amoco ran informational ads on local radio stations and in newspapers, which answered questions frequently asked by local citizens.

"The first batch of residential air monitoring, to which a lot of attention had been paid, turned out to be very good," says Wright. "There was no problem. We worked with the state health department setting up some parameters for our tests. We agreed that if we got a reading above ten parts per billion (ppb), that we would investigate that home. Interestingly, there were about ten to fifteen homes where we did get readings over ten ppb, and we traced it in every case to natural gas leaks in the homes. We set up a partnership with the local gas company to take care of that, so we killed two birds with one stone. It was very clear by the end of the January-February sampling that people living near the refinery were not being exposed to chemicals that would result in short-term or long-term health effects. By summer we knew that data from our thirty-four groundwater monitoring wells in the community that the extent of off-site migration appeared to be very, very limited, and was confined to a portion of an alley that was located next to the refinery. The containment system that rings the Amoco property had done its job. There was a small finger of migration along a utility corridor located under a city street that ran from the refinery to a former research facility that Amoco used to have in the community. That was the extent of it."

Amoco got off easy. In the end, they received only two lawsuits for property damages by disgruntled citizens and no fines from local, state, or federal authorities. Keeping everyone informed clearly defused what could have been a public relations disaster. Even the media came around: As the encouraging test results came in, news reports became increasingly glowing, praising Amoco's proactive measures.

"I think that the approach that we took was the only approach that you can take in dealing with the community. The bottom line is that you've got to build trust. Essentially, what we have come to today is a much better dialogue with the community about their concerns about the refinery, and about what we're doing at the refinery."

TRUST, IN THE ERA OF DISCLOSURE

It's a fundamental truth that the marketplace for any product, service, or idea involves a push-pull dialogue between Buyer and Seller. The Seller pushes a product (or service or idea) onto the marketplace only to the extent that the Buyer pulls it off the shelves. And the process works in reverse. If a product is inadequate, inappropriate, or otherwise undesirable, the Buyer will push it back onto shelves (or simply leave it there) and the Seller will be forced to pull it off the market. The dialogue between Buyer and Seller about most companies' environmental responsibility and performance is just beginning. And the companies that are most environmentally successful on this issue are actively keeping the conversation flowing freely and effectively.

You don't need an industrial accident—or even the threat of one—to begin a dialogue with other interested parties about your company's environmental products, processes, and performance. A wide range of firms are learning how beneficial enhanced communication can be to everyone involved. Many customers appreciate the honesty and respond with loyalty; suppliers know what your company expects, and can better deliver products and services with less waste or fewer problematic ingredients; the media, and perhaps even the environmentalists, may simply leave you alone or even give you their assistance. Investors know what they're getting into, regulators know with whom they're dealing, and members of the community can rest assured that your activities probably won't significantly degrade or destroy their homes or life-styles.

That's overly simplistic, but the point is valid: Chances are that the rest of the world will eventually learn about your environmental performance, especially if it involves bad news. But whether the news is good or bad, it's ultimately better that you be the one to tell them.

Entering into these types of dialogues is no easy matter. Everyone isn't necessarily ready to listen, at least not with an open mind. Approaching others to discuss matters of concern opens your company to criticism, further investigation, exposés, perhaps even litigation. These are calculated risks, to be weighed just as you would any other business decision. But you may find that, when these conversations and educational campaigns are done with candor and discretion, they may yield rich dividends.

It is important to ensure that the conversation flows in both directions. There's a strong temptation to attempt to make it a one-way affair—to attempt to advertise or publicize your way to an image of environmental excellence, engaging in the politics of self-belief. The reasoning goes that if you throw enough money at the right media targeting the proper demographics, you can conceivably create your own image as an environmentally sensitive, socially responsible company. But the public isn't that gullible anymore. They don't believe the ads, according to pollsters; they want to see results. According to a 1991 Hartman Group Survey, which gauged the level of trust the public has in various sources of environmental information, companies are the least-trusted information source on the environment. The percentages below indicate the number of respondents who identified a source as a "trustworthy source of information about environmental matters."

Source	Percent
Universities	51
TV/Radio News	47
Newspapers/Magazines	46
Environmental Groups	46
Government	23
Companies	13

Clearly, companies can't be trusted—at least in the public's eyes. This is not to say, however, that you shouldn't have a well-designed public relations or advertising campaign as part of your efforts, but the motivating force in all of it must be building trust. The most environmentally enlightened companies are forgoing short-term product or corporate campaigns and instead are attempting to establish solid long-term relationships with customers and others built on openness and mutual respect.

For example, Church and Dwight, the 150-year-old maker of Arm & Hammer baking soda and other products, entered the environmental consumer era with something of a delicious dilemma: how to increase awareness of its essentially environmentally benign product. Baking soda is derived from a naturally occurring mineral left behind after the evaporation of an inland lake in Wyoming fifty million years ago. The mineral is converted and purified into sodium bicarbonate—baking soda—whose basic components, bicarbonate and sodium ions, are present in significant concentrations in the human body. Sodium bicarbonate has been sold in the United States since the 1840s, and the Food and Drug Administration lists it as a "generally recognized as safe" food substance. Still, Church and Dwight, whose Arm & Hammer Baking Soda commands more than 80 percent of the North American retail market for baking soda, was dragged into the green revolution somewhat unwittingly.

It began in 1988, when Bryan Thomlison, then Church and Dwight's Canadian marketing director, was called by an environmental leader. "I think your company is irresponsible," he recalls her telling him. "The environmental community is doing so much for baking soda and you're not going out of your way to reciprocate." Environmentalists, it turned out, were promoting baking soda as an alternative to harsher commercial cleaning products. Thomlison, who had been in his job for just two weeks, invited the environmentalist to Toronto. "She showed us a whole area of opportunity that frankly hadn't occurred to us," he says.

After that experience, Church and Dwight brought in other outsiders for consultation and ideas in a way that Thomlison says "merged the complementary skills and resources of otherwise diverse groups." He goes on: "I was amazed at how much I was able to learn and how rapidly I was able to move along the learning curve by these informal coalitions that we developed to work on programs. I learned a lot about advancing and impending regulations and about the agendas of different groups that hadn't been made public but were about to be. I learned a lot that kept me from realizing or experiencing backlash from media or environmental groups that other people had experienced. I learned a lot that kept me from getting myself in trouble. Because these people were like consultants to us—almost like getting an ongoing focus group."

The results were just short of spectacular. "Baking soda sales had been flat for seven years," says Thomlison. "Within thirty-six months we had grown the brand [in Canada] something like 30 percent. It was a quantum leap." Another product, Arm & Hammer Super Washing Soda, had been the number-two brand in the laundry additive category in Canada, with about a 25 percent market share; the leading brand had 40 percent. Within a year the two brands had flipflopped, with Arm & Hammer garnering a 40 percent share and the former leader sinking to 27 percent. Moreover, the competitor had spent around $2 million in advertising; Arm & Hammer hadn't spent a nickel.

As a result, the company moved Thomlison to the United States to replicate the Canadian success. Says Thomlison: "The chairman of the board said, 'I want our company to be one of the models of corporate environmental responsibility.' He said, 'I don't want you to be worried about three-month or six-month earnings reports. I want you to look five and ten years out. I don't want you to worry about making the occasional mistake. I will tolerate errors of commission, where I will not tolerate errors of omission.' "

Thomlison redoubled his communication efforts. "I talked to everybody I could to find who could augment our efforts. I asked Burson-Marsteller to provide me with a list of key environmentalists, educators, media organizations, and like-minded companies. I asked them to match the ones that had an agenda in harmony with our products and processes and technologies. I wanted a group that was generally acceptable by the world at large. I didn't want fringe groups because I didn't want to get involved with political issues.

"I developed a list of people I could test and trust; you can't just jump into bed with anyone. I determined I could work very closely with the Clean Water Fund, the Environmental Hazard Management Institute, and Earth Day USA to get their objective analyses and critiques of everything I was doing. I told them to pull no punches. I'd rather they chastise me in the nascent part of a program than in the midst of it."

Thomlison now claims to have on his computer more than twelve hundred names of people he calls to ask questions, including regulators, legislators, environmental educators, and reporters. In fact, he says, "I'm always talking to the media—not just to get stories but also asking their advice. There are probably thirty people who I really trust that if I told them something confidential they wouldn't run out and report it. That way, when I finally do a program, if I have advice from all these sectors and representative organizations, the chance of public backlash is mitigated."

True, not every company is blessed with Church and Dwight's environmentally sound product line. But that doesn't mean companies can't engage in similar dialogues. Indeed, the greater your company's challenge is to "green" its image, the more vital these dialogues become.

THINK CORPORATELY, ACT LOCALLY

Although it may make seem to make sense to centralize your company's environmental communications efforts, the most effective environmental dialogues are usually carried on at the local level, not at headquarters. It is here, at the plant level, that companies can make or break their environmental images. After all, the executive offices don't give off much pollution; rather, it emanates from the smokestacks, drainpipes, and dumpsters of individual facilities. This is where companies must focus their environmental communications and education efforts. Unfortunately, this notion runs against traditional corporate practice, which is to create economies of scale and marketplace efficiencies. And though that's a worthy strategy for manufacturing and marketing, when it comes to the environment, the effects that company activities have on individuals' homes, children, and lives are different in every community, and must be treated that way. You simply can't lump these disparate communities together as a mass market, and hope to successfully alleviate their collective fears or anger.

Every community—whether a metropolitan area or a rural outpost—has its own demographics, its own set of interests and concerns, and its own social structure. And each community has its own methods of broadcasting or passing information along from person to person. It is simply impossible for one centralized effort to effectively address all of those various social networks. This is not to say that a company's environmental communications efforts should not be unified and coordinated. For instance, headquarters can provide training and educational materials that explain your company's operations and environmental policies. But the hands-on efforts must be implemented by the men and women on the front line who know (or should know) the local media and who better understand local issues and sensitivities.

Imagine a manufacturing plant—Mega-Spew International Corporation—in a community somewhere in middle America. The neighbors of this plant don't know or care much about the Mega-Spew corporate headquarters in some big city hundreds of miles away. They know the plant they pass by every day when driving their kids to school. This is the factory where their neighbors or relatives are employed; it sponsors the Little League team. And despite the soft-focus, feel-good commercials that Mega-Spew's parent company runs during nationally broadcast prime-time television shows, the image local community members have of Mega-Spew has far more to do with that huge plant in town than the slick media campaign on TV. When it comes to their health and welfare, the value of their homes, and the security of their jobs, those high-priced commercials are merely side shows.

For Mega-Spew to have effective environmental communications at the local level, plant and office managers must be informed and empowered to deal directly with individuals, community groups, environmental organizations, local media, and everyone else who has a stake in the environmental impact of company operations. The more proactively and less reactively this is done, the better. Even companies in nonpolluting industries can improve the quality of life in their areas—as well as their image and market share.

A good example is Puget Sound Bank (PSB), a $4.5 billion Tacoma, Washington-based institution, which has successfully helped to safeguard the magnificent body of water from which it takes its name. Over the decades, Puget Sound became Washington state's dumping ground of industrial and household waste. Companies as well as individuals routinely dumped raw sewage, waste oil, and just about anything else into one or more of its many bays. Everyone assumed that the two tides each day would cleanse the chemicals, but much of the waste settled on the bottom, where it turned into toxic muck. By the time bottom-feeding fish were discovered to have cancerous cells, the damage was done.

In the mid-1980s, Puget Sound Bank was in an expansion mode, moving beyond sleepy Tacoma, where it had a 35 percent market share, into big-time Seattle, where it was virtually unknown. "We were looking at a way to make an impact in the King County [Seattle] marketplace," recalls PSB's David Parent. "It was a copywriter looking out the window who said, 'I've got it. It's out there!' And he was talking about Puget Sound, the body of water."

Parent now heads the result of that brainstorm: Puget Sound Fund, an educational project that raises public awareness about the environmental plight of the great body of water. The bank contributes a small amount to the fund each time customers use or buy certain products or services—the ATM machine, for example, or a certain package of checks. As that list of products has grown, so has the fund—to more than $300,000 a year. The money is donated to support other organizations' education and cleanup efforts. The bank also has its own projects, including an annual beach cleanup. In 1991, that one-day event involved

2,800 bank staff and their families, who picked up 17.5 tons of trash on fifty-five beaches. In addition, PSB sponsors an annual wildlife art show, and produced an educational video, *Turning the Tide*, which was distributed to every school district and public library in the state. Such projects have helped turn bank employees into clean-water advocates—and effective PSB boosters.

One key to success is "the direction we're getting from the top," according to Parent, who says PSB Chairman W. W. Philip told him that "he doesn't want the fund to be a public relations vehicle. He grew up in this area and the health of this area's environment is very important to him. He said, 'We really want it to go out and accomplish something.' He's been our guiding voice through all this."

Even so, the fund's P.R. success continues to mount, and after four years it has taken on a life of its own. Unsolicited funds arrive from other individuals and groups. Customers, including school groups, voluntarily chip in a few dollars of their own from time to time. ("People donating money to a bank—there's a certain irony to it," says Parent with a wry smile.) And PSB has become known as "the environmental bank." In a 1991 survey, which tracked unaided name recognition of local institutions, more people were aware of the Puget Sound Fund than Greenpeace; that high-profile environmental activist group came in a distant second.

But giving away money isn't the only way to win friends and influence people at the local level (though it certainly won't create many enemies). The most effective ideas and strategies are as varied as the companies that try them, and the constituencies that respond—or don't respond—to their efforts.

Whatever you try to do, there are three principal goals of good corporate communications on the environment:

- Get the word out about your company's environmental concerns and strategies, including what it is doing to clean up its act. Be up front about things you're still working on; the public will appreciate your honesty about your ongoing problems.
- Learn what community members think about your company and its operations and answer their questions about how your operations might affect their health or well-being. Make sure you understand the modes of communication that work best in your community: media ads, community meetings, newsletters, and so on.

- Establish ongoing lines of communications with a wide range of local interests. Don't wait for them to call; make a direct effort to contact community leaders, environmentalists, and other key individuals and organizations.

KILLING THE MESSENGER

What happens when the news media have something less than flattering to say about your company's environmental record? This story is a perfect example of how *not* to communicate.

In 1988, when the Environmental Protection Agency released its first batch of Toxics Release Inventory data, the Silicon Valley Toxics Coalition called a news conference to put its spin on how local companies fared. The group reported that twenty-five major companies in the area had legally dumped more than twelve million pounds of toxic and cancer-causing pollutants into the air, land, and water. According to the data, which had been culled from the EPA's Form R, on which companies report TRI data, one semiconductor manufacturer, Advanced Micro Devices (AMD), had led the field as Santa Clara County's top polluter.

Mitchell Benson, a reporter for the *San Jose Mercury News*, dutifully reported the story and the morning after it appeared, AMD's press officer called. Benson, along with his editor and his editor's editor, met with the press representative from AMD, an AMD engineer, and AMD's corporate counsel.

"After lots of yelling and screaming, AMD admitted that they filled out the forms wrong," wrote Benson in *Chemicals, the Press & the Public*, a journalist's guide to reporting on chemicals in the community. "Where AMD officials should have noted that extremely potent acids were being neutralized into rather benign salts before being dumped in San Francisco Bay, they instead filled out the forms to show that those acids were being dumped directly into the Bay." AMD officials insisted to Benson that "they filled out the forms incorrectly because *the instructions were difficult to understand*" [emphasis is Benson's].

The story goes downhill from there. In the following days, AMD purchased a full-page advertisement in the *Mercury News* charging the toxics coalition with "Truth Pollution!" The day the ad appeared, AMD scheduled a news conference to accuse the toxics coalition of "deliberate efforts to distort the facts and misinform the public." AMD did not attack the newspaper or its reporter and took no responsibility for its mistakes. Things reached a peak—and a pique—when a local EPA official wrote a letter to AMD criticizing the company for its shoddy form-filling. That, too, made the papers, leading to still more bad press about AMD.

It doesn't take a P.R. genius to recognize that AMD probably did itself more harm than good by attacking its attacker, blaming others for its own mistakes. Rather than admitting it had made an embarrassing error, it tried to kill the messenger, blaming both the media and the environmental group for its poor performance. Like a child offering a lame excuse after getting caught with a hand in the cookie jar, it merely compounded error upon error, embedding itself ever deeper into the mire of distrust. With corporate environmental behavior, this only confirms what the public already believes: that companies can't be trusted to clean up their acts, and whatever they say isn't to be believed. These perceptions simply can't be legislated, lobbied, or advertised out of existence. If you try, you will no doubt be bypassed and outclassed by your more enlightened competitors.

In contrast, consider the experience of the Colorado-based operation of Syntex Chemicals, Inc., a subsidiary of Syntex Corporation. In 1991, it topped the list of TRI emitters in Boulder Valley and ranked second in the entire state. Just about everyone and his golden retriever in the Boulder area is an environmentalist, or claims to be. At the very least, a rather large segment of the population knows of and is concerned about earth-related issues. Clearly, this is not a good place to top the "Dirty Dozen" list.

Syntex had tried to clean up its act. As a member of the Chemical Manufacturers Association, the company had been an active player in CMA's Responsible Care program. Among other things, the 250-employee, $700 million-a-year unit had spent millions of dollars on pollution prevention measures, the result of the findings of the self-audits it had been conducting. It had stepped up its training program and changed many of its practices to reduce emissions. The company had already ingrained safety into its culture, producing a record of just one lost-time accident in nine years. Still, the TRI numbers told the story: Despite its best efforts, the company emitted large quantities of toxic chemicals.

Every year when the TRI data are released by the Environmental Protection Agency, a Washington, D.C.-based public-interest group called

Citizen Action puts on a presentation for the nation's press. First, it releases a report called *Poisons in Your Neighborhood*, detailing which companies are the biggest emitters of pollutants. On the local level, Citizen Action stages dozens of press conferences and media events to publicize who's releasing what chemicals into the local environment. The press conferences are usually well covered by local media, along with all-but-flattering quotes and sound bites from local company officials and plant managers.

Syntex anticipated Citizen Action's release of the TRI data and enlisted Environmental Communications Associates (ECA), a Boulder consulting firm, to find the best way of handling the situation.

"Through a long process of rapport-building, trust-building, and credibility-building, we got some of these activists together with the company to start a dialogue," says Dr. Robert C. Farentinos, ECA's director of environmental research.

Actually, it wasn't that simple. ECA first had Syntex invite a group of local environmental leaders to the Boulder plant to meet with Syntex management and attend a briefing on the company's environmental programs. "We wanted them to see what was happening behind the chain-link fences and ask questions about what was happening and what was going to happen," says Farentinos. "That was part of breaking the ice. It was the first time that some of these folks had ever even been approached or invited to do this. Based on that, some of these folks were able to see the direction that Syntex was going and were interested in using the company as a positive example."

Among Citizen Action's ideas was that it join with Syntex in a joint press conference on the day the TRI data were released. Syntex took an aggressive stance. At a joint media event in July 1991, Gerry Hoerig, manager of the Syntex plant, released a "Good Neighbor Pledge," promising

- to operate the facility in a manner that would protect the environment and the health and safety of Syntex employees and the Boulder community;
- to make health, safety, and environmental considerations a priority in planning for all existing and new products, processes, and facilities;
- to take specific actions to improve its management of chemicals, including reducing the total volume of air emissions by at least 50 percent from 1989 levels by the end of 1994; and

- to establish a community advisory panel to keep the community informed about environmental, health, and safety issues and concerns. The panel would be composed of residents, community and business leaders, environmentalists, students, scientists, and Syntex employees.

As part of the agreement, Citizen Action agreed to underscore Syntex's action with some encouraging words. Indeed, the press release issued that day included praise from Larry Bulling, director of the Colorado office of Citizen Action: "Syntex's actions are the kind of responsible corporate citizenship communities throughout Colorado are demanding. Syntex's willingness to look beyond the strict compliance requirements of existing law and to deal openly with the Boulder community are commitments which every corporation in Colorado would do well to copy."

Syntex's strategy worked. The following day, the *Boulder Camera* ran a front-page story headlined SYNTEX PLEDGES TO CUT ITS AIR EMISSIONS IN HALF. Denver's *Rocky Mountain News* ran a story headlined STATE INDUSTRIES STILL PUMPING TOXINS, reporting on the TRI data. Alongside was a shorter boxed article, SYNTEX LAUDED FOR VOW TO CUT POLLUTION.

The press conference had been the easy part; the hard work for Syntex came in making good on its promises. The first step was putting together the community advisory group. Setting up the twelve-member panel wasn't easy. "It took several months to set it up and to get people to buy into it," says Farentinos. "There was a good deal of skepticism of the idea. People were afraid it was some kind of public relations ploy. We had to show that it was legitimate." The first meeting of the community panel took place in October 1991, and the group continues to meet monthly.

Farentinos has seen a marked change in company relations with the community. "There's been a very interesting transformation of the panel. They are becoming more at ease with themselves and with the company. They still have their reservations and their agendas and their constituencies to please. They're sitting down with the management month after month and the meetings are at the plant, so they become more comfortable with that environment. It just breaks down the mystique and misinformation. Even some of the most outspoken critics on the panel have taken up Syntex's cause on a couple of issues, although they still reserve the right to be unhappy about other areas."

Opening itself up to environmentalists, community groups, and others was not without risk for Syntex. "There's a lot of downside," says Farentinos. "The fact that Syntex went public and said they would do all these things right away set them up for scrutiny. So anything they do now is examined under a big microscope."

But the company may have had no other choice. "Syntex realized that their link to existence is that they talk to people," says A. J. Grant, ECA's president. "These companies are no longer in the middle of corn-fields somewhere. They're surrounded by condos. It's requiring a whole new way of presenting themselves and interacting with the community. One way is to develop an outreach program and reach out to your adversaries, and bring them in and start to diffuse the aggressiveness and the uncooperative nature of the two different groups by bringing them together."

MINDING THE MEDIA

Whether dealing with community groups or reporters, diffusing aggression and uncooperativeness may not be the ultimate goal, but it's a good start. The amount of time, money, and energy wasted on name-calling and accusations of "Truth Pollution!" merely detract from each party's respective agenda. If your company is a known polluter, reporters and environmental groups are going to pay attention. Bringing them and their camera crews inside your company and sharing exactly what you're doing will increase the chances that they'll not blow the story out of proportion. You don't have to embrace every group of activists or every reporter that knocks at your door. That would be a waste of time. But Syntex and other companies' experiences make a good case for at least opening the door to find out what these folks want, perhaps even inviting them inside for a cup of herbal tea and a neighborly chat. You may not make friends, but you might just find that there are more mutual benefits to be had from cooperation than from confrontation.

Beyond that, you need to make sure your company's story gets out—and is accurate. Knowing which media outlets the public trusts most can help you determine where to focus your efforts. Of course, you should try to play all the media angles, but the better targeted your stories, the better. You might be surprised to learn, for example, that the most credible news source may not be the local paper, but a big-city one located thirty or forty miles away. Or that a short story in, say, *USA Today* may be worth far more ink than longer stories in other publications. Sometimes, *The New York Times* and the *Wall Street Journal* are the last places members of your community would find information about your company. The same goes for broadcast media. A local cable talk show could be more influential in getting your story out than making the networks' evening news shows.

Dow Chemical Company is one company that has mastered the art of working with the media. It provides the world with information about its environmental activities and performance. Since 1984, Dow has operated a twenty-four-hour-a-day toll-free media hot line and its employees are available to reporters even at nights and on weekends. The company also helps fund a University of Missouri science journalism center, which provides general science and environmental education to budding journalists. In addition, Dow hosts one- and two-day seminars for editors and reporters on topics ranging from research and development to environmental hot buttons such as waste management and toxics use reduction.

But the people at Dow don't wait for reporters to contact them about environmental issues. Since the mid-1980s, the company has conducted a Visible Scientist program, in which about fifteen scientists a year are trained to be comfortable talking to television interviewers, newspaper editorial boards, and citizens' groups. These scientists serve as spokespeople for the company and have a credibility that business executives and other lay individuals lack. "Even if at that point they're not going to do a story, if an issue later comes up they know that they can call on Dow," says Clay Allen, a Dow media representative. Nonscientists also have the opportunity to reach the public through the company's Management Speech Center, which provides training on public speaking and serves as a central clearinghouse for all Dow employee public appearances. Dow is so fierce in its resolve to communicate with the public that it publishes a quarterly in-house *Environmental Speak-Up* newsletter, which provides information and resources that employees can use in their speeches. Four times a year, Environmental Speak-Up awards are given to employees based on the number of speeches they make.

Dow's efforts are impressive, but this level of commitment to media training isn't necessary to improve your company's relations with local reporters. Sometimes, all it takes is an understanding by plant managers and others that the media isn't always an adversary, especially if you have a good story to tell. Consider an incident at a Midwest 3M facility a few years ago. After the government released its annual Toxics Release Inventory data, a camera crew from a Chicago TV station showed up outside a 3M plant to get footage for a news story, which showed that the company was among the area's biggest polluters. Normally, that would have been the end of it. Camera crews generally aren't allowed inside 3M plants, and the TV reporter hadn't asked to interview anyone from the local facility.

But the plant manager seized the opportunity. He went out, introduced himself to the TV crew, and extended an invitation: "Why don't you come inside and see what we're doing about emissions?" The company actually had a pretty aggressive pollution prevention program in place, and the manager was eager to show it off. The result: The evening news included a report on the region's TRI emissions, as well as a critical look at 3M's contribution, but it also featured a second piece showcasing the company's efforts to clean up its act. One small step for 3M, one giant leap for its local manufacturing operations.

OPENING THE FRONT DOORS

"What will the neighbors think?"

Precious few companies ask themselves this relatively simple question, yet the answer couldn't be more important. Forward-thinking companies recognize how valuable community support can be, and they pursue it aggressively.

"Ultimately, the community wants responsible corporate citizens," says David L. Trimble, corporate environmental manager at BFGoodrich Company. "We start with the premise that each one of our facilities operates with the permission of the community that we exist in. The day we lose that permission, we will no longer continue to exist."

Your company faces several factors that work against forging a positive—or at least non-negative—image among the local citizenry. One thing is that built-in public distrust of corporations, particularly about their environmental performance. Another is the public's relatively low scientific literacy. A spate of recent surveys demonstrate that Americans don't grasp the nature of most environmental problems, and that the knowledge they do possess is clouded by myths and misunderstandings. When S. C. Johnson & Son commissioned the Roper Organization to assess Americans' "Green Point Average" in 1991, it found that a cross section of two thousand adults was woefully misinformed. On average, those interviewed got only 33 percent of the answers correct, a failing grade in any classroom. One reason for this is the media: News reporters and producers try to put complex environmental issues into sound bites and short, pithy articles, which invariably oversimplify, underexplain, or simply get things wrong. That strengthens the case for your company becoming a credible source of information on the environment, and particularly about your company's performance. This may be easier at the local level, where plant managers are also members of the community and may be more effective in breaking through the public's natural cynicism.

Before you begin, it is important to know where the environment ranks among the priorities of local residents. If it is high, that would signal the need for an ongoing, comprehensive informational campaign. If it is relatively far down the list, there may be less need to pull out all the stops. Of course, any such assessment of concern is merely a snapshot in time. As the economy changes and other local and national events ebb and flow, so, too, will attention to local, national, and global environmental issues. Still, as described in chapter 1, you must keep in mind that over time the public will develop a sensitivity to environmental problems, as a result of the accumulation of small amounts of media coverage. Then, if your company is involved in an "incident"—anything from a hearing on whether to license an incinerator to a major life-threatening catastrophe—that sensitivity could be tapped, producing a public outcry that may seem out of proportion to the situation at hand.

How do you prevent that? As Amoco found out in Indiana, knowing the community is a good start, whether from a formal survey, a series of informal meetings with community leaders and citizens, or simply by assigning someone to closely monitor local media in an attempt to understand the qualms and fears of the citizenry. As Amoco learned, the more interactive the relationship, the better. The more you can become directly involved with the community, the more you will become a part of it, and the greater the likelihood that you will be understood, if not actually appreciated, should problems arise.

Some companies approach community relations with a win/win

Tips for Communicating With Stakeholders

- Let regulators know what you are doing beyond complying with the law. Show them your pollution-prevention programs, total quality management programs, and other good, green efforts.

- Treat regulators and environmentalists as you would your clients or customers. Find out their specific needs, target your messages and programs aimed at reaching them, and get feedback on your efforts.

- Educate everyone—customers, regulators, media, suppliers, community members, employees, and others—on your environmental programs.

- Pick the best people to communicate with at community and environmental groups. Make sure you're talking with people who can make decisions and influence others. It's a basic rule of sales: talk to those with the authority to buy.

- Be clear when telling your company's environmental story. Give it a beginning, middle, and end. Try to limit your message to two or three key points, even if there's much more to say.

- Respect media needs and deadlines. When fielding calls from reporters, find out as specifically as possible the kind of story they're writing.

- Admit when you've made a mistake. It builds credibility.

- Invite your company's enemies to come and see firsthand what you are doing. Many of your opponents' fears are likely based on ignorance. Share with them the things you are doing right, as well as the things you are still working to improve.

- In general, don't say anything you don't want to see repeated in the papers or on the air.

philosophy. For example, at Quad/Graphics, the Wisconsin printing company discussed earlier, local printing plants conduct what they call Operation Magacycle, a recycling collection program for glossy magazines and catalogs. Many publications—as well as so-called junk mail—have taken on a bad image among environmentally concerned citizens because very few are able to recycle them through community pickup or dropoff paper-recycling programs, despite the relatively high value much of this paper has in the recycling marketplace. But Quad provides a dropoff facility for local communities around its Wisconsin and New York printing plants. During a single five-week period in Saratoga County, New York, Quad collected some fifty-five tons of paper. This is then combined with waste paper from its own internal recycling operations. The money Quad receives from selling the waste paper is returned to community funds and agencies. The program costs the company practically nothing.

Another community eco-hero is Marcal Paper Mills. The Elmwood Park, New Jersey–based manufacturer of recycled paper towels and toilet paper had been sending trucks to make deliveries on New York's Long Island; the trucks would then return empty. Marcal decided to put those empty trucks to work, picking up undeliverable third-class mail from 175 Long Island post offices. The paper, of course, would become grist for Marcal's recycling operation. The U.S. Postal Service, for its part, saved more than a half-million taxpayer dollars in trash-hauling fees.

Besides the goodwill Quad/Graphics and Marcal engender from such endeavors, there are other potential payoffs. "We felt we had to take responsibility for the products that we produced," says John Imes, Quad's environmental manager. "And we're getting the word out there that magazines and catalogs are recyclable. One of the ideas we're trying to get across is that the catalogs you get in third-class mail aren't bad for the environment; they are as recyclable as anything else."

Therefore, Quad is acting in part out of an enlightened self-interest. Direct-mail catalogs are a backbone of its business, and these publications have come under fire recently. For instance, there is the possibility of state or federal mandates that magazines and direct-mail advertising contain a specified recycled content. One proposal by environmentalists is that recycled content be linked to a publication's bulk-mail rates. And while there are still technological obstacles to producing high-quality, four-color publications on recycled stock—among other things, inks don't dry as easily, requiring more heat, which boosts energy use and pollution—Quad and other printers are clearly recognizing that the new era of environmentalism threatens direct-mail advertising and the printers that produce and mail it. Operation Magacycle is meant to reduce this threat while also producing environmental benefits.

Quad is one of many companies that have made a habit of inviting the community into their facilities on a regular basis—in the form of plant tours, open houses, visitor centers, or events staged on company premises. This may well be the best way to facilitate dialogue and goodwill. By opening your company doors to your neighbors, you are in effect saying, "Come look for yourselves. You'll see that we have a first-rate operation here. We'll show you what we're doing to protect this community's environment. We have nothing to hide."

But simply opening the front doors may not always be sufficient if you don't have good people waiting there to meet the neighbors. Think of leaving your unruly teenage son at home alone to meet the neighbors. "We started a program to have an open house in every plant, every year," says former Ashland Chemical executive Tony Dorfmueller. "We invited the public to see what we do and how we do it, and how it affects them. But there was a reverse side to this. Many of our plant managers were chemists or chemical engineers, and they had absolutely no ability to deal with the public and with the government, other than chemistry equipment and workers. All of a sudden, there were new responsibilities thrown at them. We had to go through a whole training program for our plant managers on how to properly present things and how to think them out. It took a lot of work."

Beyond these relatively simple open-house events are more structured community advisory groups, the kind Syntex employed in Colorado. The idea is to bring a cross section of neighbors, community leaders, and citizens directly into the company, to find out their concerns and to get their advice on company environmental issues. By doing so, the company aimed to head off any potential, perhaps unanticipated, problems. Managing such groups can take a significant amount of time and resources, but the payoff can be worth it. In addition to facilitating communication between companies and citizens, these advisory committees often lead to increased dialogue *within* a community, because its members report back to their peers and neighbors about the issues and decisions discussed at the meetings. Dorfmueller helped coordinate a number of these groups at Ashland. "We didn't want them to have a group come together and hit us with something unexpected. We found that in every case we had a positive reaction from the public. It pays to have the dialogue before the problem, and then you may not even have the problem."

Eastman Kodak is another company that believes in community advisory groups. Its sixteen-member panel has met monthly since 1990. "Their input has been quite insightful," says James Blamphin, a company spokesperson. "We appear before the council and respond to their questions." He says the company can make a presentation during each meeting. "If they want a presentation on air emissions, we give it to them. There's considerable discussion. We very often follow their recommendations." Kodak supplements this communication to the community with its bimonthly newsletter, *Update*, which goes to seventeen thousand households around Kodak Park, the company's 2,200-acre facility in upstate New York.

GETTING THE TROOPS ON BOARD

Before you turn to outsiders, don't overlook the vast network of communicators you already have on board: your employees. When they get involved in and excited about their employer's environmental initiatives, they don't leave that excitement and interest at work; they take it home and share it with their families and friends. Some of their kids take it to school, showing and telling what their parents' employers are doing to "save the earth." And soon you have a no-cost grass-roots communications program. Moreover, the process has a secondary benefit: Those same people—kids, spouses, friends—can serve as an antenna to find out what the community thinks about your company—their perceptions and misperceptions. The key is to tap into that potential.

The "green team" approach discussed in the previous chapter is one means to that end, but effectively involving employees requires more than that. First, your company must take an active role in educating employees about the environment in general and in the ways that your company affects it. "One of the first places you have to start in educating employees about the environment is educating them about the commitment the company has made to the environment—the establishment of policies, principles, and goals," says Cynthia Georgeson, environmental communications manager for S. C. Johnson. Then, she says, "you have to explain to them why it is you're committed to doing that."

S. C. Johnson is committed to getting everyone thinking about the environmental impact of what they do at work and at home. In 1990, it started a comprehensive program with more than one hundred executive-directed employee environmental communication meetings at company facilities in forty-eight countries. The two- to three-hour sessions were led by senior executives—officers of the corporation—and were aimed at acquainting employees with current environmental initiatives as well as the company's goals for the future. "We told them what we're expecting to have happen in our operation," says Georgeson. "And to also begin to surface the questions that any individual would have, such as 'What can I do about source reduction?' or 'How can I, in my function, help my company achieve this goal?' "

Those efforts were backed up by collateral materials, including a brochure and video with an environmental message from the chairman and CEO. The materials have been translated into as many as twenty-two different languages to accommodate the company's diverse worldwide work force. There are departmental quizzes, which grill employees on their knowledge of specific environmental problems relating to their jobs, and guest speakers, including those from the environmental community, talking about a variety of issues, ranging from volatile organic compound emissions to understanding the green consumer marketplace. Around Earth Day, the company focuses on educating employees' families, sponsoring community cleanup days, and screening environmental videos for kids. At S. C. Johnson, Earth Day lasts a whole month.

The second phase of the program starts with office recycling. To underscore its importance, the company has set up employee recycling centers in major facilities, and allows employees to bring recyclables from home. "What we wanted to do was to provide an opportunity for our employees who were beginning to demonstrate environmental behavior an easier way to get those recyclables into recycling streams, and not into landfills," says Georgeson. Another effort involved collecting environmental success stories throughout S. C. Johnson's five operating regions and presenting them in a video that went out to all operational heads. This was done so that "others could learn about a facility in Greece that has taken processing steam that normally would have been vented out and used it as energy to heat the facility in winter and cool the facility in summer—something that was generally not done in Greece," says Georgeson. "Those kinds of initiatives are very important. And we feel that they invigorate employees and catalyze more innovative approaches. They recognize that employees have good ideas and that management is open to supporting those ideas. Dialogue is very important between management and employees in affecting environmental change. The more you see it, the more you can encourage it."

Some employees have gone beyond the company-sponsored activities. A group of employees formed an Earth Day Everyday Committee, which works directly on environmental initiatives with the community located around the company's Racine, Wisconsin, headquarters. The company actively supports this kind of community involvement, and established the Samuel C. Johnson Environmental Stewardship Awards Program to recognize employees who take an active role. Winners receive an award plaque, and $2,500 is contributed in their name by S. C. Johnson to a local organization.

Georgeson emphasizes the importance of education at all levels. "Leadership is extremely important in the environment. It's one thing to say that the chairman of the corporation believes in this. But it is critical that our mid- and senior-level executives carry on that heritage of responsible environmental decision making. And in order to be able to do so, they have to understand very specifically the implications, both environmental and economic, associated with today's marketplace. We've put together a semiannual program that's hosted by the management committee—our most senior executives. We've brought in guest speakers from the outside. We think it's important that there be an external perspective to tell us what they believe and what their expectations are, and what they see the future holding for us. We then take that information, summarize it, and put it into our employee environmental newsletter, called the *Environmental Catalyst*. And we hope that it lives up to its name—that it is a catalyst for more action."

A lot of what's needed for environmental education is a fundamental understanding of the problems and their likely solutions. Despite the vast amount of coverage the media and others have devoted to such matters recently, a great deal more is needed, as Johnson's Green Point Average study revealed.

Take the act of recycling. It's a relatively simple concept, but putting it into practice can be a challenge. Office paper recycling is a good example. For a program to be effective (*read*: profitable) employees must do more than simply lump all kinds of paper into the same recycling bins. Computer paper has to be carefully kept separate from old memos and reports; colored paper can't commingle with white; high-quality letterhead shouldn't get mixed up with junk mail and newspapers. Clearly, communicating all of this to an already harried work force takes some time and patience. When environmental coordinators try to change the way employees dispose of unwanted paper goods, they are met with everything from confusion to downright hostility. Never mind trying to take on other recyclables—glass, aluminum, plastic, laser printer toner cartridges, and all the rest.

A lot of the battle can be won by having a relatively small corps of individuals set a good example. As employees see their peers and superiors making the effort, they are more likely to do the same. "It takes a lot of positive feedback," says Glenda Goehrs, vice president for environmental affairs at GSD&M, an advertising agency in Austin, Texas. "Getting people to accept two-sided copying was a good example. There was a lot of resistance to that, especially with documents used for major presentations. I just quietly showed examples of ones that people had done that looked really sharp. I showed examples of people who made presentations on 100-percent recycled paper, saying, 'Look, this can be done.' And to the diehards—the people who just didn't want to do it—I said, 'How many books have you read that are printed on just one side of the paper?' "

Employee education efforts don't need to be formal or stuffy; they can be downright fun. At Esprit de Corp, the San Francisco–based clothing manufacturer, one basic challenge was to get employees to participate in the in-house recycling program, separating glass, aluminum, and other waste from the trash can to the recycling bins. Despite enthusiasm from the youthful work force (average employee age: twenty-seven), the compliance rate was far from satisfactory. That frustrated Quincy Tompkins, full-time manager of the company's "eco-desk," who was in charge of coordinating employee environmental initiatives.

Her solution: to produce a guerrilla video, part Monty Python, part "Candid Camera," to illustrate the problem. In the dead of night, she and a few cohorts armed with video equipment rifled through employee trash cans to find out who was throwing away recyclables. A few days later, they asked several of the unsuspecting guilty to participate in a special video project. They brought each participant onto an interview set and, cameras rolling, asked them to talk about the state of the earth.

The employees answered in earnest and the conversation would proceed apace until the interviewer pulled the rug out from under them: "We've been going through your trash and here's what we found. . . ." Realizing they had been set up and caught red-handed, the employees' reactions ranged from playful embarrassment to anger and guilt. The finished video—which featured Tompkins as an on-the-scene reporter while standing inside a dumpster—was shown on a twenty-foot-high screen at a company meeting. Though it was all in fun, it served its purpose, increasing morale—and recycling. "Now, no one throws anything away unless they call me first," says Tompkins.

Another means of getting employees involved is to encourage their financial support of environmental causes. An example is a workplace giving campaign, the kind that United Way has run for years. In 1988, a coalition of environmental groups called Earth Share created a system to do just that. The Washington, D.C.-based organization helps employees donate a few dollars from each paycheck to the fund, which is disbursed to more than forty environmental groups, including the Environmental Defense Fund, Friends of the Earth, the National Audubon Society, the Nature Conservancy, the Sierra Club, and the Trust for Public Land. It's a fairly efficient system, with about ninety cents of every dollar it receives going directly to the groups. (Most direct-mail campaigns average about seventy-five cents per dollar.) For employers, the campaigns cost little or nothing. Among the companies conducting Earth Share workplace campaigns are Apple Computer, Esprit, Kaiser Permanente, NCR, Safeway Stores, and Tandem Computers, as well as more than fifty federal, state, and local government agencies.

Earth Share's organizers believe that this process provides those who wouldn't otherwise participate a means of supporting environmental causes. And the workplace is the ideal setting for environmental groups to reach the broadest cross section of the population. The Earth Share program can also use businesses to distribute educational materials to employees on a variety of environmental subjects. The benefit to employers is that the program represents a low- or no-cost way of bringing employees into the environmental arena, and to communicate to employees the company's commitment to a cleaner earth.

THE POWER OF THE PURSE

The need for communicating openly about the environment doesn't end with employees and the public. Suppliers and customers are increasingly interested, too, not just with the products they buy from or sell to your company, but also with your commitment to environmental issues. And a growing number of companies are finding that they can use their purchasing power to pressure other companies whose environmental policies or products they don't like.

In 1988, Jacob Schnur, the purchasing manager at NRG Barriers, began beating the drum for change. Specifically, he wanted one of his chemical suppliers to switch from the fifty-five-gallon steel drums they used to deliver their product to larger plastic "totes." "We had a scrap company that was shredding our drums and recycling them," says Schnur. But before that could happen, the drums had to be pressure-washed, which produced chemical waste from the runoff. And recycled steel drums weren't available, so they had to be made from virgin steel. "I really felt an aversion to all that," says Schnur.

Each reusable plastic tote holds three hundred gallons, so Schnur could buy in bulk at lower prices. But the drums cost $1,500 each, and required the supplier to take them back for reuse, something it hadn't done with the steel drums. The problem was convincing the supplier to make the switch—and to pick up the freight costs in both directions.

After months of talking with the supplier—explaining, discussing, and cajoling—Schnur got his totes. "I figure in the last four years I've saved several hundred thousand dollars on just this one chemical," he says.

Schnur's effort is just one example of the power of the corporate purse in helping the environment. If companies are important trading partners for suppliers and vendors, they can use that clout to seek products and services that are less polluting and create less waste. In the process, corporate consumers can help "green" both their own operations as well as those of their suppliers. There's not a lot of magic to the process. "One of the ways to influence manufacturers is very simple: You have to ask for what you want," says Richard Keller, project manager of the Northeast Maryland Waste Disposal Authority.

According to Schnur, whose company makes roofing and siding panels, "You have to be a good negotiator. It helped me that I had a sales background." Schnur made an informal presentation to the supplier—what he calls "reverse selling"—showing him ads for the plastic totes and articles from trade publications. "I said, 'Here's our costs for handling. Here are the laws that are affecting our operations. It would really help us, and it would really help you.' "

Persistence paid off. "I showed it to the first guy. I went to the next guy. I refined my presentation every time. I really started working on them. I told them I was getting pressure from the state for disposal, I'm getting hit with disposal costs. You have to appeal to people on their base level." He downplayed the evidence that the totes are better for the environment. "Say to somebody, 'I can save you money.' Translate it into a language that business people can understand."

Clearly, it is easier to make demands on a supplier if you are big. For example, in 1991, Xerox Corporation decided it wanted standardized packaging, labeled with bar codes, at all its plants. The company sent suppliers a letter and information packet describing the new program, then invited them to a day-long training session, complete with brochures and a sixteen-minute video. The company had extra copies of the video on hand for suppliers to take with them.

"A few specific standard-size boxes and pallets are much easier to deal with," says Abhay K. Bhushan, manager of Xerox's Environmental Leadership Program. The company set up a program at each plant to facilitate returning the used boxes and pallets to suppliers for reuse. "While the first-time cost is slightly higher, each reuse cost is lower," Bhushan says. "Both Xerox and the supplier save money." Xerox's annual savings could reach as much as $10 million within a few years. "Companies are somewhat reluctant to change," says Bhushan. "They don't want to spend the money unless they could see the value of it. We also have to educate our employees and show them the environmental and economic benefits." Xerox's pitch used the company's philosophy of partnering, says Bob Misturak, manager of the firm's packaging commodity team. In this case, partnering meant showing suppliers that adopting a standard would result in lower costs for everyone.

Campbell Soup Company takes a somewhat harder line. The company insists that the glass jars it gets from suppliers have an average post-consumer recycled content of 25 to 27 percent, and that it sees recycled content figures at each of its suppliers' plants. "We require that they send in a corporate policy statement that details the amount of recycled in their business and what their intentions are. And if that's not

Tips on Dealing with Suppliers

- Get top management's support. This will put teeth into any policy you try to impose on other companies.

- Put the policy in writing. Send it to the CEO, VP for sales or marketing, or other top executive who can implement the policy.

- Let money talk. Promote the program on the basis of cost savings, efficiency, and market advantage.

- Make a presentation: Show costs, benefits, and laws applying to both your and the supplier's operations. The more homework you've done, the better the case you can make.

- Request a response within a given amount of time. Allow the supplier to implement the plan over a generous period. But don't let them put you off for long.

- Educate your own employees about the need for and the mechanics of the program. Offer training, support, technical assistance, and resource lists.

- Pool your resources. If your company is a small customer, work through your industry's trade association to team up with other companies in your industry to maximize your buying power.

- Play up the competitive angle. Make it known that other suppliers have already made the change, or if you believe other customers would buy the "greener" product. Let suppliers know that you are shopping the competition.

- Ask the supplier for help in coming up with solutions. Good ones will generate ideas and may have access to products you don't know about.

- Don't ask other companies to implement policies your company isn't already doing. That could backfire; you may risk being called hypocritical.

good enough, we respond," says Steve Parker, Campbell's director of purchasing.

Campbell's lets its suppliers know that "if they don't participate over the long term, they're going to lose our business. If the technology is available and they don't participate, it's their fault. If they just say, 'We're going to' or 'We intend to,' that doesn't wash." Parker says that since Campbell's instituted this policy, they have dropped several suppliers. "The essential thing is how often to remind them. 'How's your recycled rate? How does it compare with last year's? Where's it going to be next year?' You've got to keep the issue in front of them if you want to be successful." If a Campbell's supplier can't increase its recycled content, Parker says, "they better have a damn good reason. One of those reasons could be capital. Fine, put it down on a piece of paper what it is you have to do and how much time it will take. If you're not willing to put money into your business to make yourself state of the art, we don't want to do business with you."

Another hard-line company in this regard is Ace Hardware Corporation. In 1991, Thomas J. Daly, general manager of the company's paint division, sent a letter to vendors, accompanied by a sixteen-page questionnaire and an environmental policy statement. "The Paint Division will begin conducting audits of all our vendors during 1992—with special emphasis on safety and environmental issues," the statement read. "We reserve the right to immediately cancel any business awarded to a vendor found to be in noncompliance with any applicable federal, state, or local regulations, or who . . . shows blatant disregard for the best interest of our environment. . . ."

Not everyone complied; they either did not want to disclose proprietary information or didn't want to make the effort. "Some indicated that if we wanted the information, we'd have to come on site and get it ourselves," says Daly, who dropped a few suppliers in the process. Daly admits that "the communications could have been a little better. A lot of the suppliers were more than willing to provide the information and were surprised that anyone was doing this sort of thing. There aren't a lot of people who are spending the time to look at their vendors."

Ace's approach is beginning to take off in Europe, too. For example, Britain's B&Q, a division of Kingfisher, which runs a chain of 280 do-it-yourself stores, decided that its 450 suppliers must have a policy that is supported by a full environmental audit and must agree to comply with B&Q's own environmental policy. B&Q backs this up with a forty-page, detailed questionnaire each supplier must fill out. Companies that ignore the B&Q questionnaire risk being dropped from the list of designated suppliers. Among the big concerns were peat moss suppliers that get their product from environmentally sensitive areas and lumber companies whose hardwood comes from nonsustainable sources. According to Alan Knight, B&Q's environmental coordinator, the program benefits go beyond merely ensuring the environmental quality of the products sold in B&Q stores. It also opens up lines of communication with suppliers and gives them a forum to discuss environmental issues.

Meanwhile, in Germany, Computer 2000, the largest distributor of computer hardware and software in eleven European countries and the third largest in the world, announced in 1992 that it intended to sign new contracts only with suppliers that offer "recyclable and environmentally friendly" products. Although the policy applied only to new vendors, its larger suppliers—including IBM, Apple, Canon, Microsoft, and Hewlett-Packard—were beneficiaries of Computer 2000's campaign to educate vendors about new developments on packaging standards for companies doing business in the European market.

Educating suppliers about how to work with you is key. S. C. Johnson recognized that, and in 1991 held an elaborate International Suppliers' Day Environmental Symposium at its Wisconsin headquarters. The two-day meeting featured both general and specific presentations from in-house and outside speakers, including National Wildlife Federation president Jay D. Hair; Wisconsin's former U.S. senator Gaylord Nelson, who also is credited with cofounding the original Earth Day; and representatives from the President's Council on Environmental Quality and the International Chamber of Commerce. Representatives from fifty-seven of Johnson's top seventy supplier organizations worldwide attended the symposium, which also featured a lunchtime keynote speech from Johnson's president and CEO, Richard M. Carpenter. Afternoon breakout sessions focused on such things as biodegradation of products and packaging, source reduction and recycling of products and manufacturing processes, improved communication between suppliers and S. C. Johnson, and the need to reduce volatile organic compounds in the company's aerosol products.

The symposium wasn't the end of the communication efforts between Johnson's Wax and its suppliers. A summary booklet was mailed to all participants, and a newsletter, *Partners*, continues to keep suppliers and other interested parties up to speed on the company's goals and progress. As Edward C. Furey, Johnson's director of U.S. strategic purchasing, put it in the premiere issue: "From the raw materials and components you supply us to the containers in which they are packaged, your commitment to helping S. C. Johnson attain these objectives is critical. . . . Partnering together, we can and will have a measurable impact on improving the condition of the environment."

Other customer-supplier efforts are less elaborate, inspired more by communications and creative thinking between committed individuals in different companies. For example, when Digital Equipment Corporation (DEC) began recycling the plastic in old computer housings, it demonstrated how working with vendors can create new opportunities. Working with the plastic supplier, General Electric, and the University of Massachusetts at Lowell, DEC found it could process the plastic, then send it to GE, which processed it further, mixing it with 49 percent recycled material to form roofing material. That material is now on the roofs of some McDonald's restaurants.

"One of the keys was working with GE to make sure that the material could be reprocessed and there was a market for it," says Joe Collentro, DEC's purchasing manager for strategic waste management. DEC now molds codes into terminal housings. In the process, it saves 25 percent over the cost of incinerating the plastic at a waste-to-energy plant. After that experience, DEC looked at the lead content of its used cathode ray tubes—the glass monitors—which had been sent to hazardous waste sites. The supplier, a subsidiary of Corning Glass, agreed to accept the glass, but only if DEC cleaned it up first. DEC turned to Envirocycle Inc., of Endicott, New York, which also helped DEC reclaim the gold, silver, and copper from old computers. Envirocycle said it could even recycle the PVC insulation on the wiring.

Finally, Envirocycle agreed to take the entire computer. "That's pretty exciting," says Collentro. "They saw an opportunity to make a product and make a leader. It was so simple it was unbelievable. As of today, it's given us a cost savings of 43 percent." As the process is refined, he says, the company will save even more. "When you start a process, you start to see the sidelines. We showed them this was a benefit to us both."

In the end, it takes a bit of effort to move markets. "The most important thing that any organization has to do when buying an environmentally friendly product is make a commitment to the product," says Richard Keller of the Northeast Maryland Waste Disposal Authority. "If companies only buy recycled products when it's convenient, that's certainly not a policy that will encourage manufacturers to change their processes."

For smaller companies, patience may be necessary. To achieve economies of scale, suppliers may wait to see other customers' specs before making changes requested of them. But as a buyer, be prepared to change suppliers if you are dissatisfied with the response. Keller also counsels that companies stick to common specifications. "You can't have fifty different products for fifty different states. If everyone defines 'recycled' differently, then the manufacturer does not have the economies of scale."

Keller says companies must phase in new products and processes slowly. It's important to give everyone time to adjust to the change, he says. DEC's Collentro offers this advice: "Tell purchasing people, 'Go be the leader.' Go to management and say, 'We can do this.' Don't wait for somebody to tell you what to do."

WHAT'S GOOD FOR GENERAL MOTORS

No one can wield the power of the purse more effectively than a big company, and General Motors, the United States' largest manufacturer, has figured out that by leaning on its suppliers, it can save both cash and trash. In fact, some General Motors plants aim to eliminate completely all packaging material now being sent to landfills. No shrink wrap, pallets, "peanuts," cardboard boxes, or strapping tape. Nothing.

That is the ambitious goal of GM's Chevrolet-Pontiac-Canada (CPC) Group, which is made up of nineteen stamping and assembly plants in North America, plus headquarters offices in Warren, Michigan. It's all part of CPC's WE CARE ("Waste Elimination and Cost Awareness Rewards Everyone") program, which focuses on the company's efforts "as a corporate and community citizen in addressing our impact on the environment," in the words of Kathleen H. Klement, CPC's director of transportation.

In 1991, CPC distributed a letter to all its suppliers, urging them to join the campaign, and offering guidelines for making the requisite changes. For example, suppliers must use corrugated cardboard shipping pallets instead of ones made of wood. Some GM plants receive up to two thousand pallets per day; disposal may be complicated by the fact that some localities prohibit wood in landfills. When wood must be used, CPC plans to shred it, using the chips for such things as fuel, landscaping, and animal bedding. In addition, CPC facilities will no longer accept any shipment that uses wood corner supports, foam, or other materials stapled or glued to cardboard boxes. Such "foreign" materials can hinder cardboard recycling. Similarly, needless wrapping, bagging, and taping are *verboten*: Only strapping made of polyester and nylon is accepted.

One can readily see the ripple effect this one GM policy will have on the thousands of suppliers that do business with the CPC facilities. If you're a GM supplier, you will have to change the way you do business with the company. And for many suppliers, GM is probably their biggest customer.

Not surprisingly, vendor response to GM's request was "very, very enthusiastic," says Klement, and most companies expected to comply. According to Kenneth J. Horvath, CPC's senior project engineer and packaging expert, suppliers are not unduly burdened by the guidelines, which are borrowed from existing packaging techniques employed in the grocery and food packaging industries. Horvath says all the alternative packaging it recommends are off-the-shelf products, for which GM offers source lists.

GM may be the biggest but it certainly isn't the only company setting its sights on zero trash. According to Klement, CPC is part of a companywide effort, although other divisions haven't yet adopted CPC's ambitious waste-elimination goal. Another zero-trash company is Herman Miller, the Zeeland, Michigan, furniture company. By leaning on its suppliers, it has eliminated 70 percent of the Styrofoam and cardboard packaging on some products and have saved $250,000 a year in materials and shipping costs in the process. The company's goal is to eliminate all landfilling by 1995.

CPC won't say how much money or trash GM will save, but it should be substantial. Not everything it recycles will turn to gold, but GM appears to be on its way to a profitable waste-cutting venture in which both the company and its suppliers will come out winners. In this case, what's good for General Motors really may be good for the country.

THE NEW PARTNERSHIPS

This new era of corporate environmentalism has spawned a myriad assortment of new relationships and partnerships—between and among employees and employers, customers and suppliers, companies and environmental groups, even among competitors. In these new partnerships, seemingly unrelated entities—often comprising strange bedfellows—are finding that much can be gained by sharing information and other resources on environmental problems and solutions. This spirit of communication and cooperation could be vital to resolving the large and complex environmental problems we face.

These new partnerships are not easy. They can be fraught with peril, as old adversaries attempt to break down decades of mistrust to find mutually satisfactory solutions. In most cases, the relationships are double-edged: environmentalists and executives working jointly while one is watchdogging the other's performance; competitors sharing information and technologies while trying to gain competitive advantages over one another; companies pushing their customers to accept environmental changes to their products, while at the same time trying to retain their loyalty. And then there's public opinion: For example, when environmentalists and corporations get too cozy, it raises eyebrows among members, supporters, stockholders, media, lawyers, competitors, and others.

The joint task force formed by McDonald's and the Environmental Defense Fund (EDF) to find ways to reduce McDonald's solid waste makes for an excellent case study of a highly successful, win-win situation. The relationship began in mid-1989, when Fred Krupp, EDF's executive director, asked for a meeting with McDonald's executives to discuss solid-waste issues and steps that the restaurant chain might take to deal with those issues. An immediate expression of interest from McDonald's led to other meetings between the two organizations to talk about a possible relationship.

McDonald's had plenty of reasons to pursue the partnership. As environmental awareness had increased, the public had developed a strong perception that McDonald's was an environmental villain. "They hated that," says Richard Denison, an EDF senior scientist, who was part of the early meetings. "They were pretty frank about that. The letters they were getting, the pickets, and so on—they found no interest in being viewed as not doing the right thing environmentally. Clearly, they wanted to take some steps that would be viewed as credible, that would address or at least counter the negative image that they had.

"McDonald's was looking for a couple of other things," continues Denison. "One was a source of more objective information on environmental issues than they were able to get. They were basically relying on the information and perspective of their suppliers for environmental information about their practices and packaging. That, they began to feel, was not a sufficient amount of information or sufficient perspective on the issue. So I think they were very receptive, when we came along, to hearing another perspective. And they began to trust a lot of what we were saying because they perceived very quickly that we did not have a particular ax to grind. We were not trying to sell them more packaging. And in contrast to a lot of the environmental groups that they had dealt with in one form or another, we were not trying to put them out of business."

What was in it for EDF? "We approached McDonald's because of a number of things," says Denison. "We had been thinking for some time about doing some sort of project focusing on the fast-food industry, and possibly even McDonald's directly, to try to look at some new ways to solve a problem that I think a lot of people in our community were trying to solve through brute force—that is, litigation, legislation, bans on polystyrene, and so on. That would certainly serve some function, in terms of keeping pressure on them for positive change. But polystyrene was, after all, a very small piece of the industry's and the environment's problem. It was a tiny fraction of the total amount of material being used. It was symbolic, but by no means the heart of the matter in terms of the kinds of changes that were needed. And simply banning polystyrene, as a number of communities had begun to do, and as a number of environmental groups were pushing, we didn't feel would begin to solve the problem.

"We also saw some enormous potential—that if we could find some things that McDonald's could do, they would most likely be mirrored in the actions of a number of other companies, both within McDonald's business and upstream and downstream. McDonald's doing something would potentially exert a great deal of influence over its suppliers. And similarly, any changes that McDonald's made would be very visible to the eighteen million customers every day who eat at McDonald's."

It took half a year to work out the details. First, a mutual trust had to be worked out. "We got to know each other," says Denison. "A lot of the time spent before we even announced the project was critical to developing trust, to understanding enough about how each of our organizations worked and how decisions were made, so that when we did get down to work, we were able to cut through a lot of the rhetoric on both sides and home in on what we could actually do."

"We opened our doors to EDF," says Bob Langert, director of environmental affairs at McDonald's. "Anything they wanted to see we showed them, including confidential information, from sales to the way we design our restaurants. I presume that's why they trusted us. It's like having a good marriage. You've got to be very open and honest."

Denison and other EDF staffers put in many hours looking at McDonald's operations. "We spent time looking at the supply system— storage and materials going in the back door—as well as how things like the drive-through window operated. Basically looking at the operational elements of the whole restaurant team. We visited a distribution center, which supplies about a thousand stores in the Chicago area. We visited about eight or ten of McDonald's major suppliers, including food suppliers as well as packaging suppliers." On top of that, Denison and two colleagues worked behind the counter at McDonald's restaurants in New York City and outside Washington, D.C.

McDonald's executives, meanwhile, visited EDF's New York headquarters to see its operations and get a better feel for the range of issues it worked on, the kinds of expertise it had, and the type of organization it was. "We found them to be super people to work with," says Langert. "They would listen, they would relate to our business needs. And that helped them earn our trust, because we realized they're very smart people."

Another issue was the confidentiality of McDonald's proprietary data. "Our initial agreement has all kinds of language about how proprietary information would be dealt with," says Denison. Nonetheless, he says, "a decision was made that we would have access as a task force to anything we needed to know. Some of that information was clearly going to be sensitive, and we agreed that certain aspects of the information we got would be held confidential and that we would seek a way to use that information where we needed publicly in a form that did not compromise proprietary information. Far and away the most sensitive kinds of information are the unit sales and costs-per-unit information. That kind of information we had access to, to the degree that we needed it." Still, the task force's final report contains information that most companies would deem sensitive—how much waste a McDonald's restaurant generates per day, for example, or how much packaging in the aggregate a typical McDonald's restaurant uses.

To the surprise of both EDF and McDonald's, the task force became much more substantive and action-oriented than anyone would have imagined. Originally, EDF hoped the task force would develop a set of options for waste reduction, which McDonald's management would then consider. The company would be free to do whatever it wanted with those recommendations. EDF, for its part, could say whatever it wanted about the recommendations. If it thought they were feasible and should have been implemented but weren't, EDF had every right to proclaim its outrage publicly. Says Langert: "We just got excited about all the different aspects of reducing, reusing, and recycling. The momentum quickly shifted from 'These aren't just things that we should be thinking about. We're going to do these things.'"

EDF's initial proposal quickly transformed into something much more substantive: a set of actions to which McDonald's management would commit as part of the task force's final product. The new corporate waste-reduction action plan that was ultimately drafted by the task force was accepted with virtually no modifications by McDonald's management, according to Denison. And to back that policy up, McDonald's committed itself to implementing forty-two discrete actions of a Waste Reduction Action Plan over two years. In fact, by the end of the first year, not only had McDonald's completed nineteen of the initiatives, it had added twenty new ones.

Clearly, McDonald's was taking risks. Their efforts could have been panned by the press and others, viewed as anything from a public relations front to a Band-Aid solution. Indeed, the company's initiative was not universally accepted. Exactly three months after the task force was announced, McDonald's made a highly publicized announcement that it would phase out polystyrene foam packaging in all of its 8,500 U.S. stores, replacing foam "clamshell" hamburger packages with paper-based wraps. That dramatic and unexpected announcement was both hailed and reviled. Environmentalists claimed a major victory, having all but stamped out the much-hated foam packaging from the world's biggest restaurant chain. But the fast-food and packaging industries countered that McDonald's had simply caved into pressure from misinformed customers and environmentalists, making the wrong choice for the environment.

EDF, meanwhile, had taken risks, too. The group's collaboration with industry represented a sharp about-face from the motto EDF adopted when it was founded in 1967: "Sue the bastards." "We clearly had to deal with exacerbating an already existing tendency in some of the environmental community to paint a national environmental group as too compromising, too easily co-opted, and playing the insider game, which was the theme of a lot of grass-roots environmental groups' criticism of national groups," says Denison. "There was clearly a perception of McDonald's being the villain, which should be dealt with through harsh means, and the notion of trying to sit down and cooperatively work was anathema. Barry Commoner, at the beginning of this project, said that we were further exacerbating a trend by national groups to work with corporations rather than against them. And he did not mean that as a compliment."

In the end, things went better for both parties than either had expected. "We got lucky," says Langert. "It surpassed our wildest dreams." Denison echoes the sentiment: "Things went way beyond what we originally conceived to be possible, and McDonald's feels the same way. And that's a pretty remarkable statement."

McDonald's and EDF have come to symbolize the most visible and well-publicized environmental-corporate partnership, but it isn't the only one. EDF has also teamed up with General Motors to develop a plan to have companies buy and destroy older cars that produce a lot of pollution. Another collaboration involves four business and environmental organizations: the San Francisco–based Pacific Gas & Electric Company, the nation's largest investor-owned utility; the Rocky Mountain Institute (RMI), a research center and think tank founded by Amory and Hunter Lovins and based in Snowmass, Colorado; the Lawrence Berkeley Laboratory, part of the University of California; and the Natural Resources Defense Council. Their project, begun in 1989, is known as ACT², shorthand for "Advanced Customer Technology Test for Maximum Energy Efficiency," a five-year, $10-million project that aims to use an integrated approach to energy use, whether in a home or business. Amory Lovins believes that by treating energy use in a holistic manner, it is possible to design all the components to take advantage of one another's strengths in order to maximize energy savings. The project calls for retrofitting existing buildings as well as constructing new ones, then monitoring each building's energy use for up to three years, closely tracking energy use and costs.

Another example of business-environmentalist cooperation is the National Wildlife Federation's Wildlife Habitat Enhancement Council (WHEC), formed in 1988 to "promote and nurture the enhancement of corporate property—representing about one-quarter of private U.S. land— for the benefit of wildlife." The independent nonprofit works with companies, community groups, and wildlife specialists to develop "workable programs to improve wildlife habitat on corporate lands," according to Joyce M. Kelly, WHEC's executive director. Such programs, she says, "can help improve the corporation's standing among the environmental community as well as provide much-needed habitat for wild creatures." The group boasts some fifty corporate members, including Allied-Signal, Amoco, Exxon, General Electric, Honeywell, IBM, McDonnell-Douglas, and W. R. Grace. Another of its members, DuPont, Kelly calls "the driving force behind the formation of WHEC." All together, they have committed more than 130,000 acres to wildlife habitat management at 106 locations. WHEC provides technical assistance and other resources.

The National Wildlife Federation has another cooperative program in the form of the Corporate Conservation Council, established in 1982 "to bring executives from many industrial sectors into dialogue with NWF leadership," according to the group's mission statement. The group aims to "reduce or avoid conflicts" by "exchanging information and examining proposals for conserving environmental values in concert with sustainable economic development." Among the sixteen members of the Corporate Conservation Council are AT&T, Browning-Ferris Industries, Duke Power Company, General Motors, Johnson & Johnson, Procter & Gamble, Shell Oil, USX, and Weyerhaeuser.

And then there are the growing number of intra-industry partnerships, established for companies—often competitors—to collaborate on finding solutions to some of the many tough technological challenges that companies face when they try to "green" themselves. For example, in 1991, the National Center for Manufacturing Sciences (NCMS), a 140-member consortium of manufacturers, launched the Environmentally Conscious Strategic Manufacturing Initiative, which aims to pool money, expertise, and other resources to improve manufacturers' environmental performance. During its first year of operation, the group launched fourteen projects within five program areas (chlorofluorocarbon and volatile organic compound substitutes, lead alternatives, bioremediation, metal cutting fluids, and emissions from painting and plating operations), and plans to launch additional programs in such areas as life-cycle environmental design, environmental packaging, waste minimization, and energy conservation. "This thing happened so quickly, there was so much interest, we haven't had to sell it," says Donald Walukas, program manager of the initiative. He credits the success in part to the ability of NCMS to "get people together to work on things cooperatively rather than independently."

A project involving CFC substitutes demonstrates how the companies intend to save time and money by working together. In seeking CFC alternatives, "it turned out that two of our member companies were going to do nearly identical things," says Walukas. "We asked around and found that three other organizations had similar plans. We brought them together and they agreed on what to test, agreed on a testing protocol, and divided up the work." Walukas says the project costs about $750,000. "If they had done it independently, they would have spent as much as $750,000 each." And, he might have added, probably taken longer to do it.

Another impressive effort is called the Industry Cooperative for Ozone Layer Protection (ICOLP), based in Washington, D.C. By pooling resources, it hopes to find alternatives to manufacturing processes using chlorofluorocarbons, or CFCs, and to make those processes available to smaller companies as well as manufacturers in developing nations. The group has set up an online data base called OZONET, to facilitate information sharing. They have also published manuals on such subjects as CFC recycling and the use of non-CFC-based cleaning solutions. Some of the seventeen dues-paying members of ICOLP found themselves working cheek-by-jowl with some of their biggest rivals—AT&T and Northern Telecom, for example, or Hitachi, Matsushita, and Toshiba.

The partnerships extend throughout the world. In Hong Kong, the Private Sector Committee on the Environment was formed in 1991 to exchange information and resources. The group established a Centre of Environmental Technology to give advice on pollution control, environmental audits, and other topics. BAUM, the German Environmental Management Association, is focusing its efforts on spreading the word about environmental management to small and mid-sized companies in the federal states that make up the former East Germany. South Africa has an Industrial Environmental Forum, whose members share experience in environmental management. The country's Chamber of Business also has an Environmental Committee. There are green business networks in India and Zimbabwe, too, with new ones sprouting every few months.

The partnerships go on and on—from the Global Environmental Management Initiative, a coalition of companies sharing total environmental quality management techniques, discussed in the previous chapter; to the World Engineering Partnership for Sustainable Development, an initiative of the international engineering community "to provide advice, leadership, and facilitation for a sustainable world"; to the Recycled Paper Coalition, a group of seven San Francisco–area companies, including Bank of America, Chevron, Safeway, and Pacific Bell that joined together to encourage other companies to recycle; to an unnamed ad hoc task force of nineteen professionals from the advertising world, who came together to publish a brochure on "things advertising agencies can to make a positive difference" on the environment.

All of these partnerships and other activities are good efforts, but participation in them does not necessarily alleviate a company's need to get its own house in order. Your contribution to Ducks Unlimited will be mere window dressing if your operations are still fouling the air and water. The public will think your on-site wildlife refuge a sham if you haven't instigated some basic waste-reduction and pollution-prevention programs. And your green marketing claims will backfire if your factories are among the highest emitters of toxic chemicals. You must make sure that at least some of your public partnerships and charitable deeds directly address your company's environmental problems.

In the end, your fortunes live or die by the reputation you forge for yourself with your friends, enemies, and neighbors.

6

efficiency

FINDING PROFIT IN THE SOLUTION TO POLLUTION

IN CALIFORNIA'S SILICON Valley, some of the biggest manufacturing firms have turned environmental concern into a heated competition in which even the losers are winners.

To fully appreciate this statement, you have to know the bittersweet story of Lockheed Missiles & Space Company, a $5 billion a year, twenty-thousand-employee operation whose projects include the Trident submarine–based missile program and military and nonmilitary satellite systems, including parts of the space station Freedom. The company, a unit of Lockheed Corporation, is one of twenty-five members of the Santa Clara County Manufacturing Group, an industry association that promotes the interests of local industrial firms that make everything from computer chips to rocket motors to parts for the Hubble Space Telescope. In recent years this already competitive bunch has turned its energies into the area of environmental performance.

Since 1988, when the first Toxics Release Inventory was released for the area, companies have vied to outdo each other in making quantum leaps in emissions reductions. Others in the community have caught the spirit and gotten into the act. For example, each year when TRI data are released, the twenty-five companies hold a joint press conference that also includes environmental groups, public officials, and community leaders, all of whom crow about the pollution-prevention advances made over the previous year.

Pity poor Lockheed. In 1987, it ranked twenty-fourth out of twenty-five companies in TRI emissions—the second-biggest polluter of the group. Determined to do better, the entire company went to work, changing operating procedures, educating employees, developing substitutes for some of the more problematic chemicals. Three years later when the 1990 data were released, the company had managed to reduce its emissions by more than 64 percent.

The result: Lockheed dropped from twenty-fourth to twenty-fifth—last place—making it the biggest polluter of the group.

The "problem" wasn't that Lockheed was slipping behind but that its competitors were forging ahead, making dramatic improvements in reducing emissions. For example, IBM Corporation's operations in Santa Clara County reduced emissions by nearly 95 percent during that same period; National Semiconductor cut its pollutants by just over 88 percent. Indeed, the average improvement for the twenty-five companies over the three years was 74 percent. So, Lockheed's improvements were less impressive when compared with its competitors. As Dr. Thomas D. English, environmental programs director for the manufacturing group, put it, "It was kind of sad and funny at the same time."

How, in the thick of so many other economic struggles and strategies, did these companies become so pugnacious about pollution? Part of the answer, no doubt, comes from doing business in water-scarce, eco-aware Northern California. Another likely contributor is the youthful idealism that can be found at many Silicon Valley firms.

To be fair, Lockheed's operations are markedly different from most of the other in the gang of twenty-five, which includes Apple Computers, Hewlett-Packard Company, Intel Corporation, National Semiconductor, and Raytheon. Most of these companies' operations are devoted to making relatively inexpensive, mass-produced parts—at least compared with the multimillion-dollar parts typical in Lockheed's operations. As a result, "The reliability and performance standards are much higher for our products than they are for the other industries in the valley," says Mark Posson, Lockheed's manager of environmental protection programs. "If you've got a personal computer that breaks down and you've got to do a repair, that's relatively simple. But if you've got a multimillion-dollar spacecraft that breaks down in space, the repair costs are extensive."

Lockheed's products, therefore, must be cleaner and more reliable than those of their corporate neighbors. That requires far higher levels of cleaning solutions—most of which traditionally have been either ozone-depleting chemicals, such as Freon, or ones that contain high levels of volatile organic compounds, which contribute to photochemical smog. The computer firms enjoy others advantages over Lockheed. "Our life here changes very rapidly," says English. "If you have a process that's two years old, that's an old process, where in some companies that would be a brand-new one. If your processes are changing quickly that gives you the opportunity to make changes. If you make changes, you have the opportunity for improvement."

So, Lockheed must be forgiven somewhat for dropping in the ratings despite its impressive improvements in pollution prevention. Indeed, its achievements only add to the overall performance of Santa Clara County's companies.

One reason for this enviable performance by the group may be the spirit of cooperation and disclosure among the companies. "By having this annual press conference, and by publishing the information and making it available to people, the companies see what they're doing," says English. "That's the key thing behind the TRI information. In the old days, prior to 1987, nobody knew what their emissions of toxics were. They just didn't know. Because all you had to do was basically meet your permit conditions. And what you do on permits is to try to have the things show very high numbers so that you're never going to violate them. That's just the way permits are. If you're emitting ten pounds of something a day, you get a permit that allows you to emit one hundred pounds. That meant that you never really knew what you were emitting. The beautiful thing about TRI is that it basically brought to the minds of the companies precisely what they are doing for the first time. And that, coupled with this annual press conference and letting people know what's going on, provided a very powerful mechanism for change."

This Silicon Valley tale is just one part of a number of efforts by companies around the world to "green" their operations—and their bottom lines—through efficiency measures and the reduction of emissions, waste, and energy use that goes into making everything from carpets to car parts. And while some companies' efforts have received considerable attention—in the business press, if not from the public—many more have through quiet doggedness been getting the most product and productivity out of every resource.

This new corporate efficiency stems in part from environmental concerns, but comes primarily from the realization that *conservation* is no longer a dirty word. In the past, conservation meant doing without—reducing consumption and, inevitably, productivity. But today it is viewed as a means to *increase* productivity by doing more with fewer resources. And if the environment wins in the process, so much the better.

The range of company efficiency measures is almost limitless, but essentially falls into three categories:

- **Pollution Prevention** uses low- and high-tech means to prevent emissions from happening in the first place, instead of treating them after they have been created. Often referred to as front-of-the-pipe, as opposed to end-of-the-pipe, solutions, these measures are many and varied. In some cases, they involve altering processes to substitute nonpolluting ingredients for polluting ones. Other cases involve process modifications, product changes, equipment redesign, and materials recovery.

- **Waste Reduction** usually refers to cutting solid waste, often by recycling, or by minimizing the use of materials that would otherwise have required some kind of disposal.

- **Energy Efficiency** involves a wide range of measures to use less electricity, gasoline, coal, natural gas, and other energy resources.

The benefits to be gained are considerable. For example, in 1992, Inform, a nonprofit research organization, conducted a comprehensive study of waste-reduction and pollution-prevention activities in the chemical industry. It was based on a study the group had done in 1985 of environmental programs at twenty-nine chemical manufacturing plants. The 1992 study revisited those plants—large, medium, and small facilities ranging in age from twenty-five to nearly ninety years old. Inform found that the companies had achieved "dramatic benefits" by expanding their efforts to reduce waste: cost savings, rapid payback on investments, increased product yields and quality, safer workplace conditions, fewer waste-management needs, and conservation of natural resources.

In the study, Inform found that one-quarter of the forty-eight waste-reduction and pollution-prevention initiatives for which financial information was available required no capital investment at all; just under half required investments of less than $100,000. Fifteen percent of the sixty-two source-reduction activities saved $1 million or more a year, and nearly half saved between $45,000 and $1 million. A net cost increase was reported for only one of the 181 activities Inform looked at. Two of the facilities reported annual savings of $3.8 million each. Two-thirds of the projects recouped their initial investments within six months.

But Inform's findings don't tell the whole story. Arthur D. Little's Ladd Greeno, referring to the low-cost projects, points out that there are limits to such "low-hanging fruit." Eventually, he says, such endeavors will reach a level of diminishing returns. He stresses that too much emphasis is placed on incremental improvement, and not enough on quantum leaps in thinking. The greatest returns, he says, will ultimately come from significant new processes designed at higher cost and risk, but which can be highly rewarding if successful. For example, the automobile's catalytic converter was an incremental change; the electric car represents a "rethink" of the pollution problem being addressed. Arthur D. Little refers to this as the "high performance approach" to addressing environmental problems.

As a result, a new standard has arisen, which measures companies and industries by their ability to produce goods and services while creating a minimum amount of pollution. And now with TRI data, such measurements, though still relatively crude, are easy. For example, the Investor Responsibility Research Center has concocted an Emissions Efficiency Index (EEI), "to chart the progress of corporations in reducing their emissions of toxic chemicals." The index enables users to compare the relative chemical emissions of different companies and industries, and provides a measurement over time of the progress companies are (or aren't) making to reduce toxic releases. The index is expressed in terms of pounds of TRI emission per $1,000 of revenue. So, for example, based on 1990 data, the household products industry had an EEI of just 0.14—that is, 0.14 pounds of emissions per $1,000 revenue—while the paper and forest products industry had an EEI of 3.22 and the diversified chemicals sector's EEI was 12.33. According to IRRC, individual company EEI values ranged from a low of 0.0 to a high of 102.13.

Of course, such measurements assume that TRI emissions represent the best gauge of the greenest companies. Unfortunately, that's not really the case. They are essentially gross estimates of chemical use, often generated by some relatively quick-and-dirty formulas. A company might find out how much its operations purchase of a certain chemical, make some calculations based on some assumptions and rough estimates, and go with whatever number results. While there are penalties for knowingly reporting false data to the federal government, regulators conduct virtually no oversight or enforcement. It is basically an honor system. Beyond that, TRI requires accounting of only a few hundred chemicals and compounds, a relative drop in the bucket of the thousands of chemicals used in the manufacturing and process industries.

However they are calculated, TRI data don't tell the whole story about a company's performance, or its commitment to environmental quality. For instance, in 1991, 3M ranked eighth nationally in TRI emissions and is far and away the biggest emitter of toxins in its home state of Minnesota. But it has an internationally respected pollution-prevention program; more on that in a moment.

Corporate America's embracing of pollution prevention can be seen in the results of an Environmental Protection Agency voluntary program dubbed "33/50." In early 1991, EPA administrator William Reilly asked approximently six hundred U.S. companies to voluntarily release their emissions of seventeen toxic chemicals, including some of the deadliest around, including benzene, cadmium, chloroform, cyanides, lead, mercury, tetrachloroethylene, toluene, trichloromethane, and xylene. Participation in the program meant committing to reduce emissions of these seventeen chemicals by at least 33 percent by the end of 1992, and by at least 50 percent by the end of 1995. Part of the goal was to demonstrate that voluntary reduction programs could achieve targeted reductions faster than could be done by the agency's traditional regulatory approach alone.

The result: By the end of the program's first year, 734 companies had signed on, with the number approaching one thousand by the end of 1992. That's out of only 600-odd companies initially contacted by EPA. Clearly, there was a bandwagon effect in place. And it wasn't just big companies that agreed to participate. Smaller ones, like Magee Carpet of Bloomsburg, Pennsylvania, and Ultra Forge of Cuyahoga Falls, Ohio, stood up to be counted. If only Uncle Sam's other programs were this popular!

LOCKHEED: A SPACE ODYSSEY

Let's go back to Lockheed for a moment. Rankings aside, how did the company manage such significant improvements over a relatively short period?

For purposes of TRI reporting, the company's biggest emissions were 1,1,1-trichloroethane (TCE), Freon 113, and methyl ethyl ketone. All of these are solvents, used to clean plastic, glass, and metal parts during the manufacturing process. Lockheed faced some special challenges in reducing or replacing these chemicals. First, it had to convince its clients—its biggest one is the Department of Defense—that the process switch would not violate the government's strict specifications. That required lengthy and costly testing and demonstration procedures.

In the meantime, many things could be done even with existing chemicals. "We first started with operations controls," says Mark Posson of Lockheed. "We used the TRI data to help us refocus our overall pollution-prevention targets and then allocate our resources based on the emissions, the environmental effects of those emissions, and where we thought we could get the greatest reductions."

Most of the solvents are used in devices called degreasers. Parts to be cleaned are placed on racks, which are lowered into the solvent solution. The cleansed product is then lifted out. Much of the pollution takes place as a result of the solvent evaporating from the degreaser and being released into the atmosphere. Some of the pollution-prevention measures were relatively simple. For example, consolidating the operations of two degreasers into one used less solvent more efficiently. Degreasers that had historically been left on for an entire shift were operated for only an hour or two at a time. And using more care in equipment operation cut emissions even more. For example, operators used to lift racks completely out of the solvent to retrieve cleansed parts, but they now lift them only partway out, allowing more residual solvent to fall back into the machine rather than being released into the atmosphere. There were also equipment improvements. To reduce solvent evaporation they installed cooling coils near the top of the degreasers. Now, as solvent vapors rise, they are cooled, which makes them condense and drop to the bottom.

But the real goal was to stop using ozone-depleting and smog-producing chemicals altogether. "We looked at some interim substitute chemicals," says Posson. "For example, we were able to shift to lower-VOC [volatile organic compound] materials. In some cases we were able to substitute CFC cleaning with trichloroethane (TCA). TCA has a much lower ozone-depleting potential. In some cases we were able to go from CFCs to limonene, which are citrus-based solvents that have lower VOC emissions and no ozone-depleting potential." The final step was to substitute these interim chemicals with nonpolluting ones. In place of TCA and other ozone depleters, Lockheed developed water-based cleaning processes. And an alkaline cleaning process replaced TCA.

Air emissions were only one area Lockeed focused on. The company also needed to eliminate the emissions of heavy-metal-laden water into the nearby water treatment facility, which does an imperfect job of keeping these toxins out of San Francisco Bay. The company still hasn't reached its own goal of zero water-based emissions, and Posson acknowledges that it has a way to go to further reduce its air emissions.

But through gradual, incremental change—experimenting with new processes, eliminating wasteful practices, and rethinking tried-and-true methods—Lockheed has demonstrated that even in the rather slow-moving world of large-product manufacturing, pollution prevention can be both possible and profitable—even when trying to please the Defense Department, one of the world's most persnickety customers.

3M'S 3Ps

Other companies may have gone further faster in reaching their emissions-reduction goals, but none has the extensive track record of 3M, best known for its Scotch brand sealing tapes and videotapes. Pollution-prevention activities at 3M go back to the early 1970s. The company's environmental policy statement remains unchanged since first adopted by its board of directors on February 10, 1975. And even with all that's been learned about the complexities of environmental issues, its six relatively simple declarations still represent a highly evolved state of corporate thinking. Here it is in its entirety:

3M will contine to recognize and exercise its responsibility to:

- Solve its own environmental pollution and conservation problems.
- Prevent pollution at the source.
- Develop products that will have a minimum effect on the environment.
- Conserve natural resources through the use of reclamation and other appropriate methods.
- Assure that its facilities and products meet and sustain the regulations of all federal, state, and local environmental agencies.
- Assist, whenever possible, governmental agencies and other official organizations engaged in environmental activities.

Over the years, 3M's commitment has filtered through the company's ranks, becoming woven into its corporate fabric. "It's the way we approach a lot of issues in our company," says Robert P. Bringer, 3M's top environmental officer. "Whenever there's some type of issue that comes up that has a negative impact on business, we always try to turn it around and turn it into some kind of a recognition program or sort of some quasi-contest. We set a goal and everybody tries to work toward it and operating units compete. And it all ends up getting reported to management and sooner or later everybody gets on board. It's kind of a competitive thing. Even if a program doesn't have any set goals, the operating units in time set their own goals. It's kind of like nobody wants to be left out."

In this case, the program is Pollution Prevention Pays, or 3P, mentioned earlier, the program that awards employees monetarily for initiating pollution-prevention projects. The program is conducted by 3M's operating divisions, run by a coordinating committee composed of representatives from 3M's engineering, manufacturing, and laboratory organizations, as well as members of 3M's executive offices.

"In 1975, we found that we were experts in pollution control—you have a problem, we know how to fix it," says Tom Zosel, manager of the 3P program. "But we realized we knew precious little about pollution *prevention*. So, we set policy to look at the environment early on in the development of products and processes. What we did is to take the environment out of the hands of environmental professionals and put it back to the people who are running the operations and designing the products and processes. We wanted to have full corporate participation, making pollution prevention a part of every person's job, particularly the technical people. So, we empowered people to see how they were creating pollution in their area of responsibility and basically tell them to go out and do something about it."

Of course, money was a factor, too. "The whole idea of the 3P programs was to try to establish a link between pollution prevention and cost reduction," says Bringer. "Initially the program was started because there was a lot of negative reaction to the fact that under some of the new pollution laws in this country, our plants were starting to have to install equipment. Most of our plant managers—who get beat over the head all the time about costs—saw all of this stuff as being of absolutely no value in their terms. So we came up with the idea of turning this into something positive instead of something negative, as an attempt to turn that way of thinking around."

The results since the program's inception are impressive by nearly any measure, certainly by environmental ones. A Northridge, California, manufacturing plant for 3M Pharmaceuticals developed a water-based coating for medicine tablets as a substitute for a solvent-based one. The changeover cost $60,000, but 3M prevented 48,000 pounds of air emissions a year—and eliminated the need to install additional pollution-control equipment. A Hutchinson, Minnesota, videotape plant found a way to recover and reuse airborne solvents that helped apply a magnetic layer to a plastic base tape. The recovered solvents are cleansed, then distilled and prepared for reuse. Besides reducing air emissions, the process ensured 3M's ready access to methyl ethyl ketone, a critical material for its tape-making operations. A South Dakota plant that makes respiratory face masks used to landfill the resin-coated trim from the masks. A 3M team brainstormed a way to eliminate resin from the production process, enabling the excess material to be reground and put back into production.

The list of projects goes on and on. At one plant, fifty-five-gallon plastic drums that were once incinerated are now cleaned and recycled. At another, silicon carbide scrap that once had to be landfilled is now sold and formed into foundry briquettes used in making steel. All told, more than three thousand projects have been recognized under the 3P program—about a fourth from U.S. offices and the rest from overseas.

3P has by no means cured 3M's pollution problems: The company still ranks high in the nation in toxic releases and transfers, according to TRI data, even though emissions continue to drop significantly compared to earlier years. But 3M's achievements go beyond emissions statistics. Among other things, the company has established a standard for pollution prevention that many others have copied. Moreover, it has created an infrastructure and tough goals through the 1990s that will ultimately pay off in the form of lower TRI reductions. "We want to be as close to zero emissions as possible," says Zosel. That sentiment is echoed by Bob Bringer. "I just know intuitively that if we meet the goals that we've set for ourselves in the year 2000, and we are manufacturing most of our products that now use coating operations—which is a good share of what we make—with solventless processes, we're going to be making them a lot cheaper, we're going to have a lot fewer regulatory problems, we're going to have higher-quality products and processes—a lot of good things are going to happen. So that's where we're trying to drive the company through our environmental programs."

In 1990, the company announced an additional initiative: Challenge '95. According to the company's official manual on the program, Challenge '95's goal is to reduce waste 35 percent (compared to a 1990 base) by 1995 through "reformulation, process modifications, equipment redesign, changes to procedures, and similar actions." At the core of Challenge '95 is a fresh look at the definition of *waste*. Traditionally, most companies considered anything used in the manufacturing process that did not become part of the actual product to be waste. If it took two tons of goods to produce one ton of product, that excess ton was simply a cost of doing business. Under Challenge '95, the price of that waste is too high.

In examining its operations, 3M discovered four categories of manufacturing outputs, listed here hierarchically: finished goods (the final product as it goes to the customer, including its packaging), semifinished goods (partially finished material that goes to another 3M plant or vendor for further processing), by-product (material that has a potential secondary use, including those sold or transferred for recycling or reclaiming), and waste (the residual from the manufacturing site before it is subjected to any treatment process).

The goal, then, is to move materials as far up the hierarchy as possible—to turn more waste into by-product, and more by-product into finished and semifinished goods. In typical 3M style, each division and plant manager is left to figure out how to do that themselves. "Upper management has been supportive of people going out and doing things different—you run them the way you want to run them," says Zosel. "We were told that 'we want to put waste reduction into our five-year program. You guys find a way to do it.' That's basically all the direction we got."

But Zosel emphasizes that individual managers have to operate within certain bounds. "Plant managers have only a limited ability to do these things. That's one of the ways a lot of these pollution-prevention plans go awry—everything is focusing on the factory. Wrong focus; the factory can only do so much. You've got to go into research and development, you've got to go into marketing, you've got to go into other parts of the company."

As an example, Zosel remembers a situation a few years ago in which the same plant was making two products, one solventless, the other using solvent. Both products were designed to meet the same need. "We went to the marketing people and said, 'Wait a minute; why are you doing this?' They responded, 'Well, these customers want this version and those customers want that version.' We said, 'Why don't you make all the customers want this version?' 'Well, nobody asked us to.' One product created all this waste for the plant, while the other didn't. Nobody had stressed it to them not to sell this product because the other was better environmentally and would cost them less in the long run. No one had gotten to the marketing people."

Zosel's story underscores the need for big-picture thinking—corporate strategies based on full examinations of the environmental impact of each product and each product line. In 3M's case, management would have been allowed to say, "This is the product we're going to de-emphasize and eventually phase out and this is the one we're going to push." There has to be a lot of integration of people, information, and resources to get everyone moving in the same direction—not just within manufacturing operations, but within all parts of the organization.

And 3M is not the only company trying to reduce industrial emissions. Dozens of others have their own version of 3P. Dow Chemical has WRAP ("Waste Reduction Always Pays"), Chevron has SMART ("Save Money and Reduce Toxics"), Westinghouse has ACT ("Achievements in Clean Technology"), Texaco has WOW ("Wipe Out Waste"). Each works slightly differently, based on industrial sector, corporate culture, and other things, but they share a common goal: to make less waste and pollution—and to make more money.

A PROGRAM WORTH COPYING AT XEROX

Xerox captured a part of the spirit when it named one of its programs ARM, for "Asset Recycle Management." The program has less to do with the waste it generates internally during manufacturing than with maximizing the value of the things it ships to its customers: Xerox photocopiers, facsimile machines, printers, and other products.

If you've ever shopped for a photocopier, you know how fast technology changes. The exotic features of a few years ago—reducing and enlarging, two-sided copying, and collating, for example—are now widely available and can be found on some relatively low-end machines. As with computers, the state of the art is updated almost annually; unlike computers, the newest features in copiers typically can't be made by adding a new circuit board or upgrading memory. It often means you have to buy a new machine. But what happens to all those old machines? Though a small percentage of them end up in the used-copier market, the bulk are put out to pasture, where they lose all of their value.

ARM was set up to put a stop to that. "In the past, we'd design a product, manufacture it, sell it, and someday it would come back from a customer and would sit in a warehouse and collect dust," says Gail Yander, one of the ARM project managers. "Meanwhile, they were just collecting in warehouses, not generating any revenue." The longer a machine sat there, the less valuable it became. Inevitably, the machines were landfilled.

The ARM program's roots actually date back to 1967, when the company recognized the potential health hazards associated with the disposal of photoreceptor drums made from aluminum with a selenium and arsenic alloy coating. Rather than risk the hazards, Xerox decided to reclaim these parts. "What started out as a way to avoid a potential hazard became a profitable business decision," says Environmental Leadership Program manager Abhay Bhushan. "Xerox discovered that the photoreceptor drums could be remanufactured to the same quality as the new ones for a fraction of the cost." Gradually, this remanufacturing philosophy expanded to include many other machine parts. Today, Xerox reclaims about a million finished parts worldwide each year, representing a total value of $200 million.

According to ARM's official manual, the program's mission is "to maximize return on assets by increasing the velocity with which nonrevenue-producing assets are transformed to revenue-producing assets." Roughly translated, that means getting more use out of each product by designing them with parts that can easily be reused in other machines, or replaced with upgraded versions to keep current machines running longer. The result: Xerox's customers get more out of every Xerox product, with fewer machines going into premature retirement.

Take the case of Xerox's 1075 photocopier, introduced in the early 1980s. The 1075 is considered one of the classic workhorse machines—highly reliable and seemingly unstoppable. Since 1982, Xerox has sold thousands of them, many of which are still in operation.

But the 1075 is nearing the end of its life cycle; simply put, it's been outmoded. Newer models are more sophisticated, boasting an impressive array of new features. But that doesn't mean that the market for the 1075 is gone. "We have more sophisticated products than the 1075, and most U.S. customers would go with a newer product," says Yander, "but when you go somewhere like South America or some of the Eastern European markets, they don't necessarily need to have all the bells and whistles. Look at the former Soviet Union: I think they would be ecstatic to have a 1075." ARM's ability to turn these white elephants into useful products will put some of those machines back into the marketplace.

But the real impact of this program will be in Xerox's future products. The ARM team is working with each of the company's Product Architecture Teams to develop an Asset Recycle/Environmental Strategy. Among other things, that means standardizing parts for easy replacement, often using higher-quality (and more expensive) components that will have a longer life. This is a whole new approach to product design and manufacturing because it goes beyond the needs and desires of the initial buyer to those of any subsequent buyers. That will raise some manufacturing costs initially, says Yander, but they won't be reflected in the purchase price.

Indeed, Xerox believes that by reusing serviceable parts, it will lower the cost of the materials needed to build products, meaning Xerox can ultimately *reduce* product prices. Yander explains: "Say you're making 10,000 fax machines. But there's not going to be that much difference between this year's model and last year's model. So, for between 2,500 and 5,000 of those fax machines, you're going to be able to use stuff that has come back from customer sites. You're not going to have to buy every part brand-new. So the customer should not pay more; ultimately, it should lower the product cost."

With its ARM program, Xerox believes that the extra investment it is making in building machines will produce machines that will amortize themselves over a longer period of time. That, in turn, will yield big dividends for the company, its customers, and the environment.

BACK TO THE DRAWING BOARDS

ARM is just one example of a larger trend in manufacturing toward designing for the environment. Companies around the world are reexamining the beginning stages of their product cycles, taking environmental impacts into account, so they can create products that customers can use—and dispose of—with pride. Among the companies at the forefront of environmental product design is IBM, particularly in its European and Asian operations. R. Cynthia Pruitt, director of environmental affairs for IBM Asia Pacific, says her company sought information from its worldwide operations to amass the broadest possible ideas on environmental design. To do that, IBM commissioned a task force of senior vice presidents from its European operations, which already had been thinking for a few years about products that could be returned by customers and recycled. "We developed from that task force a series of technical requirements for products, supplies and packaging," says Pruitt. "We have people from each of those areas come in with their best technical expertise to at least give us a base line to start from. We originally called our task force the Task Force for Environmentally Conscious Products. Then we took all the recommendations of that task force and prioritized them in order of which ones we wanted to implement first. We came up with what we consider to be environmental design criteria for a computer."

First, the task force recommended that the computer must be designed for easy disassembly, using screws and other technology that would make it cost effective to take apart and reuse. The model for this came from some of the European automakers, particularly BMW, which have developed snap-apart technology for their cars. Also, recycled materials had to be used in a way that did not compromise requirements for durability, heat resistance, and other characteristics. And, of course, the machine had to be made of pure materials that could be recycled, and not composites, which could not. Source reduction—the need to simply use less material altogether—was another consideration. For example, rather than upgrading a computer by trading it in for a newer model, perhaps the customer could retain the housings and simply snap in new inserts. On top of all this, IBM also sought ways to lower the computers' energy use.

According to Pruitt, the information filtered down to the design groups, which embarked on a massive educational campaign. Her team created a development guide giving guidelines on product designs—everything from electrical and mechanical requirements to environmental criteria. They also set up a technical forum where engineers could seek answers to technical questions or otherwise share information. In 1992, IBM began coding the plastic computer and business machine parts by resin type, as a precursor to a recycling program that will take back computers for dismantling.

Still another tough matter for IBM was packaging. For instance, how could they cut packaging to a bare minimum while still protecting their product? Again, companies worldwide have looked to Europe, and especially Germany, which has taken the lead in packaging legislation. Following the notion that the "polluter pays," Germans have enacted a tough law that makes companies responsible for collecting and recycling the packaging used for their products. The law further requires retailers to take back packaging they sell, and to levy a fifty-pfennig deposit on nonrefillable containers for beverages and selected other products. Retailers, in turn, have to lean on their suppliers to take back the packages that consumers return, or the retailers will get buried under mountains of waste. When the system is fully implemented, retailers will have an incentive to carry only products with packages made by manufacturers that promise to pick up and recycle, thus taking package waste out of the municipal waste stream.

Packaging is also an issue with industrial goods and several companies have developed ways to minimize its use. Digital Equipment Corporation's total quality management program has been trying to find out how to eliminate unnecessary packaging in its products, with the goal of eliminating 5,400 tons of packaging materials by mid-1993, thereby cutting DEC's packaging costs by millions of dollars a year. Using a variety of measurement techniques, DEC determined that it was wasting about 27,000 tons of packaging at an average cost of $1 a pound, or an annual total of $54 million. The calculations came from measurements taken at individual facilities, such as manufacturing plants, office buildings, customer service repair sites, and other operations. When DEC management saw those measurements, which had never before been done, they charged each facility with reporting its own measurements in the future and for reviewing packaging waste performance on a regular basis. To stay within the specified goals, each facility will have to design its own ways to cut packaging use.

SILK PURSES AND COWS' REARS

As 3M, Xerox, DEC, and other companies have learned, sometimes a company's waste "assets" can be refashioned into new products, turning something that was once a cost into a profit. Export Packers Company Ltd., based in Winnipeg, Manitoba, turned the seven and a half tons of eggshells it produced every day—for which it had been spending about $41,000 a year to dispose—into "Egg Shell Meal," a calcium and protein supplement for chicken feed. Annual sales resulted in net revenue of $150,000, fully amortizing the $125,000 plant and machinery investment in under a year.

Another example comes in the form of cogeneration, also known as waste-to-energy, a century-old process in which two kinds of energy are produced from one fuel source. Typically, a cogeneration plant burns coal, natural gas, wood, trash, or just about anything else for electricity, then captures the leftover steam and uses it as a heating source. The process yields more bang for every energy buck—and reduces pollution, too.

Herman Miller, the Michigan furniture company, has had tremendous success with cogeneration since 1982, when it build an "Energy Center" at its main plant site. The Energy Center incinerates waste that would normally go to a landfill—sawdust, wood scraps, and other materials—to generate steam to heat the entire 800,000-square-foot Zeeland facility during the winter; and electricity to power absorption chillers for the air-conditioning system in the summer. According to Jim Gillespie, Herman Miller's supervisor of Waste and Grounds, the cogeneration plant has reduced landfill volume by nearly 90 percent, while reducing dependence on natural gas, fuel oil, and other fossil fuels. Moreover, the company accepts select waste from other businesses in the area—such as scrap wood from the region's many woodworking operations. These companies pay Herman Miller for the dumping privileges. Joe Azzarello, Herman Miller's plant and environmental engineering manager, says that the incinerator generates only about one-tenth of the air emissions for which it has been permitted. After more than a decade, the original one-megawatt cogeneration plant is showing its age and may be replaced by one four to five times that capacity to meet the company's growing needs.

The "cogen" facility wasn't cheap to build—about $7 million (in 1982 dollars)—but Azzarello believes it has more than paid for itself. By avoiding disposal fees, accepting others' trash, and providing heating and cooling, he figures the cogeneration plant has saved the company about $200,000 a year.

Herman Miller has made other strides in turning its waste by-products into usable assets. Strips of fabric from upholstery operations are collected and shipped via a waste broker to a North Carolina recycling operation, where the material is shredded and used for such things as insulation for automobile visors, or sound-deadening material for vehicles. In a Xerox-like asset-recycling move, the company designed its 1990s Phoenix line of office partitions to use refurbished frames from its 1980s best-selling Action Office line. All of this is aimed at meeting the company goal of being "landfill-free"—that is, producing no solid waste—by the end of 1994.

Perhaps the most intriguing notion involves a partnership between Herman Miller and a local tannery that supplies leather for the company's upscale furniture. It goes something like this: In the tanning process, machines remove hair, bits of meat, and other organic matter from the cow hides. This waste was then flushed into the sewer system at a cost to the tanner. But that organic material is rich in nutrients that could potentially be used as fertilizer. Unfortunately, it is too soupy for use on farmland, so the tanner has developed a process that mixes the animal sludge with Herman Miller's sawdust waste. If all goes according to plan, the fertilizer will be used on 1,600 acres of farmland to grow corn. The corn, in turn, will be fed to the cows, whose hides will eventually become part of Herman Miller's furniture.

In the end, it's one of those classic closed-loop deals in which everybody comes out ahead. Except the cows, that is.

PROFITS FROM HAZARDOUS WASTE

The challenge for many companies is applying this silk-purse-from-sow's-ear approach to hazardous products from the manufacturing process. Sometimes the challenge involves more managerial skills than technological ones.

An example of this is a U.S.-based multinational that must remain anonymous. In plants in the Midwest, as well as in Europe and South America, the company produced phenolic resins, which are used to bond many different types of things, from foundry sand to fiberboard to insulation. The manufacture of these resins yields a waste stream that contains phenol, a possible cancer-causing substance that can severely burn the skin and eyes; long-term exposure may damage the liver and kidneys. For a long time, that waste stream was disposed of in different ways depending on what country the plant was in. For example, in the Midwest and in Europe, it was disposed of in the local sewer system with no penalties because this was considered an acceptable waste stream. In South America, the company dumped the phenol waste directly into a river, creating adverse affects on both people and wildlife. Enforcement against this practice was as scarce as the environmental laws in that part of the world.

In the mid-1980s, legislators in both Germany and France enacted zero-discharge laws, effectively banning further phenol dumping practices. That left the company with the expensive choice of either hauling the stuff to another country or incinerating it. "The plant manager in Germany said, 'Let's look at what's in this waste stream,' " says a former company executive. "And he managed to turn that waste stream into a low-grade phenolic resin, which was sold to industries that were not very sensitive to tight specifications. For them, this material was very acceptable. So, he took a waste stream and turned it into a profit. The plant in France did the same thing. And when the South American plant recognized that the European plants were making money, they started doing this, too."

Ironically, the U.S. plant hasn't managed to change the way in which the resins are disposed, and is paying hundreds of thousands of dollars a year for the privilege of dumping the resins into wastewater. The U.S. operation is stymied because the division that creates the phenolic waste is not the same one that would be responsible for selling the phenol by-product. Without leadership from top management, it's unlikely that the two divisions will ever come to a meeting of the minds. Says the former executive: "It's a tremendous waste, for both the company and the earth."

ROLLING OUT THE GREEN CARPET

Not all the efficiency programs take place at large industrial plants—not by a long shot. For example, the hospitality industry also has recognized the benefits to be gained from waste reduction and energy efficiency. Hotel chains, restaurants and resorts, and theme parks have begun rolling out the green carpet for their guests, welcoming them to a new world of environmental consciousness and financial savings.

The Park Plaza Hotel & Towers, for example, a 977-room, family-operated hotel in downtown Boston, has become a showcase for this new consciousness. Many of the improvements are commonplace, the same types of measures taken by conservation-minded homeowners. Installing faucet aerators and low-flow shower heads in all of the guest rooms saved more than ten million gallons of water and thirty thousand gallons of heating oil a year. Energy-efficient fluorescent lighting fixtures in corridors and service areas save 25,000 watts per hour. In guest rooms, individual amenities—soap, shampoo, conditioner, mouthwash, and so on—have been eliminated in favor of refillable dispensers, saving almost two million individual plastic containers a year. Reusable china, glass, and silverware have replaced disposable tableware, leftover paints are stored and reused, educational plaques have been installed in rooms to encourage conserving energy and water. The hotel's owners have dubbed it "Boston's Eco-Logical Travel Alternative" and in 1992 claimed to increase revenue by $750,000 a year due to business from individuals and groups who appreciate the earth-conscious accommodations.

The Park Plaza is far from alone in its industry. The Stouffer Stanford Court Hotel in San Francisco recycles steam heat and uses condensation to reheat water and to replace evaporated water in the air-conditioning cooling towers. And the Hyatt Regency Chicago saves as much as $100,000 a year by recycling. Each employee is required to separate aluminum, glass, paper, and cardboard. Housekeepers have collection bins attached to carts to sort material from the guest rooms. But there's another benefit: Sorting trash has revealed that many reusable items, from spoons to coffeepots to ashtrays, had been going out with the garbage. Recovering these items saves the hotel as much as $10,000 a month.

The most integrated effort may be found at Inter-Continental Hotels, which asked its North American hotels' managers to fill out a six-page, 134-item environmental checklist. Bonuses of all general managers are tied with how well their hotels comply with the 134 items. As part of its efforts, the chain's management published a two-hundred-page environmental manual specifying measures for waste reduction, purchasing, air emissions, noise control, energy and water conservation, asbestos elimination, laundry and dry cleaning operations, and other aspects of hotel operation. At the historic Willard Hotel across from the White House in Washington, D.C., Inter-Continental Hotels has replaced more than seven thousand light bulbs in hallways and rooms with a more efficient variety and installed water-saving devices throughout. Among other things, it stopped using plastic bags to deliver newspapers and laundered shirts to guests. One of its sister hotels in New Orleans saved $79,000 in 1991 through such measures.

Resorts are facing pressure to become environmental-minded, too, as some communities recognize that unlimited amounts of tourism are not always a good thing. In the Florida Keys, whose coral reef is considered to be the most diverse marine ecosystem in the world, the Cheeca Lodge has become a leading voice for environmental protection of the fragile life forms, not just by employees and guests, but by competitors as well. In 1991, the lodge's owners, working with a conservation group called Reef Relief, gathered more than sixty area hoteliers to attend an symposium on how to run more environmentally sensitive operations. A series of environmental groups and local businesses shared secrets on everything from recycling glass to environmentally correct cleaning products.

Cheeca Lodge, for its part, has gone to great lengths to protect the fragile Keys. Aside from a comprehensive waste-recycling and water-conservation plan, the hotel's owners have banned jet skis, wave runners, and other "thrill" craft from its beaches. Renting such devices to guests could generate thousands of dollars in revenue, but their use was found to destroy the natural tidal flats and turtle grass where fish breed. The owners also have decided not to exercise their right to build thirty-two additional hotel units, which could generate as much as $1.2 million more in annual revenue, because their construction and use would further stress the region. "If we fail to protect our precious natural resources, the hospitality industry itself will wither and die," says Helmut Horn, president and chief operating officer of Coastal Hotel Group, which owns the Cheeca. "Protecting the Keys is certainly good business."

TO THE VICTORS GO THE SPOILS

There are a thousand more pollution-prevention, waste-reduction, and environmental-preservation stories waiting to be told. Even a brief survey demonstrates that the dividends reaped from these efforts can be considerable:

• Chrysler Corporation's Jefferson North Assembly Plant in Detroit incorporated a leak-detection system on all equipment located underground, such as piping, wet sumps, and trenches. According to company officials, the system virtually eliminates any possibility of materials escaping into the environment. The plant has also reformulated its painting processes to reduce or eliminate volatile organic compounds (VOCs) and other hazardous air pollutants. Among other things, Chrysler has incorporated a zero-VOC powder antichip coating and has formulated its clear-coat paints to exclude all of the hazardous air pollutants listed in the Clean Air Act Amendments of 1990.

• Kryptonics, Inc., of Boulder, Colorado, solved a difficult pollution problem by developing a new way to spray silicone mold releases that doesn't use any of the solvents that contain ozone-depleting chlorofluorocarbons (CFCs). As a result, Kryptonics reduced its CFC use from more than forty thousand pounds in 1990 to zero in 1992, without a loss in quality. Totally eliminating CFCs saves the company about $100,000 a year.

• Similarly, IBM's disk drive plant in San Jose, California, was one of the world's largest users of CFCs in the late 1980s. But by the early 1990s, the plant had nearly eliminated CFC use and cut other emissions 95 percent by substituting water-based cleaning solutions in place of CFCs. Between 1989 and 1992, that switch prevented the release of more than 2 million pounds of emissions and eliminated the need to purchase 4.3 million pounds of CFCs.

- Valley Bank in Tucson, Arizona, used a technique known as "xeriscaping" to landscape with drought-resistant plants to save water. The bank replaced water-intensive grass with native plants, cutting water use and maintenance costs by $20,000 a year. Xeriscaping is among several techniques being used by companies, particularly in the parched West, to conserve water for more vital needs.

- The Rockledge Towers office building in Boston installed 590 faucet aerators at a cost of $4,720. The devices save the building owners about 4.2 million gallons of water a year. Within three months, the investment had paid for itself in water and energy savings and it continues to save over $18,000 a year in water costs.

- Niagara-Mohawk, an electric utility serving most of upstate New York, has set up an Investment Recovery department that operates as a company within the company. Its mission is to find markets for its waste and scrap. With a $640,000 annual operating budget and a staff of about seventy-five, the department earned $7.3 million in 1991 by recycling some of its waste and selling surplus materials. The utility retains up to 90 cents of every dollar generated through Investment Recovery.

- In the mid-1970s, Mead Packaging, a division of the Mead Corporation that manufactures paperboard packaging for the beverage and food industries, decided to eliminate VOC emissions rather than just control them. Mead's VOC Reduction Program made it the first company in the carton converter industry to switch its rotogravure presses from petroleum solvent–based inks to water–based inks. As a result, Mead has reduced its VOC emissions by more than 85 percent since 1975.

- At Fairchild Air Force Base outside Spokane, Washington, a comprehensive pollution-prevention program has resulted in product substitutions, process changes, new technologies, and solvent reduction and recycling. Among other things, methylene chloride in its paint-stripping operations has been replaced with bead-blasting technology. Recycling the spent bead-blasting media has eliminated a waste stream from this operation.

- The Gillette Company incorporated a water-recirculation system into its manufacturing operation and cut the amount of water used to make razor blades from 730 million gallons to 156 gallons a year. Companywide, Gillette now saves about $1.5 million a year in water and sewage bills.

THE ALCHEMY OF WASTE EXCHANGES

One of the principal ways companies are reducing pollution and improving efficiency is by selling or giving away things that they once threw away. In an economy as rich and diverse as ours, one company's by-product or waste may well be another's raw material. In such a transaction, Company A keeps a material from being landfilled or incinerated and saves themselves the cost of doing so; Company B gets a needed resource at a below-market price. Everyone, including the environment, comes out a winner.

But finding someone who needs what you're throwing out and locating someone who wants to get rid of what you need isn't always that easy. The answer is a waste exchange, which is a kind of dating service for trash—bona fide, industrial-strength trash. A waste exchange is a listing service that matches companies with unneeded commodities—surplus materials, off-spec goods, or manufacturing by-products—with companies that can make use of those materials. There are nineteen industrial waste exchanges operating throughout North America, swapping everything from alcohol ethoxylate to zinc oxide. Materials involved are as benign as sawdust and cardboard and as hazardous as sulfuric acid and insecticides. Whatever the material, it seems someone out there wants it.

Do these exchanges work? Consider a couple of success stories.

In 1991, Planar Systems, a manufacturer of electroluminescent displays for portable computers in Beaverton, Oregon, listed twelve hundred gallons of used isopropyl alcohol with the Industrial Materials Exchange in Seattle. The listing drew a response from Western Foundries, located in Tigard, another Portland suburb. A maker of metal parts for agriculture and the timber industry, Western Foundries uses the alcohol on its molds to give a smooth finish to the castings. The foundry had been buying alcohol at $170 per fifty-five-gallon drum; now it picks up two or three drums a month for merely the cost of transportation. Planar Systems previously had shipped the used alcohol to a California incinerator at around $120 per drum. After Planar Systems was done with it, the alcohol was a flammable, corrosive waste. At the foundry, it evaporates during the casting process.

According to John Shear, a facilities technician for Planar Systems, his company saves about $5,000 a year in transportation costs alone. Western Foundries, which typically goes through four fifty-five-gallon drums a month, now saves $500 or more a month. Not a king's ransom, but still significant. "It's a classic case of a material going from a high-tech user to a less fastidious user," says Bill Lawrence, manager of the Industrial Materials Exchange.

Then there's the experience of Larry Katz, president of Graphic Arts Systems, a Cleveland-based company that is the country's largest supplier of tracing paper and plastic films for commercial artists. The company is a converter, buying large rolls of paper and plastic, then cutting them into pads and rolls. After learning about waste exchanges, Katz began leafing through a catalog, marveling at the listings. "Tons of crap," was his first reaction.

Intrigued, however, Katz ran a listing with the Northeast Industrial Waste Exchange. "After a couple of weeks, I got a call from quite a large manufacturer of paper," he says. The caller, based in Oregon, had forty to fifty tons a year of specially coated paper that was going to a landfill because it didn't meet specifications. The paper was considered a hazardous material because of its coating.

"I thought this would be great," Katz says. "We could take it out of a landfill, virtually. Some of it is dirty and gouged and wrinkled," he said, "but we end up with a fairly good product. We call it recycled. We say it's preconsumer waste. I think it has some appeal. We try to price it below a comparable first-line product." Katz gets the paper at a 60 percent savings over the cost of the new paper, plus the cost of transportation. Graphic Arts Systems carts off up to two tons of paper every other month.

Waste exchanges operate in a variety of ways. Some are supported by states or universities, others by subscriptions and advertising fees in their catalogs. Most are nonprofit, a few are for-profit. Most classify waste in eleven categories, from acids and alkalis to oils and organic chemicals, including a "miscellaneous" category that can potentially include anything from mink fat to microfiche to manure. Slightly less than half of the materials listed in the Pacific Materials Exchange are considered hazardous.

No one knows precisely how much revenue these exchanges generate; some exchanges don't even keep track of transactions. But figures on environmental savings are available for some exchanges. The Northeast Industrial Waste Exchange kept nearly 25,000 tons of materials out of landfills or incinerators in 1990; the net value of those materials was $3.5 million. Seattle's Industrial Materials Exchange helped swap 28,000 gallons of liquids and 240 tons of non-hazardous solids in 1991. And the Southern Waste Information Exchange, based in Tallahassee, Florida, helped transfer between 250,000 and 750,000 metric tons of materials in 1990.

One key issue with waste exchanges is privacy. Just like the rest of us, most firms don't want strangers analyzing their garbage. This wasn't a real problem until companies started advertising their garbage through waste exchanges. Now they are more carefully viewing their wastes. Some listers request confidentiality because they're worried about being targeted as polluters. Others are afraid of revealing their products' ingredients or processes. Buyers are similarly circumspect, not wanting competitors to know of their material needs.

Legal considerations are another factor. What are you getting into if you take delivery of someone else's trash? Companies must check out all other parties involved in a waste exchange transaction. "You have every right and you should do that," says Lewis Cutler of the Northeast Industrial Waste Exchange. As a potential recipient of a material, it's important to get an independent analysis and a representative sample, which the sender should give willingly. Check also with regulators to see if the company has problems or outstanding fines. A site visit might be a good idea, as is determining whether a company has appropriate liability insurance.

Is a waste-generating company responsible for exchanged waste the same way it is liable for landfilled waste? It depends, says Nancy Larson, an attorney with the Rochester, New York, firm of Nixon Hargrave Devins & Doyle. "I think EPA or any regulating agency would take the position that the party generating it would be responsible until its ulti-mate disposition," she says. "If the material ends up being a product used in commerce and there's a long chain from the generator, there's a less direct link to the party originally generating the material. When the second party disposes of it, your case is less and less good." As for buying or selling secondhand materials, Larson cautions businesses to use common sense about the contents.

Such problems notwithstanding, waste exchanges seem to be on a steady growth curve. The EPA has given grants to two exchanges that are trying to create a single national computerized network. "There's a principle that we're operating on here," says Bob Smee, director of the Pacific Materials Exchange in Spokane, Washington. "I call it the law of large numbers: The more materials you can identify, and the more you publicize them, the more likely an exchange is going to occur. As that number gets to be rather astronomical, then 15 percent or even 5 percent of that number gets to be rather astronomical, too."

"People are really starting to catch on," says Dan Weber, coordinator for the Resource Exchange & News of Grand Rapids, Michigan. "People are really starting to look for more ways to get rid of their waste. The costs are going up and the regulations are getting stiffer. Industry has nothing to lose by listing a waste."

Smee echoes the sentiment: "I can't understand why tens of thousands of companies aren't listing, because surely everybody generates at least one waste stream, if not multiple ones."

THE POWER OF ENERGY CONSERVATION

Energy use is another area providing companies with great potential for savings. From electric motors to electronic office equipment, corporate America is just discovering the vein of riches waiting to be mined through conservation technology and techniques. According to the Electric Power Research Institute, the savings from improved motor designs and adjustable-speed drives alone could annually save some 6.6 quadrillion BTUs, the equivalent of just over 1.1 billion barrels of oil, and could reduce carbon dioxide emissions by as much as a quarter-billion tons. Improving industrial lighting could easily double those figures, as could making heating, ventilation, and air-conditioning systems work more efficiently.

This new urge to conserve has been inspired primarily by electric utilities, which curiously have had to induce their customers to use less of their product in order to increase profits. The reasoning is that conservation keeps the utilities from having to build expensive new plants, and allows them to use only their most efficient plants to meet peak energy demands. That reduces pollution and gives them more flexibility to meet tough new clean-air standards.

The utilities' inducements have come largely through what is known as "demand-side management"—that is, managing customers' demand for energy by giving them incentives to be more efficient. In 1992, U.S. utilities poured some $2 billion into more than 1,200 demand-side management programs, and as a result energy savings allowed them to meet demand for about 24,000 megawatts, the equivalent of about twenty-five big power plants. And plans for future conservation projects look even brighter.

Lighting is one of the biggest energy gluttons, accounting for 20 to 25 percent of the electricity used annually in the United States. According to the Environmental Protection Agency, lighting for industry, stores, offices, and warehouses represents 80 to 90 percent of total lighting electricity use.

Today's newest energy-efficient lighting designs and technologies are dramatically reducing energy consumption while delivering comparable or better lighting. Consider the lowly fluorescent tube, the T-12 "cool white" bulb that populates offices, factories, hallways, and many other parts of our business and institutional world. A new breed of fluorescent tubes, known as T-8 trichromatics, can replace the T-12s and produce the same amount of light with better color rendition. Plus, the T-8s use about 20 percent less energy. Another innovation can be found in the ballast that regulates the current to the bulbs in fluorescent fixtures. The new generation of ballasts, based on solid-state electronics, is vastly superior to the old magnetic cores and coil ballasts. Not only do they use less electricity, they also eliminate the annoying flicker and hum of old-style ballasts. A third fluorescent innovation is the reflector, which takes the rays that usually shine up, sideways, and otherwise away from the work space, and focuses them downward. It is possible to use reflectors in place of half the bulbs in a four-bulb fixture without any loss in lighting. That means half the energy to get the same amount of light.

Put it all together and you've got some impressive savings. According to EPA figures, replacing four cool-white bulbs with two T-8 bulbs and one reflector, and replacing a mechanical ballast with an electronic one, costs between $60 and $90 per fixture, including labor. Based on average electricity rates, the investment has a 2.8-year payback. Equally important: The pollution prevented annually, per fixture, amounts to 537.6 pounds of carbon dioxide, 3.9 pounds of sulfur dioxide, and 2.1 pounds of nitrogen oxides, according to EPA.

You can do even better if you install occupancy sensors—which turn lights on when someone walks in the room, and shuts them off after no motion has been detected for a few minutes—in areas that aren't always occupied, such as storage rooms, restrooms, or conference areas. The pollution prevented by replacing a common light switch with an occupancy sensor for four fixtures operating at 169 watts, says EPA, is 376 pounds of carbon dioxide, 2.7 pounds of sulfur dioxide, and 1.4 pounds of nitrogen oxides. That sensor has an estimated 3.1-year payback.

When the savings to individual businesses are combined, there is the potential for tremendous environmental benefits. EPA says that installing energy-efficient lighting nationwide wherever profitable would reduce carbon dioxide emissions by 232 million tons, 4 percent of the national total—the equivalent of removing 42 million cars, or one third of all cars in the United States, from the roads. There would be similarly impressive figures for the other pollutants.

Tube fluorescents aren't the only type of energy-efficient lighting. Another is compact fluorescents, which can replace traditional screw-in incandescents in many cases. Aside from energy savings, the compact fluorescent bulbs last much longer than incandescents, resulting in reduced labor costs to change burned-out bulbs. For example, personnel at the TransAmerica Pyramid in San Francisco replaced the 50-watt incandescent floodlights around the building's perimeter with 7.5-watt compact fluorescent bulbs. The total cost, including installation of the 450 new light fixtures, was approximately $14,000. The building now saves about that same amount annually—$10,600 in reduced electricity use and $3,400 in reduced labor costs. The illumination levels are about the same.

One of the most ambitious programs to spur corporate lighting conservation comes from the federal government through "Green Lights." The EPA began this program in early 1991, calling it "a voluntary, nonregulatory program . . . to help U.S. companies realize the profit of pollution prevention by installing energy-efficient lighting designs and technologies, but only where they are profitable, and only where they maintain or improve lighting quality." Companies that join Green Lights agree to survey their facilities and install new lighting systems that maximize energy savings over five years. They agree to document the improvements as well as to use only the most current energy guidelines when building new facilities. The EPA, for its part, provides technical support to partner companies. Specifically, the agency offers an "analysis support system" that will "allow corporations to assess their upgrade options quickly." The EPA also has compiled data bases of lighting products, manufacturers, and distributors, and offers assistance to companies to secure financing for the upgrades.

What's in it for companies? EPA says the typical participant reduces electricity consumption by 40 to 70 percent, and gets a 30 to 60 percent return on its lighting investment.

For example, Southwire Corporation, in Carrollton, Georgia, a Green Lights partner, relocated its fixtures to increase the amount of available light, installed sensors in bathrooms and storage areas that turn lights off when they're unoccupied, and replaced incandescent bulbs with low-energy compact fluorescents. Their annual lighting costs have dropped by $180,000. Another partner, Citicorp, has cut lighting on average to about 1 watt per square foot in some facilities. A third partner, Boeing, upgraded the lighting in 3 million square feet of its facilities, an area equivalent to sixty-two football fields. The upgrades will save the company $1 million a year, reducing consumption by about twenty million kilowatt-hours—enough to power 2,800 homes.

The potential savings for the environment are impressive, too. Assuming that converting to energy-efficient lighting would cut energy use in half, that amounts to a savings of 290 billion kilowatt-hours (kwh), about 11 percent of total U.S. electricity use. At an average commercial rate of 7 cents per kwh, a successful Green Lights program could save American companies more than $20 billion a year, according to the EPA. The agency calculates its program has the potential to prevent 232 million tons of carbon dioxide emissions (about 4 percent of the total), 1.7 million tons of sulfur dioxide (1.7 percent of total), and 900,000 tons of nitrous oxide (4 percent of total).

The program has been received enthusiastically. By the end of the first year, more than 400 participants—companies, government agencies, lighting manufacturers, and utility companies—had signed up, including Arco, Bellcore, Boeing, Chevron, Digital, Duracell, Gerber, Gillette, Goodyear, Marriott, 3M, Polaroid, TransAmerica, and Xerox. In addition, the state governments of California, Florida, Maryland, and Oregon volunteered. According to EPA, the program's participants collectively own or lease 2 billion square feet of space—the equivalent of all the leasable office space in and around Chicago, Dallas, Los Angeles, New York, Philadelphia, San Francisco, and Washington, D.C.

To join, companies must sign an eight-page Memorandum of Understanding that spells out the obligations of both the company and the EPA. There are no costs to join the program. Then, companies are asked to conduct surveys and make those upgrades that will yield profitable returns through energy savings.

"We encourage companies to take a step-by-step process," says program director Bob Kwartin. "Pick a facility, do a lighting survey, and do some trial installations to learn how to apply the technology. What are the best ways of purchasing materials, the best ways of identifying and selecting contractors, and structuring an internal team that will work with an external team? We ask companies to start small, learn, and do another piece."

For those concerned with the idea of forging a partnership with the government's lead environmental enforcer, Kwartin offers assurance: "We are not an enforcement program. We're not going to be sending in the rapid deployment force in the middle of the night. We want people to do well."

COMPUTING YOUR PROFITS

Lighting is just one glaring example of how businesses waste energy, but other areas aren't that easy to see. For example, it's hard to spend more than a few minutes at work without flicking at least a few electronic switches—computers, printers, copiers, fax machines, and, of course, phones. We do this without thinking. These are the indispensable tools of our workday, as much a fact of life as coffee breaks and quitting time. All these devices afford us remarkable capabilities, the impressiveness of which seems to improve by the month. But as more and more of these new and powerful machines come onto the market, they are consuming increasing amounts of energy—both in the electricity it takes to operate them and in the air conditioning needed to remove the excess heat they create. Consider:

- In one U.S. Department of Energy study, computers and related equipment were found to consume, directly or indirectly, about half of all energy used in a modern office building.
- Almost all the electricity used by office equipment ends up as heat within a building. When a full complement of office electronics is added to an old building whose air conditioning was sized for older equipment such as typewriters, the building's air-handling capacity is often overtaxed.
- Electricity use in office buildings is expected to grow steadily. A

study of buildings in the Pacific Northwest projected increased energy growth of about 75 percent between 1986 and 2000.

The good news is that any investments in new office equipment shouldn't raise your company's energy bill. In fact, developments in technology and management techniques can actually reduce energy consumption of office equipment by up to 70 percent in the short term, according to the Rocky Mountain Institute (RMI), and by as much as 90 percent over the long term. RMI's findings are contained in a proprietary technical report issued by Competitek, its information service on advanced techniques for electric efficiency. According to Amory B. Lovins and Richard Heede, the report's authors, "Careful attention to electric efficiency in office equipment can already save American business about $2.5 to $4 billion worth of electricity per year, and during the 1990s can save U.S. utilities tens of billions of dollars' investments in power plants." Moreover, they say, in many existing buildings, "reduced plug loads can avoid costly expansions of chiller, air-handling, and wiring capacity. In new buildings, coupled with advances in lighting and window efficiency, they may even eliminate major mechanical systems altogether." The potential savings, they say, "corresponds to at least nine giant (1,000-megawatt) power plants in the United States, and several times that in avoidable growth during the 1990s." If these were coal-fired plants, they would emit 45 million tons of CO_2 per year.

Much of our wasteful energy habits, it seems, has to do with letting electricity-draining equipment run day and night, without regard for its actual use. For example, RMI found that up to 70 percent of computers and related equipment are left on all the time, even though they're used infrequently. That mid-sized copier, quietly standing by, waiting for someone to push the PRINT button, may be consuming five hundred or more watts an hour. If left on day and night—as many such copiers are, if only out of neglect to turn them off—they can consume over four thousand kilowatt-hours a year, costing around $350 at typical utility rates.

The results can be even more dramatic for personal computers. Though they consume far less electricity—typically, around 150 watts per hour—their sheer quantity, combined with employees' tendency to leave them on all the time, makes them big energy eaters. (Even when turned off, some computers, such as the Macintosh IIcx, consume as much as thirteen watts to facilitate maintenance of clocks, calendars,

Power-Saving Tips

■ Turn off computers and other equipment if they won't be used for at least fifteen minutes. Contrary to popular belief, turning machines off won't harm hard disks or other components.

■ Use master-switched power strips that can turn off a computer's peripherals (printers, monitors, modems, external disk drives) at the same time.

■ Consider abandoning late-night backups altogether. Low-cost back-up systems, such as "tape streamers," can back up a large hard disk in just a few minutes.

■ If a large photocopier is used only occasionally, consider buying a smaller tabletop copier to perform small jobs. Many of these inexpensive machines require little warm-up and use far less energy when running. By keeping the larger copier turned off until needed, the energy savings could eventually recoup the price of the smaller machine.

■ When purchasing a copier, look for one that has an energy-saving "standby" switch. But some such features save very little energy; ask your dealer for exact specifications.

■ Plug copiers and other equipment into timed switches to ensure that they are turned off at night and on weekends. They can still be used if needed by flicking a switch.

■ Consider laptops or other portables instead of desktops. They use far less electricity.

■ Turn off computer monitors, even if only for a few minutes. That can save up to fifty watts an hour and extend the life of the screen itself. Don't rely on screen savers, which only save the screen, not energy.

■ Choose ink-jet printers over laser printers. Ink-jets are cheaper to buy and use far less energy to operate, though they are not as versatile as laser printers.

■ When possible, use solar-powered desktop calculators instead of battery or electric ones. They cost nothing at all to operate.

and other gizmos. Generally, however, Macs use less energy than IBM and compatible PCs.) Printers, especially laser printers, are even bigger energy gluttons. Laser printers use about as much standby power as computers, and up to four times more when printing. The energy is required to keep the fuser lamp at the desired temperature. Ink-jet printers, in contrast, use far less energy—up to 99 percent less when printing, according to RMI.

It is only recently that computer makers have begun to recognize the energy-saving potential of their products. Their efforts were aided in 1992 by the EPA's creation of the Energy Star Computers Program, a Green Lights–like program to certify computers and related products designed to reduce energy use by "powering down" or turning off when they sit idle. EPA estimates that such innovations could save 25 billion kilowatt-hours of electricity every year.

Perhaps the most impressive energy-saving potential comes in the fast-growing world of laptop, palmtop, and notebook computers. These devices, in case you've missed all the hoopla, are by far the fastest-growing segment of the computer industry. This new generation of portable computers are tinier, easier to use, and far more powerful than any of their clunky predecessors.

Laptops' most impressive—and least advertised—feature may be their energy-saving potential. Through such innovations as low-power disk drives, flat-panel displays, energy-conserving chips, and built-in power-management systems, these battery-powered machines use up to 99 percent less energy than their desktop counterparts. Moreover, the new portables do not require cooling fans, so they consume almost no standby power.

Laptop computers often cost more than desktops, but when considering the two machines' life-cycle costs, they are competitive. According to RMI's Lovins and Heede, "The extra cost of the laptop machine can often be repaid just by its energy savings, especially in new buildings." Compared with the energy and building air-conditioning requirements for a typical IBM AT-class computer, Lovins and Heede calculated that a single laptop can save as much as $950 in direct costs. Operated about 2,500 hours a year, that one laptop can save roughly one ton in carbon dioxide emissions annually, about four times as much CO_2 as is saved over several years by replacing a seventy-five-watt incandescent light bulb with an eighteen-watt compact fluorescent one.

The energy consequences of portables could be even greater if portable computers permit more employees to work at home, thereby cutting commuting. The savings could be enormous: In 1992, AT&T's Business Network Sales Division had plans to evict ten thousand of its salespeople from their offices, issuing them laptops and basing them at home. The plan would cut the division's office-leasing costs by 50 percent.

The performance of these micro-microcomputers seems to get more mind-boggling by the minute. In 1991, for example, Hewlett-Packard Co. announced a tiny, eleven-ounce, checkbook-sized computer that comes with a built-in version of the popular spreadsheet program *Lotus 1-2-3*. Compatible with most XT-class computers, the $700 device includes a calculator, calendar, Rolodex, and other features. It runs on just two "AA" batteries. The new generation of hand-held "personal digital assistants" from Apple Computer and related products from other companies promise to further enhance computing power from minimal energy resources.

In the end, when you look at computers and other office equipment from an energy perspective, the purchase price is only a fraction of what it will ultimately cost in the energy needed to operate them. And those energy costs can vary widely, depending on how the machines are operated. Opting for energy efficiency not only conserves natural resources and reduces the pollution the machines produce, but it can significantly extend a product's life.

It doesn't take a mainframe—or even a palmtop—to calculate that the benefits to both companies and the earth can be well worth the effort.

SHIPPING FOR A BETTER WORLD

You never know where you'll find savings in your company. Sometimes, the most seemingly insignificant parts of your operation can be the basis for dramatic reductions in waste and costs.

For example, consider the lowly shipping pallet. These are the workhorses of industry, on which most goods are transported from factory to market. American companies send a half-billion wooden pallets into landfills every year in the process of getting things from here to there. Stacked on top of each other—this is one of those great eco-statistics—these half-billion pallets would reach more than 3,617 miles in the sky, the equivalent of 14,146 World Trade Center towers. In addition, U.S. companies spend well over $1 billion a year just to throw wooden pallets into landfills. And two-thirds of those pallets are used only once before being tossed out.

As anyone who's ever been in a warehouse knows, most shipping pallets are made from wood—usually oak and other hardwoods, between 18 and 20 board-feet worth each. In fact, more hardwood goes into pallet production than into papermaking. According to one estimate, a tree must grow for about ten years before it can yield enough lumber to manufacture just one wooden pallet.

As they are constructed now, wooden pallets are built stronger than necessary for one-time use and not built sturdy enough for multiple use. So, wood is an inefficient choice. A better choice for one-time use may be recycled corrugated cardboard, which can itself be recycled. For multiple use, there are plastic pallets, usually made from recycled plastics, which are durable and can be readily repaired with epoxies. Of course, wooden pallets can be repaired, too, and some companies—Quad/Graphics, for example—have set up pallet repair stations at facilities to do this. Some companies also send their unrepairable pallets through chippers, which turns them into mulch for use in gardens and on walkways.

What about costs? Cardboard pallets cost about the same $6 or $7 as a wooden pallet and are rated to hold up to three tons. The plastic ones cost up to $55, which means they must outlast a half-dozen or so wooden pallets to be amortized. However, the real cost savings come in disposal costs. General Motors, which had been discarding 36,000 wooden pallets a day—most after only one use—switched to cardboard in its North American operations. This change could potentially save the company $100,000 in disposal fees, and earn them $40,000 more from reselling the used cardboard—*every single day.*

Savings like that make being environmental—well, palatable.

PAPER CUTS

One of the most visible signs of any company's wasteful habits is how it uses office paper. By this point in the twentieth century, we shouldn't be using much paper at all. Computers and other technologies were supposed to have created an "office of the future" that made paper obsolete. But the opposite happened: Computers enable us to print things six ways from Sunday. As automation consultant Amy Wohl once put it, "The paperless office turned out to be as practical as the paperless bathroom."

According to the American Paper Institute, the total supply of office paper in 1989 was 23.8 million tons. Some of that paper is thrown away and a lot is filed away, taking up valuable office real estate for storage. Wohl says U.S. companies file 120 billion new sheets of paper annually, which means that by the year 2000, they will have squirreled away the equivalent of all the office space in Pittsburgh. Some business sectors are particularly paper intensive. After government, the legal profession is the second largest consumer of paper in the United States, according to the American Bar Association, with each lawyer using about a ton of paper a year. About 300 million sheets are filed annually in California courts alone, enough to bury San Francisco in a layer of paper ten sheets deep.

A growing amount of that paper is being recycled—not just by lawyers but in most industries—thanks in part to the efforts of the National Office Paper Recycling Project, begun in 1990 by a coalition of city and state government agencies and such companies as Boise Cascade, Eastman Kodak, Fort Howard Corporation, IBM, and Xerox. The project's members have made great strides in helping stimulate interest in paper recycling. In 1991, American companies managed to save just over 15 percent of office paper from the waste stream, up from practically nothing a few years before.

But recycling alone isn't enough. A growing number of companies are finding ways to tame the paper tiger by using less paper. Doing so addresses several key issues: It reduces paper costs, decreases the environmental impact of paper manufacturing, reduces printing and photocopying costs, cuts down on the amount of paper that must be discarded or recycled, lessens the amount of filing space needed, cuts labor costs for filing and other paper-pushing chores, and most likely improves efficiency and productivity. Exactly how you tame the tiger depends on what business you're in and the size of your company. Many of the most effective paper-cutting strategies require significant investments, although they can pay a handsome return. Others are decidedly low-tech and can be put to work today.

First you need to understand exactly how much paper you're using, and exactly who's using it. That's how AT&T began when it set a corporate goal of reducing waste paper by 15 percent (from 1990 levels) by 1994. It is also aiming to recycle 35 percent of the paper it uses. "We identified the major purchasers of paper," says Barry Dambach, senior engineer with AT&T's environment and safety organization. To no one's surprise, the big copier centers were among the largest paper users. AT&T owns seven thousand copy machines. A study revealed that AT&T makes forty-six million copies a month, less than a fourth of which were made on both sides of the paper, known as "duplexing." The company set a duplexing goal of 50 percent, which could eliminate 6.44 million pages a month, saving $385,000 annually. In addition, AT&T is making greater use of its on-line information exchange system, which can electronically send updates to environmental managers at sites around the world, further cutting paper use. "We no longer make copies of memos and send them to three hundred people," he says. The company now advertises job openings electronically within the company. That alone saves 2 million pieces of paper a month.

One aspect of any campaign to reduce a company's paper consumption is getting people to adjust to it. "There's a lot of cultural change that's slowly beginning and going in the right direction," Dambach says. Cutting paper usage can't be an absolute mandate, he noted, but getting them to think about it is. "If a person needs a hard copy for a specific reason, they should go ahead. A lot of it's not rocket-scientist stuff, but sitting down and having people focus on it."

Another paper cutter is Nordstrom Inc., the Seattle-based fashion retailer, which had seen paper use escalate. In five years it witnessed a 21 percent increase in paper consumption at one facility, a rate that outpaced the company's growth, according to information manager Chris Adkisson. Adkisson and others at Nordstrom discovered some fairly low-tech solutions. For example, they discovered that its sales and inventory reports, which are sent around the country, could be printed in a smaller typeface, combining two and in some cases four pages of data on one sheet of paper. In addition, it puts historical sales information on its IBM mainframe rather than printing it out. "Everyone has access to information sooner and we reduce our courier costs," says Adkisson. Twelve months of sales reports are stored on-line. "It's like a filing cabinet. If they need to print a page or two pages of it, they can do that locally," he says. One of Adkisson's tasks is to persuade people to use the system. He reminds employees that the 160 million pages of paper saved, or 778 tons, works out to thirteen thousand trees that aren't cut down. The savings for the company are projected at more than $2 million a year. Kmart Corporation had a similar experience. The mass-merchandiser put its sales records on-line for 3,600 workers at its Troy, Michigan, headquarters, and placed older information on microfiche. Now, managers print only what they actually need. "The storage has reduced the number of file cabinets necessary," says Jan Potter, a Kmart spokesperson. In 1990, Kmart saved 250 million sheets of paper, says Potter, or about twenty thousand trees.

Those paper-saving methods are relatively simple. Many companies are extending their paperless practices outside company bounds—to customers, suppliers, and others. The most widely used process is known as electronic data interchange, or EDI, which is basically a standardized computer format that allows firms to electronically communicate sales, billing, and inventory information. EDI is already widely used in the auto parts industry, in trucking and rail, the petroleum and chemical industries, and by retailers such as Sears, Wal-Mart, and Kmart. A 1993 edition of the *EDI Yellow Pages*, published by the Dallas-based Interlink Resources, lists some 31,000 companies worldwide that are using EDI to eliminate paper, up from 21,000 from the previous year's edition. About two-thirds of the companies are in the United States.

"The real issue is the paper between us and our vendors," says Lance Dailey, director of EDI for Sears Roebuck & Co., which has converted all of its vendors to EDI. Sears started the program in 1989. Since then, paper use has decreased substantially. "In 1989 Sears sent 21 million purchase orders," says Daily. A one-page purchase order consists of three copies. That in turn generated 21 million invoices, packing slips, and bills of lading. He explains that EDI cuts the cost of handling paper and entering paper-based information into computers. EDI also has helped streamline the ordering process. For starters, it eliminates the need for humans to type an order into a computer. Instead, computers automatically issue standing orders when inventories reach a preset level.

Another high-tech strategy is to put information on compact

disk, or CD-ROM, the same technology used to play high-quality music. Already, CD-ROM disks can store libraries full of reference material that can be accessed by personal computers. But they can store much more.

MCI Communications Corporation's largest customers receive monthly phone bills of ten thousand pages or more. That requires a great deal of paper, printing, and shipping costs. Moreover, customers have difficulty analyzing their bills in this form. MCI can also send a bill on magnetic tape, but that takes a lot of mainframe computer time to analyze the data. As an alternative, MCI asked Eastman Kodak Co. to develop a better way. Now, the company's hundred largest customers can get their bills on an eight-ounce disk, and analyze them using off-the-shelf software. A CD-ROM drive for a personal computer costs about $300.

Larry Boden, head of Nimbus Information Systems, a CD production company in Rickersville, Virginia, says that any company can put information onto a disk rather inexpensively. The cost of manufacturing disks starts at around $1,400 for the first disk, plus $2 per additional copy, with discounts for quantity orders. Also required is software to make the data CD-friendly, which can cost up to $2,000. A single CD can hold roughly 700 million characters, the equivalent of about 250,000 pages, or six trees' worth of paper.

If the start-up costs are too high, National Computer Solutions in Danville, Virginia, offers a cost-share CD, where up to thirty users can utilize a single disk, sharing production costs. "Anybody who routinely sends out more than five megabytes"—about 1,700 pages—"can do it less expensively and more efficiently with less impact on the environment by using CD-ROM," said Stephen Keel, the company's president. The data are coded so that others can't read your data, and vice versa. Though prices vary, five discs holding five megabytes (approximately five million characters) each of data would probably cost less than $300. There are some one-time startup costs, however.

Other companies have become hooked on fiche—microfiche, that is. Anacomp Inc. of Atlanta makes a system that converts computer-based data to microfiche, complete with an index. Mark Woods, executive vice president, says microfiche costs about $2 for the original, and 10 to 20 cents a copy. "A computer-output piece of paper costs a company about a nickel," Woods said. "We're putting one thousand pages out for 20 to 30 cents. As a rule of thumb, we'll save a company 80

Paper-Cutting Tips

Here are some low-tech, low-cost ways to cut your company's paper use:

- Edit documents thoroughly on computer before printing.
- Use a smaller typeface so that more type fits into less space. (But make sure it's still readable.)
- Similarly, use narrower margins.
- Single-space (or use 1.5-line spacing) instead of double-spacing.
- Be brief. Keep letters and memos to just one page.
- If you must print a rough draft, use the back side of waste paper. Use the back side for informal memos, too.
- Use waste paper for scratch pads. A local print shop will cut your paper to any size and glue one edge, making a pad.
- Photocopy documents on both sides of the page, which can cut your paper consumption in half.
- Rather than distributing a memo, post announcements in a central area—in the coffee room, bathroom, by the elevator, copier, or water cooler, for example. Or circulate a few copies.
- Print summaries of reports and let people know where they can get the whole document if they really need to see it. Make reports and historical information available on-line.
- Use half-page cover sheets for faxes rather than full-page sheets. Better yet, don't use any cover page.
- Redesign and rewrite forms to reduce paperwork and form length. Get rid of unneeded duplicates.
- Avoid making too many "extras"—additional copies of a document you make "just in case."
- Ask yourself: Do I really need to print this out?

percent against paper." A microfiche reader costs about $250; versions that also print cost about $2,000.

The paper-cutting possibilities go on and on. Here's a sampling of solutions:

- Andersen Consulting developed for BFGoodrich a software package for Goodrich's vinyl-making division that allows plant managers to schedule plant time for production runs, as well as to synchronize ordering ingredients for each batch. "Typically, that was done on the back of an envelope," says Andersen partner David A. Crow. The program, *PROCESS/1*, also automatically produces Materials Safety Data Sheets required for hazardous materials. (More on this in chapter 7.)
- MCI's small- to medium-size firms can receive on-line billing. Designed for companies that have monthly long-distance bills of between $1,500 and $50,000, it lets them examine their phone bills via modem, and generates reports on calling patterns.
- United Parcel Service developed an electronic clipboard to record pickups and deliveries for its seventy thousand drivers. Each driver generates an average of six pages a day—a cumulative total of about 105 million sheets a year. The new device enables drivers to punch in numbers and delivery information, even digitize signatures.
- Alacrity Systems Inc. has introduced a Desktop Document Manager, which combines the functions of a fax machine and photocopier in a personal computer. The paper savings comes from being able to send a fax without printing it first; to copy a book or magazine electronically before faxing it; or to read and discard faxes without having to print them. The price: $1,995.

And then there's the good old Internal Revenue Service, which has offered taxpayers the option of filing returns electronically since 1989. Until 1992, when around ten million forms were filed electronically, only taxpayers due refunds could file in this manner; now it's open to all. But all these paper-saving benefits may be offset somewhat by the agency's *Handbook for Electronic Filers*, which is a hefty 248 pages long.

Sometimes you have to kill a tree to save a tree.

excellence

THE SEARCH FOR TOTAL ENVIRONMENTAL QUALITY

"QUALITY" HAS BECOME one of the most vibrant buzzwords of the business world. Since the mid-1980s, companies around the world have embraced some or all of the precepts of the so-called quality movement, all aimed at improving productivity, lowering costs, attracting and retaining valued employees, and generally achieving peak performance.

There are at least two good reasons for quality's popularity boon. One is that these challenging times require bigger, more systemic thinking, and that happens to be a cornerstone of total quality management (TQM) programs. Also, TQM, though made in the U.S.A., was tested in the Japanese corporate world. And its successful results there have been the envy of the business world.

When you examine the links between corporate environmental concern and the movement to achieve total quality management, a number of things begin to fall into place. Consider for a moment the evolution of how companies have delivered quality to their customers over the past few decades, especially in the United States. In the 1960s and 1970s, businesses focused primarily on customer *compliance*, a reactive stance. Simply put, it meant getting the order out the door—more or less on time, and more or less the way the customer had in mind. Any small mistakes, inexact quantities, or shoddy workmanship was overlooked as an acceptable price customers paid for doing business in booming economic times. If you didn't like American products, you couldn't do much about it. When it came to manufacturing efficiencies, America was pretty much the only game in town.

In the 1970s and 1980s, company focus shifted to customer *satisfaction*, a more proactive stance in which the goal was to produce defect-free goods and services. "Quality Is Job One" was Ford Motor Company's slogan, though any of a number of firms could have used it as they felt the growing global competition for goods and services. Suddenly, geting the order filled correctly and on time was no longer enough; it had to be the best it could be.

In the 1990s, the ultimate quality stance became customer *success*, with companies working hard to make their customers winners in their respective industries. By helping customers succeed, the reasoning goes, you ensure their loyalty and longevity, two commodities in extremely short supply nowadays. That, in turn, ensures your own company's success.

When you think about it, going from customer compliance to customer success in two short decades is quite a turnaround.

The growing efforts by companies to play a proactive role in the environment reflects this same progression, albeit at an accelerated pace. As noted earlier, until recently most companies had focused almost exclusively on environmental *compliance*, a reactive stance in which companies strived merely to earn a clean bill of health from regulators—or at least avoid government and public wrath for the pollution caused by their products and manufacturing processes. However, today the trend has shifted to environmental *satisfaction*, which includes molding one's corporate image, perhaps even one's policies, to reflect a concern for the planet's future. This was important because even the "little" bits of pollution that a company's earlier behavior produced became an unacceptable price. "Environment Is Job One" never exactly made it into anyone's corporate advertising campaign, although some companies' efforts have come pretty close to that sentiment.

Now, a few cutting-edge companies are beginning to set their sights on the goal of environmental *success*, in which they effect a positive impact on the environment through a shift in management policy and style. Environmental success embraces the TQM notion that a company can thrive only when it acts as a whole system that includes not just executives and workers, but customers, suppliers, and neighbors. This holistic perspective brings together a wide spectrum of individuals and interests.

In the late-twentieth-century hypersonic business environment, this evolution from "compliance" to "success" on the environment is happening much more quickly than the quality movement. Where the latter took a decade or more, the former will likely take a few short years.

The above "compliance," "satisfaction," and "success" designations are simplistic, to be sure; any particular company could be found straddling two, perhaps even all three, of them. For example, as stated earlier in this book, 3M may be at the cutting edge of some environmental policies and practices, but it is still among the nation's top ten emitters of toxic chemicals. While the company may be in the "success" mode in some ways, it clearly remains in "compliance" when it comes to reducing emissions. Even so, these three categories offer a convenient handle on the direction in which the bulk of business is headed, and on some of the parallels between the environment and quality movements.

The links between the two movements do not end there. Consider for a moment the organizational changes each demands. When companies strive for TQM, they often find it necessary to restructure their bureaucracies, their communications styles, and their decision-making processes. Some of the changes involve integrating functions across departmental lines. For example, TQM companies must ensure that communication moves in all directions—up, down, and across, internally and externally. To do so often requires consolidating various duties and departments so that all report to a vice president for quality assurance, or some other such title. With environmental quality, many firms are finding it similarly necessary to restructure various parts of their organizations, allowing the formulation of new alliances and partnerships, new avenues of communication, and a revamped decision-making structure—headed by a vice president for the environment, or some similar senior executive.

Quality and the environment share another important link. One of TQM's principal aims is to eliminate defects. Indeed, "zero defects"—or at least continuous improvement to eliminate defects and mistakes—is the holy grail of most quality-based organizations. Defects point up inefficiencies in the system and the need for changes. Under a quality-based environmental program, waste, including pollution, is reviled for the same reason—it reveals inefficiencies in a company's operations. So, "zero discharges," "zero waste," and similar corporate goals put its environmental initiatives squarely in sync with the goals of total quality management.

It's very simple: Waste is a defect. "Zero defects" means "zero waste."

All of this explains why a submovement has emerged out of TQM in the early 1990s calling itself "total quality *environmental* management," or TQEM. Already, you can find TQEM seminars, conferences, and publications, and more than a few consultants bandying about the term. According to the Investor Responsibility Research Center, 54 out of 100 Standard & Poor's 500 companies surveyed said they apply TQM to the environmental principles and practices of their business. And with good reason: At its best, TQEM brings together the best of both worlds—better-run companies operating in more environmentally responsible ways.

UNDERSTANDING TQEM PRINCIPLES

To understand further requires a brief primer on TQM principles and how they apply to environmental management. Total quality management has its roots in the United States during World War II, when a statistician named W. Edwards Deming applied his craft to improve the production quality of war materiel by American workers. Deming and his colleagues taught some 35,000 industrial engineers and technicians to use statistics to get higher-quality results in manufacturing. But after the war, Americans embarked on an unprecedented baby boom and buying binge, and the manufacturing focus shifted quickly from *quality* to *quantity*. It seemed that the public would buy just about anything companies could make.

Deming's theories were basically spurned by the Americans following the war. However, the Japanese found them extremely useful in building a new economy in their ravaged cities. Deming went to the Far East, where his lectures and writings on statistical quality control became gospel among Japanese business leaders. And while American companies were distracted by the economic explosion and social upheaval of the 1960s and 1970s, the Japanese embraced and applied the theories of Deming (and several other quality gurus, including Joseph Juran and Philip Crosby) to become a manufacturing force in the world's economy. In return, they named their highest award for corporate quality the Deming Prize. Over the years, a few U.S. firms dabbled with quality concepts. For example, Crosby initiated the "zero defect" movement at Martin Marietta in the 1960s, popularizing the concept "do it right the first time." Finally, around the mid-1980s, American business leaders began to catch on to the "quality challenge," and Deming's and others' principles were not only accepted, they became vogue. Deming emerged as something of a mythical folk figure in international business.

Subtle but significant differences distinguish the leading schools of quality-management thought, though Deming's has emerged as the dominant version. Even so, many of today's quality consultants preach a gospel that borrows liberally from the work of Deming, Juran, Crosby, and others, focusing on some basic themes that are common to all:

- **The Customer Is Always Right.** First and foremost, quality is customer-oriented. It begins with the notion that the customer is king—that his or her needs always come first. Of course, as we've learned throughout this book, "customers" are not just those who buy a company's product or service. They also include colleagues, superiors, subordinates, regulators, neighbors, environmentalists, media, and others. Unfortunately, their collective needs are many, varied, and often conflicting.

- **Prevention Is Cheaper Than Cure.** Preventing defects costs a lot less than solving problems once they occur. At Philips Petroleum, they refer to the 1-10-100 rule: If you catch and fix a problem in your own work area, it costs $1; if you catch it internally but beyond your area it costs $10; and if you have to correct the error after delivery to the customer, it costs $100. Some version of that is certainly true with pollution and waste: Dealing with symptoms—disposing of hazardous materials, "scrubbing" dirty air emissions, and so on—usually costs far more over time than preventing the problems in the first place. Crosby popularized the notion "Quality Is Free," meaning that the costs of implementing quality controls at the front end of an operation are usually more than paid for by the savings in not having to fix defects—including the price of poor company image and loss of customer loyalty—at the back end. And so it could follow that "Environmental Excellence Is Free."

- **Everything Is Part of a System.** The systems of business—people systems, money systems, information systems, and the like—can be charted and quantified, so that efficiency can be maximized and waste can be minimized. This systemic approach to business demands thinking, communicating, and acting across departmental and divisional lines. Doing so brings as many individuals as possible into the decision-making process, which can increase empowerment and motivation throughout the work force. Quality-based companies think systemically, resolving problems not by blaming individuals, but by focusing on the workings of the entire organization.

- **What Gets Measured Gets Managed.** TQM relies heavily on quantifying systems, processes, and companies to determine their most efficient and inefficient parts. Quality-measurement tools include a variety of statistical analysis charts, which help visualize and identify principal problem areas. Among other things, doing such analyses requires accurate information and efficient and accessible information systems.

But measuring has its limitations. Richard Wells, vice president of Abt Associates, a Cambridge, Massachusetts, consulting firm, offers what he calls a "cautionary tale" about measurement: "It is said of the former Soviet Union that when central planners measured success by number of units produced, producers of nails delivered huge numbers of very small tacks. When success was measured by volume of production, many fewer but very large spikes were delivered. What central planners forgot, and producers had no incentive to learn, was that success must be measured in terms that are relevant to customers. How we measure environmental performance will determine the kind of performance we get. The measures we select must reflect the demands of internal and external customers for a corporate environmental policy."

- **Continuous Improvement Requires Total Involvement.** Under TQM, top management spreads its vision throughout the company, getting everyone into the act of identifying problems and making improvements. One principal tool for achieving that is training, making sure that the entire work force knows what quality is, how to achieve it, and why it is important. Teams are another important part of the process, letting participants capture the collective energy that exists when people pool their resources and creative efforts. Ultimately, any

TQM success is directly linked to the kind of leadership—both top-down and bottom-up—devoted to the quality process.

• **The Process Never Ends.** At the heart of both TQM or TQEM is the notion of "continuous improvement," which means that nothing in business is ever so good that it can't be improved upon, and that even the best-performing companies should constantly fine-tune their products and operations to keep up with changing conditions and technologies. TQM stresses the need to refine, re-refine, and re-re-refine a company's goals, and the processes used to reach them. TQM gurus like to say that achieving quality is a journey, not a destination. No one ever really gets there, but the best companies are the ones that keep trying. Another favorite TQM saying is, "If it ain't broke, fix it!"

Hudson Whitenight, corporate quality consultant at ICI Americas, Inc., likens quality to gardening, which, to be successful, requires more than just plants. You have to test and work the soil, provide proper nourishment, and manage the growth. He says that at ICI in the 1980s, "We tested the soil and found it was somewhat deficient in nutrients essential for growth in a changing environment. Global competition required a new approach—new ingredients, such as customer focus, employee involvement, and a commitment to the big 'Q' of quality—in other words, total quality as a total organizational process. Just as in gardening, however, before planting the seed or implementing total quality, the proper tools and nutrients must be applied to the soil to prepare it and provide the best opportunity for the seed to take root. This is a top-down responsibility. Management gave the continuous improvement wheel a push. They prepared the soil by first preparing themselves and then the organization." From there, the company's senior management formed a business team to "cultivate" the quality process by getting people involved throughout the organization. That helped stimulate bottom-up growth. Eventually, Whitenight says, "bottom-up employee involvement and ownership seedlings began to break the surface," until the blossoms of quality—communication, measurement, teamwork, and recognition—flourished. "As these systems grow, they will strengthen the roots of service excellence, and a never-ending process of continuous improvement will become self-sustaining."

Whether you subscribe to Whitenight's metaphor isn't important (although it is certainly appropriate for the greening of business). What's important to understand is that quality involves equal parts art and science, and a seemingly endless array of tools, the appropriateness of which will vary from company to company. Just as with gardening, achieving the greatest benefits requires constant tinkering, along with ample doses of persistence, pampering, and patience. And maybe a little passion.

The gardening metaphor has its limits. For example, little about growing plants will prepare you for the tremendous amount of measurement and analysis involved in total quality environmental management. "Ultimately, any TQEM program must begin with the definition of waste," says David L. Trimble, corporate environmental manager of BFGoodrich Company. Trimble's definition of waste is "anything other than the minimum amount of equipment, materials, parts, space, and worker's time which are absolutely essential to add value to the product." So, according to Trimble, the beginning of the TQM journey, "starts with inventorying the waste, then looking at ways to recycle, treat, or eliminate it, and maybe as a last step modifying the process." That sounds simple enough, but it's not so easy to do. At Goodrich, Trimble set out to identify and measure the material losses at his plants. A simple inventory identified at least eight categories:

- Underdelivery: things paid for but never received
- Handling losses: things broken, spilled, or otherwise destroyed while getting them into the production area
- Cleaning losses: bad housekeeping procedures that result in damaged goods or materials
- Process losses: manufacturing inefficiencies that result in unused and unusable materials
- Stack losses and evaporation: materials emitted into the atmosphere
- Scrap, rework, and samples: wastes resulting from production errors, as well as excessive batch samples
- Overspecification: giving customers more than they really needed
- Overfill: giving customers more than they asked for

Most of these losses result from small things, but they add up. For example, at one plant, Trimble found that employees were taking five-gallon bucket samples out of a batch of chemicals for testing. "The reason they were doing that is they had to drain it off the bottom of the reactor to get a thoroughly mixed sample and that required a five-gallon bucket. Five gallons multiplied by the number of batches they were running over a year was a significant amount of waste. We looked at alternatives to pulling samples and managed to reduce their annual waste disposal costs from $400,000 a year to $60,000 a year—just by modifying how they pulled batch samples. Small things like that have major impacts."

THE GREENING OF AUDITS

You don't get to this level of specificity of a business operation just by hanging around the plant. You've got to take a systematic approach—measuring, compiling, quantifying, analyzing, and, of course, doing—to get results that will lead to genuine efficiencies. Inevitably, that requires some kind of an environmental audit.

As much as it is bandied about these days, the word *audit* is really rather vague, particularly when applied to the environment. The word itself stems from the Latin *auditus*, "a hearing," from *audire*, "to hear." Originally, the audit "hearing" was a financial one, in which officials or their representatives compared charges with supporting documentation, often supplemented by statements from key individuals. Then this was all summarized and detailed in an audit report. These days, the process takes place within well-established guidelines of the accounting profession, some of which date back to the fifteenth century.

But that financial auditing model is scarcely relevant in the late-twentieth-century world of corporate environmental analysis, in which money is only one of many primary determinants of a company's greenness. As we learned in chapter 2, ecological inputs and outputs—the use of resources to create products, by-products, and waste—must be quantified, analyzed, and integrated into the model to get the most accurate possible portrait of the environmental impact of company operations. But numbers alone aren't enough; they can belie the need for companies to make larger policy or organizational shifts. What's needed is a big-picture view of an audit's findings.

While nine out of ten large companies now conduct environmental audits, according to IRRC, the meaning of the word *audit* differs from company to company. For some, it's what you do at the beginning of

245

your greening efforts to get a sense of where you are and what you need to do. (Some professionals prefer to call that exercise an *initial assessment.*) For others, an audit monitors compliance with existing rules and regulations. One reason for the variety of definitions may be in the different backgrounds that environmental auditors bring to their profession. They range widely in educational levels and academic interests, from bachelor's degrees in fine arts to Ph.D.'s in engineering.

Some help in defining the current state of the art comes from the International Chamber of Commerce, which has defined an environmental audit as "a management tool comprising a systematic, documented, periodic, and objective evaluation of how well environmental organization, management, and equipment are performing with the aim of helping to safeguard the environment by (1) facilitating management control of environmental protection, and (2) assessing compliance with company policies which would include meeting regulatory requirements." But even that definition is extremely broad—purposefully so, no doubt, to encourage the broadest range of implementation.

"Environmental audits are tools for measuring a company's adherence to health, safety, and environmental requirements, whether government requirements or internal requirements," says J. Ladd Greeno, vice president and managing director of the worldwide environmental, health, and safety practice at Arthur D. Little, which has pioneered the environmental auditing process. He explains that in the mid-1980s, environmental audits were used strictly to identify problems, but as they became more sophisticated they were able to verify a company's compliance status. Now, a few cutting-edge companies are using their audits to confirm the effectiveness of management systems. In other words, instead of simply finding problems, today's audits help determine the absence of problems.

That distinction may seem like an exercise in semantics, but in fact it points to a more forward-thinking trend, one more consistent with TQM principles. If a company had a policy not to keep hazardous waste on site for more than ninety days, a traditional audit would determine that the waste either was or wasn't ninety days old. As part of a TQM mandate, a plant manager might decide to remove all stored hazardous waste within seventy days so that he wasn't bumping up against his deadlines. An audit that took management controls into account as well as regulatory requirements would identify waste that was over seventy days old, but still under the ninety-day limit. A mere compliance audit wouldn't have caught that. And so, little by little, the plant manager gets ahead of the curve, incrementally improving the plant's environmental performance. Eventually, as part of the continuous improvement process, that plant manager might move his internal standard to sixty days, or even fifty, gradually lowering the plant's environmental risk.

In Europe, environmental auditing is broader and more complex. In 1991, the European Community proposed a voluntary "Eco-Audit" scheme that will likely shape similar policies around the world. The plan asks companies to establish a formally documented "internal environmental protection system," and to conduct periodic formal audits of their sites, prepare audit reports, and manage the follow-up of all findings. Moreover, they must submit validated environmental statements to EC authorities. Companies that pass muster are entitled to display a special Eco-Audit logo on their products and plants.

Even this level of audit isn't enough for some camps in the environmental debate. "American corporations still tend to see auditing in a relatively legalistic and narrowly technical perspective," write Ernest Callenbach, Fritjof Capra, and Sandra Marburg in *The Elmwood Guide to Eco-Auditing and Ecologically Conscious Management*, "as a means of fending off fines and lawsuits, and as a means of preparing to deal with government regulations which may require high-level management attention and sometimes serious corporate investment. People working in the auditing field sometimes speak of aiming to improve management 'comfort' through assurance that systems to monitor and control defined environmental impacts are in place and operating well." The Elmwood guide is an instructive document, even for companies that don't subscribe to its deep-ecology perspective. Filled with checklists and action plans, which are shrouded somewhat in New Age/new paradigm jargon, the book tackles both the pragmatic and the idealistic aspects of business policy and operations.

The authors, whose Elmwood Institute, based in Berkeley, California, was formed in 1984 "to facilitate the cultural shift from a mechanistic and patriarchal world to a holistic and ecological view," believe there is a difference between *environmental* auditing, which they consider a comparatively shallow perspective, and *ecological* auditing, which they see as having more profound implications. They say their ecological audit is nothing less than "an examination and review of a company's operations from the perspective of deep ecology, or the new paradigm. It is motivated by a shift of values in the corporate culture from domination to partnership, from the ideology of economic growth to that of ecological sustainability. It involves a corresponding shift from mechanistic to systemic thinking and, accordingly, a new style of management known as systemic management. The result of the eco-audit is an action plan for minimizing the company's environmental impact and making all its operations more ecologically sound."

Such a philosophy likely won't mesh with some companies' agendas, but Callenbach and colleagues have made their point: Whether it originates in a philosophy of deep ecology or in more "shallow" levels of ecological concerns, there is no singular type of environmental audit, and no single set of standards and guidelines on which one can be based. The styles, sizes, shapes, and scopes of audits currently undertaken by companies around the world are many and varied. A brief sampling:

- **Compliance audits** evaluate whether a company (or division or plant) meets the full complement of federal and local environmental regulations, as well as internal corporate policies and standards. This audit most closely resembles its financial counterpart, focusing mostly on issues where criteria have been established. It is a fundamental building block for further corporate environmental initiatives.

- **Waste audits** analyze the nature of a waste stream, quantifying the items present. The purpose of the audit is to provide the information a company needs to reduce or eliminate those waste outputs, either by recycling, reusing, or by turning them into energy or secondary products.

- **Product audits** examine the environmental impacts of a product's cradle-to-grave life-cycle so that opportunities can be identified to reduce toxicity and waste, and increase reusability or recyclability.

- **Energy audits** are precursors to energy-efficiency initiatives, involving highly detailed analysis of how all types of fuels are used. More sophisticated versions may examine the energy embodied in a company's goods and services, assigning values to individual units. Such audits will be increasingly important if governments enact so-called carbon taxes based on fossil-fuel use.

That barely scratches the surface. There are many subcategories and variations on these basic themes. Among them: transportation audits (a subset of energy audits, aimed at finding ways to use company vehicles and delivery systems more efficiently), supply audits (a subset of waste audits, aiming for efficient materials use), supplier audits (examining the policies and practices of vendors), ethics audits (a catch-all look at company values and beyond-the-law compliance with community and customer concerns), communications audits (looking at how information is shared both internally and externally), prepurchase audits (examining the environmental risks and liabilities of potential real estate or equipment purchases), and management audits (determining whether a company's organization and structure adequately address its environmental missions and goals).

Whatever its name and intent, an effective audit has several important components and considerations. For example:

1- **Planning.** The most effective audits are the best thought out. Among the many initial considerations:

- What is the specific scope? Will it be comprehensive or cover a single topic? The whole company or specific facilities, departments, or product lines?
- Who is the ultimate consumer of the final report—the CEO, department heads, customers, employees?
- Who will conduct the audit—company employees, outside consultants, or a combination? If employees are involved, will they need special training?
- What resources will be needed—financial and otherwise? Is the company willing to make such a commitment?

2- **Goals and Objectives.** It's also important to know early on what you are trying to learn. What's key here is understanding the often difficult trade-offs between environmental performance and cost considerations. There are usually four basic questions:
- What do we do to help or harm the environment?
- What can be do better?
- What can we do more (or less) of?
- What can we do at a lower cost?

At this point, it's crucial to identify existing environmental policies and programs, so that the auditing team can reconcile them with actual performance in the field.

3- **Priorities.** You generally can't cover all aspects of company operations in a single audit, even when tackling a single facility or a portion of the company. To increase effectiveness it may be necessary to identify the highest-priority concerns—toxic wastes, for example, or opportunities to optimize assets by reusing and recycling used or outdated goods.

4- **Selecting a Team.** A knowledgeable and unbiased audit team is essential to success. Ideally, the team should be familiar with the processes and technologies of the facilities they're auditing. Members also must know existing regulations and legal issues. They must also be impartial and have no hidden agendas or a financial stake in the findings. Admittedly, it is rare to find such ideal candidates within the company. A workable mix often includes employees and outside auditors.

5- **Reporting.** Once the audit is completed, the audit report is vital to ensuring that the findings are read and that recommendations are implemented, or at least considered. A number of existing report formats can help shape the information into a usable format, depending on the type of audit involved. In some cases, a checklist format is appropriate, while other audits are better suited to in-depth discussion and analysis.

Beyond that, the specifics will depend on the organization and its own needs and style. Allied-Signal Inc., for example, forgoes a single comprehensive health, safety, and environmental audit in favor of four specific audits: environment, health and medical programs, safety and loss prevention programs, and product safety programs. Each year, it conducts about eighty audits at 50 of its 240 facilities; about half the sites get more than one kind of audit. Each typically takes four days.

Ann C. Smith, Allied-Signal's manager of health, safety, and environmental audits, emphasizes that a good audit is not a slice in time. "If you do a snapshot, by and large any plant, given sufficient warning—and sufficient can be as short as three days—can make itself look pretty darned good," says Smith, who also chairs the Environmental Auditing Roundtable, an international professional society of environmental auditing. "And that doesn't do you or management any good to know that they can clean up in a hurry. What you want to know is on an ongoing basis, are we doing what we're supposed to be doing?" Smith's four-day audits look at company operations over an eighteen-month period. That enables the team to examine more than a year's worth of compliance, report submissions, record keeping, and so on. "There is a kind of routine approach to these things. You find out what the requirements are of the location that you're going to look at. You look at what systems exist to achieve those compliance objectives. You evaluate the efficacy of the system to do that, and whether it is in fact achieving the compliance objective by means of interview, observation, lots of documentation review, sometimes supplemented by calls to the local agencies and discussions with neighbors. And then you make a judgment."

Perhaps most important is what happens next. "The whole premise behind the audit program as first conceived is to find out what's wrong before the government comes in—the people who can come in and fine us for no good reason," says Smith. "In my mind, fines don't buy a whole lot for you. You might better use the money cleaning things up beforehand. It's a lot cheaper, for one thing. The premise of our program is 'Let's find it and fix it.'

"Now, if the fixing starts slipping, that's not a very desirable thing to do from two standpoints. For one thing, you're not achieving the goals of the program. The second is, you're laying a trail, potentially available upon discovery, which doesn't speak very well. So we have multiple follow-up mechanisms. We at corporate write the findings, but the ownership of the fix lies with the business group. We do not get involved in demanding quarterly reports, progress tracking, and that sort of thing. The only thing we're interested in is that an effective action plan is written to address the deficiencies that we found, and that business management does the follow-up and ensures that those action plans are completed."

Smith's office has a sophisticated computerized system that keeps track of findings and responsive actions from audits—as well as from insurance inspections, peer reviews, and various other inspection and evaluation modes. For example, if an action item is more than sixty days overdue, the computer issues a report to the company's chief operating officer. "As you might imagine, nobody wants the COO to get word that his actions are behind schedule. So, none are." says Smith. "It's very simple."

Arthur D. Little's Ladd Greeno believes that the responsibility for turning audits into action is moving simultaneously up and down the corporate ladder. "More and more companies have come to the point of view that it's line management who is responsible for achieving these results," says Greeno. "Having a SWAT team of some sort to come in and fix things isn't the way they want to do it. They want an audit team to find out what the facts are and report them internally and then expect local management to deal with it, rather than have the team from headquarters go in and implement all the fixes. Historically, these things started out being reported pretty far down the line. One of the more recent phenomena is that they've started sending them up the line, and you find higher and higher levels of management are interested in what the environmental auditors are finding."

According to Smith, it's important to emphasize that an audit should be no more than 5 to 10 percent of an environmental management system. "Auditing is not a stand-alone function. It can't operate in the absence of strong compliance management systems and programs. And if anybody tries to make it do that, they're spinning their wheels. The people who get enamored with audits and get all big-eyed about it when they first hear about it, tend to think that it's going to be some kind of panacea. They tend to think that it can supplant strong management programs. It can't do that."

Like Greeno, Smith finds that the most forward-thinking audits go well beyond compliance. "We find an awful lot of stuff in our audits that has nothing whatever to do with regulatory compliance. We find a lot that we call management- or control-systems-oriented matters. It's a matter of 'Have you got a sufficient handle on this stuff to be able to react to potential or likely future regulatory or industry change? You may be in compliance now, and may have managed to stay in compliance for ten or twelve months, but are you going to be able to continue that given your resources, given your training levels, given the fact that you haven't done adequate maintenance on the plant for five years?' "

Employee training makes for a good example, says Smith. "Take hazard communications. There is nothing in the hazcom regulation that requires periodic training. It requires training for new employees and for transferred employees. But if the same employee sits in the same location for seventeen years, it's possible that over time he's forgotten his new-employee training about the chemicals around him. So it would be desirable to have some kind of periodic training refresher course from time to time. Our management-control audit would pick that up."

A good case for taking your audit program beyond mere compliance was made in 1991 by the Justice Department. In a fifteen-page memorandum it offered some insight to the following question: What happens if your voluntary audit turns up some horrible problems, ones for which you or others in your company could be criminally liable? It's a compelling quandary. After all, what incentive is there to uncover problems that will only get you into trouble? The Justice memo offered an escape hatch—and a window of opportunity. By laying out the four principal considerations used in determining whether to press charges, the department in essence issued a set of guidelines encouraging companies to ferret out their own environmental problems:

- voluntary disclosure—with consideration to "whether the person came forward promptly after discovering the noncompliance, and to the quantity and quality of information provided"

- cooperation—"the violator's willingness to make all relevant information . . . available to government investigators and prosecutors"

- preventive measures and compliance programs—including "the existence and scope of any regularized, intensive, and comprehensive environmental compliance program"

- additional factors—including the pervasiveness of the noncompliance, any internal disciplinary action taken, and subsequent compliance efforts

The memo emphasizes that these factors "do not constitute a definitive recipe or checklist of requirements. They merely illustrate some of the types of information which is [sic] relevant to our exercise of prosecutorial discretion."

In any case, whatever an audit turns up, one thing is clear: Companies that aren't already engaging full-tilt in comprehensive environmental auditing programs risk being left in the dust by their competitors. Already, the Chemical Manufacturers Association's Responsible Care program mandates auditing for its members, as do the Ceres Principles, which are being foisted on many companies' annual shareholder meetings. And eventually, the European Community is likely to mandate some version of its proactive Eco-Audit among its member countries. That means if you want to export your products or services to the EC's 350 million or so residents, or to set up manufacturing operations in their countries, your firm may have to comply with those standards. That alone makes environmental auditing a force to be reckoned with.

BENCHMARKING

These days, it's not enough to know only what your own company is doing environmentally. You must also be aware of what improvements your colleagues and competitors are making in environmental performance. The goal in watching them is to ensure that your own programs represent the best available knowledge and technological expertise.

In the past, you had to do something sneaky, of questionable ethics, perhaps even illegal, to check up on other companies. That may still be true if you're trying to pilfer the top-secret recipe for Coke or the technology behind Reebok's latest sneaker, but it is far easier than ever to find out who's doing what for the environment, and how you can do it, too. The process is called *benchmarking*.

Webster's New Twentieth Century Dictionary defines *benchmarking* as "a standard or point of reference in measuring or judging quality, value, etc." It derives from the worlds of geography and cartography, in which surveyors inscribe a permanent landmark that has a known position and altitude. That mark is then used as a reference point in determining other positions and altitudes. That's not far from what benchmarking is in business: trying to determine the state of the art of a given company operation so you can tell whether your own is up to snuff. Benchmarking is by no means limited to environmental matters; it is widely used in many other areas, particularly in management programs and employee participation programs. Whatever the topic, benchmarking in essence is a sophisticated game of "Follow the Leader," in which companies gauge the competitiveness of their strategies, processes, and procedures in order to keep them at the leading edge.

This is particularly appropriate when it comes to environmental quality, where the leading edge is a constantly moving target. From purchasing to personnel to public relations, corporate environmental policies never seem to remain stagnant for very long, as one company or another finds a way to turn some new aspect of environmental responsibility into a competitive advantage.

Most companies are surprisingly willing to share information about their operations, especially about environmental programs, which don't seem to be as proprietary as other parts of their business. "There are just certain things worth sharing," says Art Soderberg, manager of corporate environmental and safety quality for AT&T. "When it comes to pollution or accident/injury [prevention], I'm not sure that anybody will see that as competitive." One benefit of benchmarking, Soderberg notes, is that it forces companies to examine their own operations more carefully. "You have to understand your own process before you start, because you won't understand what questions to ask, areas to probe, or elements to improve. That's key."

Soderberg describes the joint benchmarking effort AT&T took with Intel Corporation. "I got the subject matter experts in a room, and we came up with about twenty-five issues. Then we decided to say on a scale of one to five what was very important and what was less important. One of the areas that we came up with was pollution prevention. How does corporate roll out a pollution-prevention program?"

The group then identified a number of companies that had state-of-the-art pollution-prevention programs, continually narrowing the list to select comparable companies, including those with relatively new programs, so the managers had them fresh in their minds. "We developed a set of one hundred questions on various topics," ranging from culture, management responsibility and accountability, and auditing, to numbers, training, and media. "Then we started setting up interviews," Soderberg says.

The two firms, working with a team of six, benchmarked five companies against their own: Dow, DuPont, H. B. Fuller, 3M, and Xerox. Their questions focused on three major areas: accident/injury reduction, energy management, and pollution prevention. After the interviews, which included site visits, "we had a one-week skull session," says Soderberg. "We rated all the categories, all the elements that were important and not important. We developed a compendium of best-in-class practices for a corporate program to roll out. At this stage, we have prepared for our management the dollars, the resources, and the time frame for a pollution-prevention program."

AT&T and Intel worked on their study for a year, but the process need not take that long, says Abhay K. Bhushan, manager of the Environmental Leadership Program for Xerox Corporation. "It can take anywhere from a few days to a few months," he says. Bhushan, whose company is a pioneer of the technique, has benchmarked a number of different processes, including redesign of products to be more environmentally friendly, energy conservation, recycling, and environmentally responsible publishing practices.

For example, in 1991, when Xerox failed to win the Environmental Conservation Challenge Award, issued each year by the White House to companies with standout environmental programs, he was determined to find out why. He conducted a general benchmarking exercise to analyze what qualities the companies that did win the award had in common, and how Xerox measured up to those qualities. "I wanted to know what were the things that made them an award winner," says Bhushan. "What were the things that were extra special?"

Of the three winning companies—Pacific Gas & Electric (PG&E); Times-Mirror, publisher of the *Los Angeles Times*; and 3M—Bhushan decided to focus on PG&E and 3M, which most closely resembled Xerox in a variety of ways. Bhushan called on Claude Poncelet, PG&E's chief environmental executive, and Tom Zosel and Bob Bringer, 3M's environmental leaders, to get more information. "I wanted to find out what they did and look at it in more detail as to what was unique about them, and what would it take to get to the same level of excellence. What would it require from us? What could we learn from them? I found out that in some areas we were doing better, in other areas we had a lot to learn." Bhushan discovered that the winning companies had three things in common: They had visible top-level CEO commitment, they had made a major change to a product or process, and they had well-developed employee-awareness programs that included reward and recognition for environmental performance.

In comparing those traits to those of his own company, Bhushan first concluded that Xerox's top management hadn't been visible on the environment. While company chairman Paul A. Allaire had been pressing forward on a number of environmental programs, says Bhushan, "our employees weren't convinced that our CEO really cared about this issue as a top priority."

And though Xerox was well on its making product and process changes, the most significant programs—Asset Recycle Management, for example—hadn't been fully developed. Most of its benefits were a few years away. The company's conservation programs paled when compared with those at PG&E or 3M, for instance. The same was true for Xerox's employee reward and recognition programs: They were just gaining momentum, a far cry from PG&E's and 3M's, which were several years old and going full steam.

Bhushan presented this information to the company's Environmental Leadership Steering Committee, a policy-level committee made up of people from various Xerox divisions and operating companies. "We

Benchmarking Tips

- When approaching other companies, counsels AT&T Bell Labs benchmarking consultant Brenda Klafter, simply "call them up on the phone, explain who you are, that you've read something about them. Also let them know that you're going to share something back with them. I think we've only been turned down once," she adds, and that was because the firm just couldn't spare the time.

- Keep things simple. Rosemarie Fiorilli, a financial analyst at Nestlé Chocolate and Confection Company, cautions against attempting too much. "You have to be careful not to benchmark too many processes at one time. It becomes a mess."

- Have a high-level manager on your benchmarking team, says Klafter. "Pull in people who are involved on the operational level." Some firms plug just anybody into the benchmarking process. "It doesn't work."

- Get specific, says Intel's Terry McManus. "You really need to understand what was successful in assisting a company to be best-in-class." Find out what attributes apply to your company.

- Harry Artinian, Colgate's vice president of corporate quality, says, "The first tendency is to try and take what you see and insert it in your own company. That inevitably leads to failure because your own systems are different. You have to understand your own system and what your objectives are. Align your strategies and objectives across and down the organization so that what comes out the end will be better than what you had before, whether it's packaging, formulation, plant and facilities, or whatever."

- Xerox's Abhay Bhushan sums up the process as simply looking at the rest of the business world. "There are people out there to help you, and they feel gratified when you call. If somebody has done well, they feel proud to talk about their accomplishments. And it takes a heck of a lot less time than reinventing the wheel."

looked at ways to make changes," says Bhushan. "So, for example, we now are developing a program to make our CEO and Xerox more visible on the environment." And the company donated three hundred photocopiers, laser printers, and facsimile machines, and eight million sheets of 100-percent recycled paper to the 1992 United Nations Conference on Environment and Development in Rio de Janeiro. As for the Environmental Conservation Challenge Award, says Bhushan, "we're going to apply every year until we get it. And we'll keep doing the benchmarking every year, too."

Bhushan is quick to point out that this was a relatively quick-and-dirty benchmarking exercise, limited by time and budget constraints to one person over a few weeks. "The overall benchmarking only gives certain broad policy direction, meta type of information. The most important information we get comes from the detailed benchmarking—on remanufacturing, for example: how other people are doing it, what can we do better."

Bhushan offers advice for those who want to get a sense of where their programs stand. For recycling, it helps to benchmark other companies in your region. To do this he had an employee at Xerox's Palo Alto facility call recycling coordinators at other nearby high-tech firms. "We developed a set of questions to ask," Bhushan says. "We assigned an employee to take three or four days. They got some very good answers. They are site-specific to the Palo Alto area." It also helps to use measurements in making comparisons, he says. "If you don't measure it's hard to see how you're improving." So when benchmarking a recycling program, "I was looking at what goals people were setting," such as recycling 30 percent of the firm's paper, or setting a minimum recycled content level by a certain date.

There are many ways to benchmark your firm against others. You can do it privately, or as part of a group, or a coalition like the one formed by AT&T and Intel. Industry groups are also forming benchmarking committees and clearinghouses, in which companies share their studies.

Best in Class?

Who's got the best-in-class environmental programs? In 1991, attendees at a Global Environmental Management Initiative conference were asked which part of their operations they felt could be considered "best in class"— that is, reflecting the state of the art for that operation. Keep in mind that in giving these answers, customers were judging themselves. Here is how they answered:

- Audit systems: Procter & Gamble
- Basic assessment of environment around facilities: Duke Power
- Communication with regulatory agencies: Colgate-Palmolive
- Community involvement groups: Vulcan Chemicals
- Computer tracking of chemical usage: AT&T
- Corporate environmental policy development: Browning-Ferris Industries
- Developing corporate environmental programs: Booz-Allen & Hamilton
- Development of chemical accounting systems: Boeing
- Environmental and safety training: DuPont
- Environmental auditing: Texaco
- Environmental leadership in hazardous material problems: Xerox
- Environmental, safety, and health task force: Lockheed
- Fugitive emissions monitoring: IBM-Endicott
- Groundwater program: Rohm and Haas
- Internal audit program: Alcoa
- Recycling programs: IBM-Yorktown
- Solid-waste reduction: Milliken and Co.
- Toxic use and waste reduction: Polaroid
- Underground storage tank program: Eli Lilly

THE INFORMATION CHALLENGE

By the time you begin to pull together the many things needed to create a quality-based environmental program—education and training, regulatory compliance, statistical measurements and analysis, pollution-prevention techniques, and a host of efficiency measures—you can easily become overwhelmed by the sheer volume of information involved. The simple task of computing what's known as a mass balance—the raw inputs and outputs of chemicals and other materials at a given plant—can involve thousands of products and tens of thousands of pieces of data. The bigger challenge is turning all that data into something useful, whether mandated compliance reports, internal health-and-safety measurement systems, or environmental and energy-efficiency plans. As the graphic opposite reveals, environmental information comes from a wide range of places, and all of it must be massaged and integrated if these myriad facts are to be conscripted into the TQEM battle plan. Says Arthur D. Little's Ladd Greeno: "The whole environmental field is one that has enormous information needs, and most companies are not very far along in handling it elegantly. There's a lot of room for improvement."

But some companies are closer to transforming all this information from an organizational nightmare into a useful environmental management tool. Part of the challenge is simply appreciating the problem. "We go into companies and draw spaghettilike diagrams of where their information is going," says Karl Newkirk, an Andersen Consulting partner specializing in the process industries. "Until you can chart their flows and their data-capture methods, management really hasn't yet realized that this is a problem."

The principal finding of this pasta-on-paper exercise is that there is usually a great deal of costly redundancy and inefficiency in the way companies collect environmental data, and a lot of the information they compile isn't even accurate. At one company, Newkirk found thirteen people, "each with their Lotus spreadsheet and their little PC system, or even just a manual system, collecting information—punching it into their own computer, printing it out, trying to get it as accurate as possible, then sending it on." Many of these individuals were inputting the same data, though they were using it differently.

This is expensive information to capture, says Newkirk, and the way companies capture it makes accuracy questionable. "It's hard to

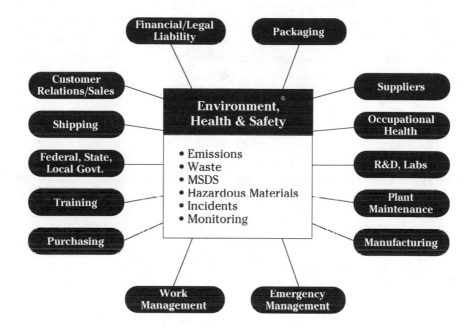

know which employees are exposed to which materials and how much of those materials are going into the environment," says Newkirk. "How does the guy after the fact understand what happened in today's batch run and how much of the input material must have gone into emissions, then enter that into a data base?" The solution, says Newkirk, is to build a system that captures that information automatically as part of the production process. The one Newkirk and his colleagues at Andersen designed is called *PROCESS/1*, an integrated data base that allows companies to capture the information they need as a natural by-product of the manufacturing and materials management systems.

The program's proving ground is the Cleveland-based Geon Vinyl Division of BFGoodrich Co. The division is more than fifty years old and is credited with inventing polyvinyl chloride (PVC), which was originally used in making better automobile tires. But Goodrich got out of the tire business in the 1980s, and the market for PVC became glutted. Therefore, the company refocused its strategy by becoming a value-added custom maker of specialty plastic compounds. That involved a major reengineering of many of its processes. Andersen installed *PRO-CESS/1* to create a system that would automatically keep track of what chemicals were going into each production line, and exactly how much of them were going into the air, land, or water. The result: The information needed to fill out compliance reports can be gotten from a single data base. Even better, management can tap into that same system to get a better handle on things such as production efficiency, emissions, and waste.

But efficiency alone isn't what drives top management to do this, says Newkirk. "Top management more and more wants to be able to assure the community that they're doing everything in their power to have good information about what's going on—just in case. Clearly, the P.R. importance of that is only increasing. And as more and more communities come up with community-action groups that insist upon meeting with the local plant management and reviewing information, plant management is going to have to be able to trot out credible information that's regularly reported on emissions and other things."

An operation like Goodrich's presents massive environmental, health, and safety information challenges. For starters, each made-to-order product requires its own Material Safety Data Sheet (MSDS) to protect employees and surrounding communities in the case of accidents involving chemicals. Among other things, an MSDS describes the hazardous components of a product, and how to treat leaks, spills, fires, and improper human contact.

Creating an MSDS can be a laborious process, requiring toxicologists and chemists to retrace their steps in creating a product. That's all fine and good, except that companies like Geon Vinyl can create thousands of new recipes a month, each with its own information needs. "We've got a client that does a lot of tweaking of their standard products all the time, to the tune of probably ten thousand new recipes per month," says Newkirk. "Imagine the paperwork department. The compliance question is whether you give the customer a generic, standard MSDS, or issue a new MSDS every time you tweak the product. When you have those kinds of situations you have no choice but to stay with the generic MSDS, even though that little tweak you just made may have changed the chemical properties sufficiently so that it needs to be handled differently in case of fire or spillage. You need a system that can flag that for you—to say, 'Oops, you just altered the basic chemical properties sufficiently so the handling procedures on this slightly modified product have to be different in order to be safe.' "

Newkirk has worked with Geon Vinyl and other companies to develop what he calls a "knowledge-based system"—in effect, artificial intelligence—that can automate MSDS generation, making the information more accurate, efficient, and timely. In the process, Andersen has helped the Goodrich unit cut the work-flow steps needed to create MSDS from eleven to seven, and the number of personnel involved from six to two. There were even greater efficiency improvements in the area of chemical inventory reporting, another requirement of SARA Title III: In performing that task, work-flow steps decreased from seven to one, and the number of personnel required dropped from ten to one. In some cases, the personnel savings involved not just keyboard inputters, but valued knowledge employees. "If you argue that a good toxicologist is an extremely rare and expensive person, then trying to leverage him is a very good benefit," says Newkirk. *PROCESS/1*, he says, lets toxicologists be toxicologists, and not pencil-pushers.

The future of environmental information management may be found in the electronic byways of the Boeing Company. Slowly but surely, the $29 billion aerospace company is fitting the pieces together to create a highly integrated system that could eventually do as much for company profitability as for the environment. David Smukowski, Boeing's corporate manager of environmental operations, emphasizes that though all of what he describes is in place somewhere in the company, every component is not there companywide, nor will it be for years.

The process begins when a material comes into a plant. "Take paint, for example," says Smukowski. "We have a building where all materials coming on to the site have to go through, and the people in that building actually distribute the products throughout the factory, so they know exactly what is where and where it went. All the material is bar-coded so we can capture the information efficiently. And we have some people controls: We know who has been trained to handle, move, capture, collect, store, and utilize any given material.

"So the paint comes into this facility. It is recorded to make sure it has the proper information—both chemical-component information and safety information. That's typically through a Material Safety Data Sheet. If the material arrives without an MSDS, then we check it against a computer data base to see if we have an active MSDS in our data base. We have a centralized MSDS system that's part of the information system. If we don't have the MSDS, the product stops. It doesn't move further until we get an MSDS.

"From that point, the paint moves to the shop—hopefully, on a just-in-time basis, so we don't have an oversupply or an undersupply. The reason is that with hazardous material, you don't want to have more material on hand than you need because it has a larger potential for a spill or being lost or misplaced. And it can go out of specification. Our materials are all controlled by very rigid aerospace specifications as to the quality of the material, and shelf life is a critical factor. So, when the paint first comes in, we make sure it meets our specification and then we put a shelf-life expiration date on it.

"At that point, since we know where we disbursed it to, we know what kind of training and what kind of medical surveillance we have to do, so we can tie the people to it. Training records are a very important issue. They're required by law and people that are working with different types of material require certain types of training. So, we have a system for employee records that captures the training data and assures that they've been trained appropriately to handle those materials.

"The next step is trying to discern where the paint goes—on the actual part, out as hazardous waste, or air emissions, or wastewater. We have broken company operations up into twenty-three basic processes, which also have subprocesses. For example, there are a lot of different ways to do painting. You can put paint on with a roller or with a brush, you can spray it, dip it, or electrically charge it. Each of those processes has a different factor associated with it as to what kind of emissions it creates. If we put paint on with a roller we get a lot fewer emissions than if we put it on with a spray gun, because the gun is going to have a lot of particulate overspray and go other places; we can't control it quite as much. We'll use more paint and create more emissions. So we have emissions factors established and in our data bases.

"Now we know how much paint arrived in the shop, we know what's in the paint, and we have emissions factors, depending on the physical process. From that point we can determine how much went out as emissions. We know that for a given process, how much of every gallon of paint will end up in which places.

"So, for example, in a can of paint you may have three or four different types of solvents, some different metals, some pigments. You could have ten or twelve toxic materials in a single can of paint. And you have to report on each one. So you have to have 10 or 12 different line items for each paint.

"If the waste happens to go into the water supply, that waste stream can either be treated as wastewater or as hazardous waste. We sample the waste. If it meets a certain criteria, we may discharge it as wastewater and send it to our wastewater treatment plant. If it exceeds a certain level, it must be shipped off as hazardous waste. From the sample, which we call a profile, we'll know how much of which chemicals are in the water. That information, the profile, which is also computerized, allows us to know the best form of treatment, recycling, or disposition of that material. Certain things have to be incinerated by law. The profiles will tell us what to do with that. Sometimes we prefer to recycle than dispose of something, so the profiles will also tell us that.

"All of this ties into the final systems, which are the reporting systems. We have one for air, called the Emissions Data Management System, and another for hazardous waste, the Hazardous Waste Profiling System. The hazardous waste system keeps track of everything and where it ultimately went—if we took it to recycling, and what the recycler did with it, all the way to its final destination, wherever that may be. We have continuous monitoring on the wastewater streams, and that is computerized as well. That one's easy; it's almost completely automated. It just takes a sample every fifteen minutes or so."

So far, Boeing's information system merely determines what materials have gone into its manufacturing system and where they've ended up. That's useful, but what about using all that finely honed data to foster quality improvements? Smukowski continues: "Based on the information about what emissions we have, what wastewater we have, what hazardous waste was generated, we can estimate costs, track employee overexposures, and anticipate health problems. We put together a matrix of all of our waste streams—air emissions, wastewater, etc.—and where they're coming from. Then we can take a look and compare an emission from paint—say, methyl ethyl ketone—with all the regulatory requirements for methyl ethyl ketone. We'll compare it with employee records—people who have medical surveillance for overexposure to methyl ethyl ketone. We'll compare it with the cost of disposal of anything that contains methyl ethyl ketone, which happens to be effluent waste, which must be incinerated at about $600 a drum.

"We're also starting to capture other costs—the cost of electricity used in the painting process, the cost of transportation to and from the painting shop. So everything that feeds into paint—moving the materials in there, the cost of the materials, the cost of the waste, the cost of the electricity to do the painting, the cost of the water coming in, the cost of the wastewater going out—gets factored in.

"Based on that, we can make risk decisions and prioritizations. We use those to determine where we're going to spend our funding for pollution-prevention activities. We'll rank these things—a weighted average, based upon laws, regulations, employee health, community needs, changeability, toxicity, volume, cost—and find out where can we get the biggest bang for the buck. We can present the information to our research organization so they can try to find alternatives—chemical substitutions, changing how we paint, changing shop practices. We might change how we clean up the tools we use to paint. Do you just wash them down with solvent, or do it in an encapsulated booth and recover the solvent? In that case we'll need a solvent-recovery system. We can make educated decisions on how to best manage those systems at the best price."

Putting this process together has been no mean feat, says Smukowski. At times, the information requirements seem mind-boggling. "I think there's a great misunderstanding by the lay public and the unregulated community about environmental numbers in general. They look at a SARA toxic emissions report and see a specific chemical, methyl ethyl ketone. But we don't buy methyl ethyl ketone. We buy paint, which has paint thinner in it, and paint thinner happens to contain methyl ethyl ketone. So we have to determine what the content of methyl ethyl ketone is, and extract that amount. To do all that—to purchase a can of paint, to get the information from the vendor or supplier of what components are in there, which is a tough, difficult process, because they don't necessarily want everybody to know that; it's proprietary information. We have 125 different qualified paints. They could come from as many as 125 different suppliers, which could mean 125 different MSDS. All of our suppliers use a different format MSDS. Getting the suppliers to give us the information has been a nightmare."

But when the nightmare stops, the benefits of the system begin to look promising. "Our hazardous-waste disposal costs alone have gone from about $2 million a year to about $50 million a year since 1983," says Smukowski. "Our air emissions are a concern, not because of costs so much as operability—whether we can continue to operate facilities. The cost of air-pollution abatement equipment is starting to become very large as well. We figure that if we don't start doing something to re-manage these wastes, it could—by the time the Clean Air Act is fully implemented—cost about $60 million. So the reason we're implementing all these things is to first try to contain the costs, and then try to lower them. Because right now, all they're doing is escalating."

There are less-tangible benefits, too, says Smukowski. "All of this takes communication and education for our employees. Everybody must know what their functions are, be trained for them, and understand everything from the chemicals' personal health effects to what they might be doing to the community if we don't reduce the use of these things. So it's improving morale, the workplace certainly is becoming safer, and it's becoming less risky to the environment."

The benefits of integrated information don't even stop there. "One element of our Continuous Quality Improvement efforts is that we're trying to recognize the regulatory agencies as our customer," says Smukowski. "That's a little foreign for a company like ours. But the reality is that we provide a lot of reports that they require. And if they're lousy reports, the customer isn't satisfied and we're at odds. Our customer might respond by going to Congress and saying, 'They need more regulations because they don't report properly.' So information becomes vital in meeting their needs. We're starting to work hand-in-hand with the agencies about, 'What do you need this information for? What's going to be of value to you?'

"And what's going to be *mutually* of value is even more important. If we can capture information that suits their needs while at the same time helping us apply measurement to our continuous-improvement activities, it's a win-win. If we're capturing information just for their use, it doesn't do us any good and we're not assuring our profitability goal. If we're capturing information that costs us a lot of time and money but doesn't really benefit the environment because it's just information for information's sake, the environment isn't winning. So the information system in essence becomes a tool. It doesn't solve anything, it doesn't help us comply. We don't need computers and things to comply. It's just a tool to make us more efficient."

Amassing all of the data needed for such a system may seem formidable, but it's not as difficult as you'd think. For example, Tom Zosel, 3M's pollution-prevention director, found that all of the data he needed already existed somewhere in the company, but no one had put it all together into one system. "We had kept track of pollution prevention on a project-by-project basis," says Zosel. Tracking the major projects was easy enough, "but there were also a lot of little things that were continually being done. Some guy would decide to change a little thing over here to prevent some waste from being generated. That wasn't really being picked up in the system. So management said, 'Can we develop a better way of tracking all of this?'"

They needed a system for tracking waste. But existing methods—government-approved methods for measuring hydrocarbons, for example—weren't particularly accurate; they could easily be off by as much as 15 percent. That simply wasn't close enough for 3M's needs. "We needed to come up with something that had a higher degree of accuracy," says Zosel. "We got together people who knew a lot about what happens within 3M plants. We realized that there was a lot of information that was available that we could use. A lot of the information was not environmental information—it was production information, laboratory information, process engineering information, purchasing information. Once we got all these people together, one would say, 'I can get you this piece of information, but I don't have this one over here.' Someone else would say, 'Well, that's pretty easy for me to generate. I just pull it out of here and with a little manipulation I've got it.'" Before long, Zosel and colleagues were able to cobble together the kind of information they needed.

Of course, that didn't solve all their problems. "The hardest part was getting the software," says Zosel. "Everybody's system wasn't speaking the same language." That required integrating and interfacing systems written in different languages. But when it all came together, 3M had created an information system that revolutionized the company's ability to manage waste.

Another data base has helped the Lawrence Livermore National Laboratory identify and report on health, safety, and environmental (HS&E) problems, as well as their root causes. The $1 billion-a-year, eight-thousand-employee lab is operated by the University of California for the U.S. Department of Energy. Known as the Deficiency Tracking System (DTS), the aim of the data base is to provide logical and convenient mechanisms for defining and tracking environmental and health-and-safety deficiencies, to verify that corrections were made, and to assess how the system works. Unlike Andersen Consulting's *PROCESS/1*, which operates on a high-end computer system, this one works on a desktop system—in this case, off-the-shelf Macintosh computers; the program fully supports the Mac's easy-to-use graphical interface. The data base can run either as a single-user, stand-alone program or as a multi-user data base on a Macintosh network.

The DTS process begins when an inspection team identifies one or more deficiencies in the field—anything from a minor risk to life-threatening dangers to both human health or the environment. Each deficiency is assigned a code from a list of compliance criteria and is ranked a priority, from 1 to 4. These data are routed to a manager, who reviews them and assigns responsibility for corrective action. The data are then entered into the data base. At this point, the data base generates a detailed report to the responsible individual, who then must take corrective action. That action is then recorded in the data base, which periodically transmits reports to the corporate assurance office. Whenever necessary, management can access the data to produce trend analyses or other reports.

There is no great magic to this—it is the kind of operation for which data base programs were invented—and perhaps that's the point. The beauty of its simplicity may be in the system's ability to push the data down to the lowest level of responsibility, where the broadest possible spectrum of employees can have direct involvement in HS&E issues.

That's exactly how it should be, says Goodrich's David Trimble. "One of the TQM principles is that we want to put the output of the data closest to the person who generates it. That's total empowerment. We want the employee to generate the data, have it be manipulated by the system, which feeds it back to the employee. So the employee is not mailing data off to some place in the sky and it just disappears. The employees are running the system and management is managing the system."

MAKING QUALITY WORK

The success of TQM, like most other widely embraced business trends, is spotty. There are countless success stories, but also tales of firms whose TQM programs foundered and died. As with so many other programs, a lot of it depends on top-management commitment. "We see companies that have quality programs, with special logos on their cards and everything, and you talk to these guys," says Richard O. Toftner, president of Cincinnati-based EnviroAudit Services, and a former EPA official. "They think it's a joke. Because it's all cosmetic, for marketing purposes. And there's this head guy who really doesn't subscribe to it. He tells his marketing department, 'We need to get these blue ribbons and stamp them on our cards so that we look like a quality company.' And it really doesn't come from the top down. They still pretty much govern by the carrot-and-stick method of management—do it or else. The majority of the companies are like that. They use the old bureaucratic, hierarchical model that goes back to the Chinese at least five thousand years ago. It defines the lines of communication, but it doesn't give you that level of quality."

Other evidence shows that despite the almost cultlike embracing of TQM programs by thousands of companies, their effective implementation remains to be seen. For example, a 1992 survey conducted by Ernst & Young and the American Quality Foundation found that many companies are stumbling in implementing TQM programs, particularly in American companies. Among the findings of the study—which surveyed nearly six hundred companies in four industries in the United States, Canada, Germany, and Japan—was that only 26 percent of U.S. companies use customer complaints to help identify new products, compared with 73 percent surveyed in Japan and 60 percent in Germany.

The problem, say experts, is that companies tend to see TQM as a discrete program within the company, isolating it from day-to-day operations. That, of course, misses the intended mark of quality programs by 180 degrees. The whole idea is to incorporate TQM thinking into everyone's daily job. Another problem is that many companies try to take on too much at once, sometimes making hundreds or even thousands of small changes all at once, some superimposed on others, then get embroiled in the organizational gridlock that ensues. Indeed, the Ernst & Young study found that the surveyed companies used a total of 945 different quality-management tactics. A third problem is that quality programs take time—sometimes years—to show results, a time period that outlasts many managers' and executives' patience. And when results do come, they often seem trifling, at least compared with the time, energy, and money invested in the process.

With sufficient commitment and patience, TQM—and TQEM—

Tips for Successful TQEM Programs

- Identify the various "customers" of your environmental performance, and each party's needs. That includes both internal customers (other departments, divisions, or management levels) and external customers (customers, environmentalists, legislators, regulators, media, community groups).

- Maximize communication throughout the organization—top-down, bottom-up, and cross-departmental—about environmental problems, programs, and processes. The greater the sharing of ideas and information, the better. Create cross-functional "green teams" to tackle one or several specific environmental challenges.

- Amass and analyze information about your company's environmental performance, and make the information available to a wide range of parties in a simplified manner. The result will be to pinpoint opportunities and challenges for making improvements.

- Use benchmarking to compare your environmental programs and performance with other businesses in your industry, as well as those in other industries. Learn what places them at the top of the class and how you can achieve similar goals.

- Understand that the goal is not to reach environmental perfection, but to make gradual and continuous improvements on your company's environmental performance.

- Bring everyone in your organization into the process. There is no department, division, or job description that shouldn't be conscripted into the battle for total environmental quality.

can work, as evidenced by a host of companies. But it takes hard work, commitment, and more than a little time, to make happen. "The way we're approaching TQM, it's probably a five- to seven-year transition," says David Trimble. "It's not today's program. We intend to start out slow and shift a culture so that it's a permanent shift. That's what will make it work. It's a long-term cultural commitment."

That's exactly the recipe—for fostering not only quality, but environmental excellence as well.

afterword

MAINTAINING PERSPECTIVE

IF YOU'RE EVER in Saint Paul, Minnesota, stop by 3M headquarters and ask Tom Zosel about the future. Specifically, ask him what tools he and his company use to stay ahead of the environmental curve, to anticipate future regulation and changing customer demands, and to be prepared for the challenges both present. A slight smile will form on the face of 3M's pollution-prevention czar. Then he'll turn around and grab a small round object sitting on a velvet cushion next to his computer terminal. And he'll present it for your inspection:

A crystal ball.

Zosel's ploy is more respite than response, of course, a mere break in the action from discussing a subject about which he is so clearly energized and enthused. But his point is well made: No one, except maybe a clairvoyant, really knows where all of this is headed. To some cynics, corporate environmentalism is yet another well-intended but misguided management fad, a mere distraction from the business at hand, no less ephemeral than dozens of others that have preceded it—and dozens more that no doubt will follow. Over time, the reasoning goes, this one will quietly join the others by fading into the corporate wood-work.

Perhaps. But this "fad" may be different. For one thing, it involves more than a mere change in management style. Its adherents are spending billions in capital investment, writing thousands of pages of new regulations, making untold organizational shifts, and reengineering countless products and processes. There is also the gravity of it all, the knowledge that without some kind of constructive action, any number of unpleasant fates may await us—or if not us, our progeny. And there is the personal and universal nature of the subject, that all of us, from top executives to entry-level clerks, will suffer the same environmental fates—or celebrate the same environmental victories.

So, all of this probably will not simply fade away. More likely, corporate environmentalism will become woven into the fabric of commerce, a routine way of doing business, no less revolutionary someday than ethics workshops or electronic mail. No doubt, a generation from now, we will wonder how we managed to do things any other way. The E-Factor—the Environment, Economics, Empowerment, Efficiency, and all the rest—is destined to become part of our daily business lives. The question is how to make it happen as efficiently and as effectively as possible.

That's the challenge nearly every forward-thinking company will face in the coming months and years, as demands for more environmentally sound business practices creep into every industrial sector. The companies that embrace the challenge will be best positioned to claim competitive advantages in the decades ahead.

Make no mistake: It is easy to quickly become overwhelmed with the idea of tackling the environment in your company. With so many possibilities, all of which require investments of time and resources, there simply aren't enough hours in the week to deal with them all and still carry on the day's business. What's important is to maintain perspective—to step back from time to time and view the bigger picture. That's easier said than done, of course, but it is imminently possible.

Here are some essentials to keep in mind:

Don't try to become perfectly green. This applies to individuals and households as much as to managers and companies.

You simply can't do it, and if you try you'll make yourself—and everyone around you—frustrated and discouraged. You'd be surprised how often this happens: A company executive gets newly found religion on the environment and decides to overhaul everything and everyone—today. As anyone familiar with change management knows, such dramatic quick fixes are inevitably ineffective and short-lived. And too many factors—and too many unknowns—are involved in greening your operation to take on everything at once.

2 **Start somewhere.** On the other hand, don't be stymied simply because you feel your company can't "save the earth" all by itself. Clearly, doing something is better than doing nothing, especially if that "something" will lead to other somethings down the line. Start with a project that is likely to yield a success, then build on that success. Abolish foam cups. Recycle paper. Bring in a speaker. Turn off machines that aren't in use. Conduct a modest waste audit. Do whatever you can do. Over time, as you gain confidence, experience, and enthusiasm, you can take on bigger challenges.

3 **Get the boss on board.** Without top-level approval, little of substance will get done. There is no question that the most environmentally forward-thinking companies have a mandate from the CEO and the board of directors to incorporate green thinking throughout the organization. Still, if the boss isn't yet a believer, don't abandon the whole idea. You can still launch effective environmental initiatives. Keep senior management apprised of every development. Send copies of memos showing how much trash you've saved from the waste stream. If you can attach a dollar savings to it, so much the better. If you get press attention for your efforts, make sure the boss sees it. If someone from your company gives a speech to a civic group and receives a thank-you letter, send a copy upstairs. Let it be known the number of employees involved and the enthusiasm generated by environmental programs. Eventually, the message will sink in.

4 **Involve everyone.** The more people who are in on the process, the better. An environmental initiative that involves only the top people—or only the rank-and-file—is doomed to fail. Each individual has the potential to bring his or her enthusiasm, creativity, and work

experience to the situation. The more each individual has the chance to participate directly in designing or fine-tuning your company's environmental programs, the greater the chance he or she will buy into it. And the greater the chance the program will succeed.

⑤ **Leverage your actions.** As you begin to take on significant pollution-prevention and waste-reduction efforts, encourage others to do so, too. Challenge your suppliers and competitors to meet or beat your goals. Help employees to incorporate some of these same greening activities into their home lives; that, in turn, will further increase their environmental awareness at work.

⑥ **Talk to everyone.** Fulfilling all those customers' demands and needs takes a great deal of two-way communication, something most companies are not naturally suited to do. That means it may be necessary to create some specific mechanisms to facilitate information flows between and among employees, customers, community members, environmentalists, regulators, suppliers, stockholders, and other interested parties. The more you know about their environmental needs, and the more they know about your environmental efforts, the greater the chance for mutual satisfaction. Much useful research is being done in the field of communication today, and its results can assist your efforts in this area.

⑦ **Tackle the substantive as well as the symbolic.** It's easy to do otherwise, to initiate a highly visible but hardly meaningful campaign to, say, stamp out disposable coffee cups or initiate a modest paper-recycling project. These are worthy pursuits, but if you believe your company is "green" as a result, you're missing the bigger picture. For example, for all the waste paper an employee can rescue from the waste stream for purposes of recycling, the environmental impacts of that effort are likely obliterated by the mere act of that same employee driving to and from work alone in a poorly tuned, gas-guzzling car with underinflated tires. So, whatever greening efforts you take on should go beyond the superficial in an effort to foster genuine behavioral change.

At the same time, the actions you take should be appropriate to your company and industry. A campaign to team up with a national environmental group to save endangered turtles off the Maldive archipelago will be meaningless—and, no doubt, will be viewed by some with suspicion—if your company doesn't address its own solid-waste or air-emissions problems.

(8) **Don't rest on your laurels.** It's easy to do: Your company meets or exceeds an environmental goal, and the program is over. Without continuity, all the enthusiasm, creativity, and hard work that went into meeting the goal will be lost and you'll have to fire it up again the next time. The most successful companies are those that maintain an ongoing series of challenges—setting tough, long-term goals, and revising them up if they seem too easy.

(9) **Give credit where credit is due.** You can't continually push employees to excel without giving them proper recognition and rewards. The acknowledgment needn't be financial—although money is clearly the most powerful motivator—but it should be more than a token gesture. What's key here is that employees get recognized for their good, green work, and understand that it is appreciated far up the chain of command. That means that top management would benefit by *personally* thanking employees for their deeds, not delegating the task to a department head, who will in turn delegate it on down the line to a supervisor. The mere act of a corporate officer personally thanking an employee or group of employees sends a powerful message about company commitment to environmental goals.

(10) **Don't underestimate the power of what's going on here.** As companies incorporate the E-Factor into their daily operations, their employees will be more likely to express these same ideals in their private lives—through voting, investing, and educating their kids. In that light, green businesses take on a greater importance: If we can't sell the environment to secretaries, salespeople, supervisors, and senior executives, we probably won't be able to sell it in society at large.

Over the past few years, I've told countless consumers, "Every time you open your wallets, you're casting a vote for or against the environment." And I believe that. What's most stimulating about this notion is that the marketplace is not a democracy: It doesn't take 51 percent of people "voting" in any one direction to effect environmental change. Far from it: Just a small percent of consumers changing the way they shop can move markets, shake up corporate environmental policy, and otherwise send shock waves through boardrooms. A relatively small number of consumers can make a big difference.

But all the power consumers possess doesn't hold a candle to the clout businesses can wield in dealing with environmental issues. Businesses spend far more money, use far more resources, and create far more waste than do individual households. When companies change the way they do these things, the impact can be felt from Main Street to Wall Street and around the world. And the actions companies take go far beyond the direct deeds they do for the environment. They send a loud and clear message to employees, customers, neighbors, suppliers, competitors, and others.

We'll end this book as we began it: There are opportunities and challenges before us. The opportunity is to help turn this new green consciousness into good, responsible business practices by incorporating the E-Factor in appropriate ways throughout your organization. The challenge is to do so deliberately and carefully, with an aim toward long-term cultural change, always with an eye toward the bottom line, lest you get frustrated and discouraged in the process.

With everybody's hard work, some creative thinking, and a little bit of luck, environmentally responsible businesses can be both possible and profitable.

resources

Organizations

- Business Council on Sustainable Development, 1825 K St. NW, Washington, DC 20006; 202-833-9659
- Buy Recycled Business Alliance, c/o National Recycling Coalition, 1101 30th St. NW, Washington, DC 20007; 202-625-6406
- Coalition for Environmentally Responsible Economies (Ceres), 711 Atlantic Ave., 5th Fl., Boston, MA 02111; 617-451-0927
- Competitek, c/o Rocky Mountain Institute, 1739 Snowmass Creek Rd., Snowmass, CO 81654; 303-927-3128
- Corporate Conservation Council, c/o National Wildlife Federation, 1400 16th St. NW, Washington, DC 20036; 202-797-6870
- Corporate Environmental Data Clearinghouse, c/o Council on Economic Priorities, 30 Irving Pl., New York, NY 10003; 212-420-1133
- The Elmwood Institute, P.O. Box 5765, Berkeley, CA 94705; 510-845-4595
- Environmental Information Service, c/o Investor Responsibility

Resource Center, 1755 Massachusetts Ave. NW, Ste. 600, Washington, DC 20036; 202-234-7500

• Environmentally Conscious Strategic Manufacturing Initiative, c/o National Center for Manufacturing Sciences, 900 Victors Way, Ann Arbor, MI 48108; 313-995-0300

• Global Environmental Management Initiative, 1828 L St. NW, Washington, DC 20036; 202-296-7449

• Industry Cooperative for Ozone Layer Protection, 1440 New York Ave. NW, Ste. 300, Washington, DC 20005; 202-737-1419

• International Society for Ecological Economics, P.O. Box 1589, Solomons, MD 20688; 410-326-0794

• Management Institute on the Environment and Business, 1220 16th St. NW, Washington, DC 20036; 202-833-6556

• National Association for Environmental Management, 1440 New York Ave. NW, Ste. 300, Washington, DC 20005; 202-737-3415

• Northeast Industrial Waste Exchange, 90 Presidential Plaza., Ste. 122, Syracuse, NY 13202; 315-422-6572

• Recycled Products Information Clearinghouse, 5528 Hempstead Way, Springfield, VA 22151; 703-941-4452

• Wildlife Habitat Enhancement Council, 1010 Wayne Ave., Ste. 1240, Silver Spring, MD 20910; 301-588-8994

Publications

• *Beyond Compliance: A New Industry View of the Environment*, edited by Bruce Smart (Washington, D.C.: World Resources Institute, 1992)

• *Beyond the Limits: Confronting Global Collapse, Envisioning a Sustainable Future*, by Donella H. Meadows, Dennis L. Meadows, Jorgen Randers (Post Mills, Vt.: Chelsea Green Publishing Co., 1992)

• *Business Guide to Waste Reduction and Recycling* (El Segundo, Calif.: Xerox Corp., 1992)

• *Business Recycling Manual* (New York: Inform, 1991)

• *Changing Course: A Global Business Perspective on Development and the Environment*, by Stephan Schmidheiny with the Business Council for Sustainable Development (Cambridge, Mass.: The MIT Press, 1992)

- *The Corporate Environmentalists*, by SustainAbility (London: SustainAbility, Ltd., 1991)
- *Costing the Earth: The Challenge for Governments, the Opportunities for Business*, by Frances Cairncross (Boston: Harvard Business School Press, 1992)
- *Earth in the Balance: Ecology and the Human Spirit*, by Senator Al Gore, Jr. (Boston: Houghton Mifflin, 1991)
- *Ecological Economics: The Science and Management of Sustainability*, edited by Robert Costanza (New York: Columbia University Press, 1991)
- *Environmental Dividends: Cutting More Chemical Wastes* (New York: Inform, 1992)
- *50 Simple Things Your Business Can Do to Save the Earth*, by the Earthworks Group (Berkeley, Calif.: Earth Works Press, 1991)
- *Green at Work: Finding a Business Career That Works for the Environment*, by Susan Cohn (Washington, D.C.: Island Press, 1992)
- *Green Is Gold: Business Talking to Business About the Environmental Revolution*, by Patrick Carson and Julia Moulden (New York: HarperBusiness, 1991)
- *The Greenhouse Gambit: Business and Investment Responses to Climate Change*, by Douglas Cogan (Washington, D.C.: Investor Responsibility Research Center, 1992)
- *Greening Business: Managing for Sustainable Development*, by John Davis (Cambridge, Mass.: Basil Blackwell, Ltd., 1991)
- *In Search of Environmental Excellence: Moving Beyond Blame*, by Bruce Piasecki and Peter Asmus (New York: Touchstone Books, 1990)
- *Management for a Small Planet*, by W. Edward Stead and Jean Garner Snead (Newbury Park, Calif.: Sage Publications, 1992)
- *Managing the Global Environmental Challenge* (New York: Business International Corp., 1992)
- *One Earth One Future: Our Changing Global Environment*, by Cheryl Simon Silver with Ruth S. DeFries for the National Academy of Sciences (Washington, D.C.: National Academy Press, 1990)
- *Paradigms in Progress: Life Beyond Economics*, by Hazel Henderson (Indianapolis, Ind.: Knowledge Systems, Inc., 1991)
- *Prosperity Without Pollution: The Prevention Strategy for Industry and Consumers*, by Joel S. Hirschhorn and Kirsten U. Oldenburg (New York: Van Nostrand Reinhold, 1991)

company and organization index

Ace Hardware Corporation, 144, 146, 182
Advanced Micro Devices, 163–164
Alacrity Systems, Inc., 236
Alcoa, 259
Allied-Signal Inc., 138, 192, 250–251
American Airlines, 116–117, 141
American Telephone & Telegraph Company, 137, 138, 192, 193, 229, 232, 254–255, 257, 258, 259
Amoco Corporation, 137, 138, 149–155, 170, 192
Anacomp, Inc., 234
Andersen Consulting, 236, 260–263
Apple Computer, 138, 144–146, 147, 178, 183, 196, 229
Arco, 131, 224
Arthur D. Little, 47, 67, 127, 129, 199, 246, 251–252, 260
Ashland Chemical, 41, 173
Ashland Oil, 100, 131
Atlantic Richfield Company, 131, 224
Bank of America, 94-95, 96, 194
Bellcore, 224
Ben & Jerry's Homemade, 136
Boeing Company, 138, 224, 259, 263–267
Boise Cascade, 231
Booz-Allen & Hamilton, 124–125, 259
Borjohn Optical Technology, Inc., 69
Bristol-Myers Squibb, 72
Browning-Ferris Industries, 60–61, 137, 138, 192, 259
Burson-Marsteller, 159
Butterworth Hospital, 146–147
Campbell Soup Company, 180, 182
Chapman and Cutler, 76
Cheeca Lodge, 215–216
Chevron Corporation, 111–112, 132, 137, 194, 206, 224
Chicago Board of Trade, 51
Chrysler Corporation, 216
Church and Dwight, 157–159
Colgate-Palmolive Company, 257, 259
Computer 2000, 183
Conference Board, The, 126
Coopers & Lybrand, 125

Corning Glass, 184
Cray Research Inc., 144
Deloitte & Touche, 10
Digital Equipment Corporation, 138, 184, 210–211, 224
Walt Disney Company, 127
Domino's Pizza Distribution Corporation, 137
Dow Chemical Company, 10, 101, 138, 168–169, 206, 255
Duke Power Company, 192, 259
DuPont, 10, 85, 138, 192, 255, 259
Duracell, 224
Eastman Kodak Company, 85, 109–110, 138, 144, 174, 231, 234
Electric Power Research Institute, 221
EnviroAudit Services, 270
Environmental Communications Associates, 165–167
Ernst & Young, 270
Esprit de Corp, 177–178
Export Packers Company Ltd., 211
Exxon Corporation, 12–13, 102, 131, 192
Fairchild Air Force Base, 217
Financial Accounting Standards Board, 91
First Brands, 21
Fleet Factors Corporation, 85
Ford Motor Company, 238
Fort Howard Corporation, 231
H. B. Fuller, 255
General Electric, 98–99, 184, 192
General Motors, 185–186, 191, 230
Gillette Company, 217, 224
Goldman Sachs, 144, 146
B. F. Goodrich Company, 169, 236, 244, 261–262, 269, 271
Goodyear, 224
W. R. Grace, 138, 192
GSD&M, 127, 177
Hale & Dorr, 75
Henkel KGaA, 127
Herman Miller, 63, 119–120, 186, 211–212
Hewlett-Packard Company, 183, 196, 229
Hitachi, 193

index

Resolution Trust Corporation, 86
Resource Exchange & News, 221
Responsible Care, 133–136, 164, 253
Robertson, Thomas A., 37–38
Rockwell International Corporation, 73
Rocky Mountain Institute, 191, 226
Rocky Mountain News, 166
Rohm and Haas, 259
Roper Organization, 20, 22, 98, 170
Rosen, Robert H., 142

Safeway Stores, 178, 194
salaries, environmental links to, 60–65
San Jose Mercury News, 163–164
Sander, David, 112
Santa Clara County (Calif.) Manufacturing Group, 195–196
Sara Lee Corporation, 104
Sawhill, John, 131–133
Schnur, Jacob, 179–180
Scudder, Stevens & Clark, 113
Sears Roebuck & Co., 233
Securities and Exchange Commission, 71, 90, 92
senior environmental executives, 123–129
Sentencing Reform Act, 75–76
shareholder initiatives, 136–138
Shell Oil, 192
shipping pallets, 229–230
Shopping for a Better World, 67, 108, 111
Sidley & Austin, 71
Sierra Club, 98, 99, 178
Silicon Valley Toxics Coalition, 163
Skinner, David, 145, 147
Smart, S. Bruce, 132
Smee, Bob, 220–221
Smith, Ann C., 250–251
Smukowski, David, 263–267
socially responsible investment, 137
Soderberg, Arthur, 254–255
South Coast Recycled Auto Project (SCRAP), 59–60
Southern Finance Project, 86, 96–97
Southern Waste Information Exchange, 220
Southwire Corporation, 224
stakeholder relations, 22–23, 27–28, 271

Stanford University Graduate School of Business Public Management Program, 10
State of the World, 53
State Street Bank & Trust Company, 85
Stouffer Stanford Court Hotel, 214
sulfur dioxide emissions, 48–52
Superfund, 16, 71, 82–89, 90, 92, 106
Superfund Action Coalition, 88, 101
supplier relations, 179–186, 271
Surma, John P., 90–91
surveys of corporate environmental programs, 124–125, 131
sustainable development, 55–57
Sweden, 131
Sweeney, Kevin, 138
Switzerland, 131
Syntex Corporation, 164–167, 173

Tandem Computers, 178
taxes, environmental, 48–55
telecommuting, 228–229
Tennessee Valley Authority, 50
Texaco Corporation, 206, 259
Thomlison, Bryan, 158–159
3M, *see* Minnesota Mining & Manufacturing
Three Mile Island, 9, 13
Times-Mirror, 256
Toftner, Richard O., 128, 269–270
Tompkins, Quincy, 177–178
Toshiba International Corporation, 103
total quality management (TQM), 6, 117–118, 210, 237–245, 246, 260, 267, 269–272
  history of, 237–240
  links with environment, 239–240
  measurement tools, 242
  tips for success, 271
  see also benchmarking, information management
Touche Ross & Co., 131
toxic emissions reduction, 133–136, 200
toxic waste contamination, 149–155
Toxics Release Inventory, 23–24, 107, 108, 163–167, 195–196, 197, 199–200, 201, 266
TransAmerica, 223, 224

acknowledgments

Though the subject of this book is business and the earth, it is really about people striving for ways to lessen the impact of their companies and their jobs on the environment. As such, credit for this book must be shared by the dozens of people who related the stories, experiences, and expertise that can be found in these pages.

Several individuals deserve special recognition and thanks. Gail Ross was one of the earliest supporters of this project, and her friendship and professionalism have helped me see it through to fruition. Henry Ferris of Times Books, the most patient and hardworking of editors, took on this book with a level of enthusiasm and commitment that never wavered.

Simultaneous to the researching and writing of this book I had the pleasure to work with a number of people at Andersen Consulting, including Tom Christel, David Crow, Ellen Johnson, Helene Love, Karl Newkirk, and Chuck Pisciotta, all of whom provided support or helped to shape the ideas behind this book. Through Andersen Consulting, it was also my pleasure to meet Tony Dorfmueller and Dick Toftner, both of whom shared their wisdom and stories from the trenches.

Special thanks to those who took time from busy lives to read all or part of the early drafts and provide comments, including Abhay Bhushan of Xerox Corp., Ladd Greeno of Arthur D. Little, energy consultant Tom Robertson, Ann C. Smith of Allied-Signal, Mark Starik of George Washington University, and Bryan Thomlison of Church & Dwight.

I am indebted, as always, to my staff at Tilden Press and *The Green Business Letter*, who provided a wide range of logistical and editorial assistance, including Jamie Queoff, Ilyanna Kreske, Nancy Thenvlerl, Alex Friend, Norman Meres, Anna Mulrine, and, of course, Shayna P. Rosenberg. Thanks also to Geneva Collins, who contributed research assistance, and to Felicia Tiller, for her transcribing help.

Others who provided generous assistance include Bob Bringer, Tom Zosel, and Rick Renner of 3M; Leslie Ratay and Kelly Smith of Quad/Graphics; Susan Cohn of New York University's Stern School of Business; Robert Costanza of the University of Maryland; Carl Frankel of *GreenMarket Alert*; Alice Tepper Marlin and her staff at the Council on Economic Priorities; A. J. Grant of Environmental Communications Associates; Bruce Piasecki of Rensselaer Polytechnic Institute; Richard Wells of Abt Associates; designer Robert Bull; and production assistant Mary Ann W. Bruce.

Finally, and most of all, to Randy Rosenberg, whose love and support have provided the foundation for this and so many other personal and professional adventures.

THE GREEN BUSINESS
Letter

To obtain subscription information and a
sample copy of THE GREEN BUSINESS LETTER, a
monthly newsletter edited by Joel Makower,
write Tilden Press Inc., 1526 Connecticut
Ave. NW, Washington, DC 20036. Or call
800-955-GREEN (202-332-1700 in
Washington, D.C.).